CW01336347

Disgust
The Gatekeeper Emotion

Disgust
The Gatekeeper Emotion

Susan B. Miller

THE ANALYTIC PRESS
2004   Hillsdale, NJ   London

Copyright © 2004 by The Analytic Press, Inc.

All rights reserved. No part of this book may be reproduced, stored, or transmitted in any way whatsoever without the prior written permission of the publisher.

Published by
The Analytic Press, Inc., Publishers
101 West Street, Hillsdale, NJ 07642
www.analyticpress.com

Designed and typeset by
Christopher Jaworski, Bloomfield, NJ
qualitext@verizon.net

Typeface: Baskerville 11/13

"Personal Helicon" by Seamus Heaney is used with kind permission of Farrar, Straus & Giroux.

Library of Congress Cataloging-in-Publication Data

Miller, Susan B. (Susan Beth)
Disgust : the gatekeeper emotion / Susan B. Miller
p. cm.
Includes bibliographical references and index.

ISBN 0–88163–387–9
1. Aversion.   I. Title.

BF575.A886M54   2004
152.4–dc22
2004043780

Printed in the United States of America

10 9 8 7 6 5 4 3 2 1

To Marlene and Gail
for being there

And in memory of Cyrus,
who knew no disgust
and when I wrote the
book on shame,
he ate it

Contents

	Acknowledgments	ix
Chapter 1	Entering the World of Disgust	1
Chapter 2	The Body and Mind of Disgust	23
Chapter 3	Nature and Its Excesses	47
Chapter 4	Varieties of Disgust	59
Chapter 5	Disgust Syndromes	79
Chapter 6	Sex, Procreation, and Human Intimacy	97
Chapter 7	Disgust Within Family Groups	125
Chapter 8	The Artistically or Scientifically Creative Individual and Freedom from Disgust	137
Chapter 9	Group Identities and Hostility Across Borders: Affairs of Ethnicities, Classes, and Sects	153
Chapter 10	Disgust and Horror	171
Chapter 11	Concepts of Disease and Health	177
Chapter 12	Final Comments	191
	References	197
	Index	205

Acknowledgments

More than any previous writing project, this one brought input from a great many people. I believe the explanation lies in the topic. Although I had great difficulty interesting any of my graduate school professors in the unsavory topic of disgust, many years later, returning to it, I have found it a topic that evokes curiosity and lively engagement from others, certainly more so than my previous subject, shame. My own engagement with disgust has been enlivened by many discussions, often humorous, with friends, family, and colleagues. A great many people shared their disgust experiences or those of acquaintances. Others contributed more formally.

Lois Kuznets, Judy Gray, Ann Pearlman, Howard Erman, Kathy Tuta and Rose Everett all invested hours and effort reading and critiquing large portions of the manuscript. The final manuscript benefited from their astute reading and skillful editing in a great many places and I am grateful to each of them for his or her special contributions and generosity.

Support, a listening ear, and personal anecdotes and ideas came from many other friends and family members including Gail and Allan Shiner, Judith Saltzman, Irv and Nancy Leon, Cecily Legg, Michael Harrington, Colleen Archibald, Moses Everett, Jack Novick, Hitomi Tonomura, Stephanie Platz, Peter Gray, Jim Dowling, Michael and Deb Jackson, Kelly Askew, Wendy Cheng, Jay Radin and Edith Britt.

Thanks go as always to my family for their love and support and, in this instance, for specific input on a number of occasions.

Though a cliché, it is nonetheless true that this book would not have been possible without the learning gained from my practice. I feel special gratitude to the many clients whose experiences and insight helped me frame and embody the ideas presented in this book.

Working with the staff at The Analytic Press has been a pleasure during the production of three books. I am especially appreciative of Paul Stepansky's editorial guidance from the initial book proposal through to the near-finished manuscript. Paul was enthusiastic about the topic and consistently engaged with the evolution of the book. Nearing completion, the manuscript moved into Nancy Liguori's able and practiced hands.

Chapter 1
Entering the World of Disgust

Personal Helicon

As a child, they could not keep me from wells
And old pumps with buckets and windlasses.
I loved the dark drop, the trapped sky, the smells
Of waterweed, fungus and dank moss.

One, in a brickyard, with a rotted board top.
I savoured the rich crash when a bucket
Plummeted down at the end of a rope.
So deep you saw no reflection in it.

A shallow one under a dry stone ditch
Fructified like any aquarium.
When you dragged out long roots from the soft mulch
A white face hovered over the bottom.

Others had echoes, gave back your own call
With a clean new music in it. And one
Was scaresome, for there, out of ferns and tall
Foxgloves, a rat slapped across my reflection.

Now, to pry into roots, to finger slime,
To stare, big-eyed Narcissus, into some spring
Is beneath all adult dignity. I rhyme
To see myself, to set the darkness echoing.

—Seamus Heaney, for Michael Longley

It seats itself at the dinner table, slithers into the bathroom, cozies up to us in bed, and makes itself at home in family relations and national politics. As an emotion of our intimate lives, disgust has stirred the interest of psychologists, philosophers, novelists, poets, and anthropologists. Yet, with a few notable exceptions, disgust has been shunned as a subject of serious inquiry, no doubt in part because its unsociable stink threatens to transfer to those who study it. Important questions remain concerning the functions of disgust and how it gained its stature as one of the six basic emotions Darwin (1872) catalogued: Is disgust a remnant of our animal past or is it a uniquely human parsing of events? How does disgust show its face in the consulting room? Is it widely distributed clinically or allied primarily with particular syndromes? Is it pathognomonic for any single syndrome? And what variant forms or affective kin does disgust have? These questions and others will be considered as we examine disgust's place in diverse contexts ranging from the vegetative profusion and gaseous decay of the swamp, to the infected sneezes and festering wounds of the sickroom, to the ethnic slurs of the backroom and battleground, to the "you stink" salvos of brothers and sisters at home.

Many observers center their understanding of disgust in the body and its innate biology. Some see disgust as inextricable from the world of food and ingestion (Rozin, Haidt, and McCauley, 1999) or that of malodorous body waste (Angyal, 1941). Others understand the drive to flee from carriers of infection (Curtis and Biran, 2001) as the basis for an emotion that discriminates between unwholesome and benign contacts. Rozin and Fallon (1987) observed that disgust itself is contagious: whoever touches something disgusting becomes disgusting and untouchable. Hygiene researchers Curtis and Biran see this transmissibility of the fouled, disgusting state as advancing disgust's ability to protect us from physical infection. They refer to Pinker's (1988) concept of "intuitive microbiology" (p. 22) as an explanation for why we label as disgusting whoever or whatever comes into contact with something disgusting. They believe we understand instinctively that touch or proximity may communicate biological dangers.

Differences exist among the biological theories in that one person may emphasize protection from germs (whether these are transmitted through the air, the skin, or the mouth), while another focuses exclusively on oral intake, and a third focuses on the risk of contact with animal waste. In each of the biological theories, however, disgust operates as an instinctive response genetically maintained because of its protective value for the body: it makes us want to cease smelling, ingesting, or touching whatever substance arouses it. Biological theories also establish the protective value of one person's disgust being detectable to another. An adult wearing disgust on the face cautions others about the unhealthy contact that stimulated the emotional reaction. A feeding infant with what appears to be disgust tightening its face or food pushed from the mouth signals the parent to stop feeding the baby a displeasing substance. Interactions between babies and older people suggest some degree of innateness in food aversions, but also demonstrate transmission of disgust across generations as adults consciously and unconsciously model disgust for certain things put into the mouth. An adult may deliberately teach a child disgust over dirty coins while unwittingly modeling disgust for Brussels sprouts.

Curtis and Biran (2001) offer an interesting theory about the relative absence of disgust in the early months of life (pp. 27–28). They see disgust as unnecessary in infancy, a period during which the baby is protected from dangerous contacts by the attentive parent's disgust. Absence of disgust in infancy is viewed as offering developmental advantage because it promotes a baby's willingness to sample varied food offerings, which can result in good early nutrition and also in the biologically advantageous ability of the adult to recognize a great range of edible substances as acceptable. We also know that somewhat older children, now operating outside constant parental surveillance, can become extremely cautious about their food choices and subject to true disgust over many foods. One child becomes known in the family for eating only French fries, another for living on hamburger and bread. What happens then to the advantage conferred by the infant's comfort with varied foods? Is it lost altogether or does it impact later life food choices? These questions await research.

With the exception of the infancy hypothesis, the biological theories generally do a better job of explaining the evolution of disgust as a protective mechanism than of accounting for people who never experience disgust, are slow to arrive at disgust, or overcome disgust readily. The biological theories also have difficulty explaining adequately things that are disgusting due to context, meaning, and history. A friend recently showed her intuitive grasp of the contamination concept by commenting, "Some things are gross by association." Interestingly, she meant mental association, not physical touch; therefore, her intuition did not seem rooted in "intuitive microbiology." In fact, her comment was intended to explain why a perfectly clean, even sterile, object could be disgusting. She found her explanation in the associations linking the clean object to a disgusting one. Another friend wrote, "When I was a kid, both terrified and grossed out by insects, I was unable to touch the can of Raid my mother kept under the kitchen sink because it was associated with the disgusting bugs it was supposed to kill."

A second group of theorists argues that an adequate depiction of disgust must go beyond the physical body to emphasize the self. It is the self, not the body per se, whose vulnerability to invasion and degradation is at issue when disgust arises. The self is vulnerable to agents as diverse as foodstuffs, feces, slimy messes that touch the skin, disturbing ideas and visions, immoral acts, and repellent people (see Miller, 1986, 1993). These theorists argue that, had nature cared only to equip us with an instinct to avoid rotten food or nonnutritious waste, simple distaste would have sufficed, as it likely does for dogs and cats; disgust would not be needed. According to these authors, the true defining characteristic of disgust is its protection of self boundaries, not body boundaries, whether represented by the shut mouth, the pinched nostrils, or the hastily wiped skin surface. Some writers and researchers (Rozin et al., 1999) see disgust as a response clearly evolved to reject bad food; they believe, however, that the disgust response has been exploited over time by our interpersonal and self-protective needs so that its functions have expanded greatly.

Although Freud could be single-mindedly focused on the libido as the primary mover of every human action, he did not reduce the libido to a purely biological drive but saw it operating within a complex psychological field that is rich in human meanings and motives. Similarly, disgust as he described it is a psychological force, not a manifestation of nature providing us defense against germs. This psychological perspective on disgust is conveyed well when—considering disgust over anal sex—Freud (1905) asserts that "people who try to account for this disgust by saying that the organ in question serves the function of excretion and comes in contact with excrement—a thing which is disgusting in itself—are not much more to the point than hysterical girls who account for their disgust at the male genital by saying that it serves to void urine" (p. 152). Freud also understands that oral revulsion has little to do with hygiene and much to do with context and meaning. He states that "the limits of such disgust [over "perverse" practices] are, however, often purely conventional; a man who will kiss a pretty girl's lips passionately, may perhaps be disgusted at the idea of using her tooth-brush, though there are no grounds for supposing that his own oral cavity, for which he feels no disgust, is any cleaner than the girl's" (pp. 17–18). Freud is attuned to the biological needs of the human organism; however, he does view disgust as managing defensive needs of the *psychological* self. He fits better with the self-oriented group within those considering disgust than with those whose emphasis is on biological dangers related to ingestion, inhalation, or touch.

My own thinking leads me to understand disgust as fundamentally about protecting and maintaining the self. One branch of its root system may have evolved for the purpose of avoiding or disgorging toxic organic substances, including waste and spoiled food. Its roots may also extend to the need to evade toxic skin contacts and bad air. However, these roots alone do not seem adequate to support the development of disgust. Other species share with us these biological needs, but not even monkeys, our close relatives, have developed disgust. Rozin, Haidt, and McCauley (2000) argue strongly that disgust is a food-directed response, but see disgust as forming fully only in childhood (between four and eight). They do not adequately explore why an emotion that has evolved to protect the body from noxious food would appear so late in a child's development. Even Curtis and Biran's hypothesis regarding maternal responsibility for infantile food choices would not obviously predict so late an appearance of disgust.

Food rejection occurs in various species and in human infants, either without emotional awareness or with simple distaste, but once we enter the world of fully formed disgust, we are dealing with a complex emotional commentary oriented toward promoting the safety of the uniquely human self. Even when operating to protect the body's health, disgust functions by way of the self, which mediates many contacts between person and environment. That mediation involves assigning significance to elements of the environment and deciding how to interact with them. The chapters to follow will show disgust fulfilling a variety of self-protecting functions and will also examine how disgust differs from horror—a neighboring emotion that is the subject of chapter 10—in its use of self-boundary reinforcement and good–bad division.

While protecting the self, disgust also operates to define individuals' concepts of self and body and to establish relationships between the two conceptual realms. Variations exist across time and among individuals with regard to the sense of connection with the body self. One person may feel a sense of unity with his body, as if no duality or estrangement exists. Another person (or the same person, at another time) may experience her body as taking care of much of its own business, running its own shop, doing its own thing. She can go to sleep and the body carries on with its breathing, its chemistry, its circulation, its getting sick or getting well. It may be seen as having its own wisdom (e.g., about what foods it needs), its own motives (e.g., to trip us up, to make us slow our pace), its own culpability (e.g., in hosting cancer), or its own personality (e.g., persistent or accident-prone). A menopausal woman of Buddhist bent talked of conversing gently with her organs and getting to know how they were feeling and faring. She did not see herself as unusually alienated from her body. On the contrary, she felt able to achieve more feedback from these normally mute organs than most do. Another woman referred with disdain to her breast, which had twice been afflicted with cancer, and said it had "a mind of its own," was unconcerned about her, and thus the surgeon "could have it." An elderly man commented that, as far as he could see, his immune system "did nothing but sleep on the job," whereas a younger, fit man said, "My T cells are world class . . . they're champions."

Even the mind can feel apart from the "me," subdivided so that a person can say, "part of my mind is gone on vacation today," due to hormones or medicines or something outside awareness. Mental disturbance can have a not-me feel to it that can be unsettling or reassuring, as when someone concludes, "that's not me, that's the depression talking" or "I didn't choose to gamble away that money—my addiction took over."

How does disgust impact these internal subdivisions, especially with respect to the self–body conundrum? Disgust promotes certain self-conceptions, certain illusions even. The idea, for example, of using disgust to protect my body by keeping certain things distant is in part a protective fantasy, because much of the time disgust is actually protecting my *sense* of security rather than any true physical security. Disgust does not consistently serve the microbiological security of the corporeal body, but it does consistently promote psychological security, a mission that includes security-seeking for the imagined body. Disgust asserts: "We have a well-coordinated system in place here in which the senses operate like sentries and give the self information about what to keep away from the body." While much in this conception is largely nonsense, the reassurance it offers is part of the mind-set created by disgust. Moments of sharp disgust reinforce the sense of self–other boundary, of inside and outside, of body under the protective watch of consciousness. They also work to protect the spiritual integrity of the individual or the group, either of which can insist that something is morally, ethically, or aesthetically unacceptable.

As we develop beyond earliest infancy, the body in many ways becomes a symbol of the self. The body stands alongside other self-symbols, such as one's house, one's car, or one's wardrobe. Wrye and Welles (1998) capture this symbolism in describing the skin—a physical organ—as something that "denotes the boundary *between the psychic outside and inside* and is also the symbol of containment" (p. 97, italics added). As explored further in chapter 11, adult concerns about the body, and the role of disgust in protecting the body, are complex amalgams of intuitive and learned health consciousness relating to the actual body together with reactions to perceived threats to the symbolic body.

What we experience as worries "about the body" may actually concern our feelings about self-security masquerading as interest in bodily safety. For example, when an effluvium of body odor offends my nose, one must ask if it is in fact the nose twitching in disgust that has initiated the response, or is it my class sense, which detects beggary in what it smells. If we do not want our skin to touch something slimy, our concern may be less about skin infection than about associating the self with such a mess. In the evolutionary background of fearing to touch or otherwise contact a "mess" may be the intuitive microbiology Pinker discusses, which may shape our ideas of what constitutes mess.

Many disgust experiences arise in response to sensory input. This pattern does not, however, belie the self's position at the center of disgust. The self begins its development with body experience and such experience comes to signify much about the state of the self. We will also see, in chapter 2, that the senses all generate disgust according to the *meaning* of the stimulus that provides the sensory information. Among the senses, smell, taste, and touch associate most strongly with disgust. Vision is less critical and hearing least of all. The senses most liable to carry information that provokes disgust are those associated with close contact between the body and the outside. The idea of something very close to the body or touching it conveys risk that puts disgust on alert.

Because the experience of tasting signifies something soon to become part of the body, the sense of taste is keenly attuned to the need to reject what is foul, an observation that may suggest biological roots for disgust but may also signify the self in action protecting both bodily and psychic integrity. Smells enter the body imperceptibly through the air, making them potent invaders; they also activate ingestion impulses and that capability gives them disgust power. Things that touch the skin are close at hand and have potential to penetrate the skin surface, sometimes through dangerously imperceptible absorption, a process so incremental and undetectable that it creates unsettling doubt about the very concept of a firm body–environment boundary.

Texture deserves special attention as an important source of disgust. Unnerving textures (sliminess, for example, or gumminess) stimulate disgust whether on the body surface or on the mucosal surface of the mouth. Since many food aversions are responsive to texture even more than to taste or smell, one can regard them as expressions of the sense of touch. They differ somewhat from disgust over substances on other skin surfaces because our fantasy is of swallowing whatever is in the mouth, not absorbing it or sticking to it, surface-to-surface. As texturally disturbing foods are chewed, they become a familiar, generic mush, now hard to discriminate from other foods and less disgusting. Unfamiliarity, which connotes danger, is often a factor in heightening sensitivity to texture.

Tactile characteristics of disgusting skin contacts may differ for oral and nonoral skin surfaces. In the mouth, substances that contain lumps or seeds—especially slippery seeds—sometimes disgust. These substances have nonuniform texture; they contain objects of hard consistency within a softer substance. The hard substances get the attention of the tongue and mucosa and perhaps raise questions about what is slipping down the gullet along with the softer substance. An amalgam of instinct and associations may be at work here. Babies sometimes instinctively find the nuts in soft bread and spit them out, perhaps biologically programmed to sense danger in such hard or embedded objects. Older children and adults may associate seeds with something reproductive and gross, especially slimy seeds like those in a watermelon or tomato. Slimy seeds also threaten to slip down the throat without one's deciding to ingest them. Mixed consistency substances on the skin are unlikely to evoke the same disgust as those ready to slide down the esophagus.

Sight often concerns objects that keep their distance. Although vision spans that distance and makes remote objects accessible, the distance nevertheless works against disgust. Looking at objects close at hand facilitates disgust, because the object will seem real, three-dimensional, and near enough to pose danger. More distant objects seem two-dimensional and may feel more like pictures or visions than real objects with mass. Distant objects lack detail and often give only visual information (and perhaps auditory information), unalloyed with smell, taste, or touch, and thus they will disgust only if substance and detail is provided by the imagination or by previous close contact.

Like sights, sounds can carry over considerable distance. Details and volume diminish with increasing range, but, close or far, sound seldom disgusts. Only when steeped in personal associations or cultural and class meaning does it arouse disgust. Listening to a National Public Radio piece on the practice of noodle-slurping in Japan (Weiner, 2001), I felt mildly disgusted by the audio of noisy noodle-slurpers at a public eatery. I started to attend to the piece and culled a few excerpts. A young Japanese woman is quoted saying, "Listening to these middle-aged men slurping, I find it offends my ears." Later in the narrative, a woman from the older, noodle-slurping generation says, "I can't believe these young people find it disgusting . . . [it's part of being Japanese]. What are they talking about?" The reporter describes a young person twirling his or her noodles Italian-style and an older person says, "I was appalled. Nothing is sacred." Here is an intergenerational war of disgust, focused on disgust as a culturally loaded response to a food-related sound.

Sometimes actual sense experience elicits disgust; at other times, the idea or the imagining of such sense experience does the evoking. As indicated earlier, the danger is as frequently to the self or to the conception of the body as to our actual physical status. Body-symbolization protects us from knowing what actually is at stake psychologically. Hearing is no different from the other senses in these respects. It differs only with regard to the restricted domain in which it conveys the disgusting essence of an object. Sounds also seem less likely to redintegrate the organic processes that stimulate disgust than visual images do (rotting food, for example, is silent, but visually and olfactorily rich). When on occasion sounds do connote such processes—farting, belching, or clogged, labored breathing, for example—disgust may follow.

Disgust likely has some rudimentary manifestation in infancy. The infant's spheres of intense activity revolve around sense pleasure (and displeasure), social engagement, and development of coordination and strength. Within those areas of activity, tasting, smelling, and touching—the senses of close contact—till the ground for various aversive reactions. The earliest visible suggestions of anything akin to disgust often come from the infant's reaction to foods introduced into the mouth. Babies may spit out food with a facial expression suggestive of disgust. Whether the baby actually feels disgust as adults do—or feels some partial, rudimentary form of the emotion—we do not know for certain. It is difficult though to conceive of the affective complexity of disgust—especially the idea of contagious badness (see Rozin and Fallon, 1987)—in infancy. In an earlier paper (Miller, 1986), I discussed the likelihood that early negative response to foods lacks aspects of the psychological content we associate with adult disgust and remains an immature form of the emotion until the self as a center of activity and response takes shape.

Paul Rozin, who, with colleagues, has done the majority of psychological research on disgust, suspects that disgust matures into its final form somewhere between the ages of four and eight, with a more recent, Australian study suggesting the earlier time point (Rozin et al., 1999). Rozin et al. (1997) see the commonly observed disgust-like facial expression of the baby[1] as expressive of "distaste," an early occurring "proto-emotion" on a developmental line with disgust. Rozin (1999) sees the contamination property of disgust as late appearing and definitional. He states that "this property sharply distinguishes disgust from rejection based on sensory properties (distaste), because distasteful foods are generally not contaminating" (p. 23). Various writers, including those emphasizing the biologically protective aspects of disgust and those emphasizing protection of the self agree that the infant's facial expression of distaste is distinguishable from fully formed disgust.

To suppose a developmental line from early distaste for food to true disgust need not imply that, without distaste, disgust would never develop. We cannot assume, for example, that an infant who is tube-fed

---

[1]Rozin, Haidt, and McCauley (1999, p. 430) tell us: "The disgust face is familiar and recognized in many and perhaps all cultures (Ekman, 1984; Ekman et al., 1987; Izard, 1971; Haidt and Keltner, 1998). The three major muscle groups involved (Darwin, 1872; Ekman and Friesen, 1975; Izard, 1971) are the gape (lowering of the jaw), with or without tongue extrusion, the nose wrinkle, and the upper lip raise. The gape and nose wrinkle are most associated with disgust situations related to food. The upper lip raise, the movement least related functionally to eating or rejecting food, is most associated with what we call elaborated disgust (elicitors like dead bodies, physical contact with strangers, and certain moral violations) (Rozin, Lowery, and Ebert, 1994)."

and hence lacks the experience of early food rejection would fail to develop later disgust toward food or other unacceptable contacts. Likely, the internal structures that promote so fundamental a category of emotional life as disgust are quite robust and will manifest even if particular experiences are missed. In addition to early ingestive experience, unpleasant nonoral contacts of infancy (e.g., being held too tightly) are also likely contributors to the development of disgust. Interestingly, a study of feral humans showed that people lacking *social* interactions, not ingestive experience, failed to develop disgust (Malson, 1964).

Organizing behaviors characteristic of infancy may make a contribution to the eventual consolidation of disgust responses. For example, it is common to see young toddlers display sustained interest in separating complex materials into components, sometimes choosing one element and not another to eat or to admire or derogate. Babies can take great care separating their diced carrots from their peas, perhaps to eat one and not the other, perhaps to eat both but separately. One toddler I observed studied her belly button and dug out any dark specks she could find with her little fingers, then she held them up and pronounced them "dut" (i.e., dirt). In these instances, the toddler seems invested in keeping things pure. Certain things shouldn't intermingle or touch. They should keep their individuality and purity. It is by no means clear that the toddler who removes the dirt from her belly button finds the dirt disgusting. She does, however, seem to want her belly button clean. The behaviors described fit within a larger category of order-establishing, compulsive behaviors of young children who are establishing some control over the environment.

Cognitive maturation may influence the evolution of displeasure into true disgust. The child's recognition that the feeding parent is a separate being who is responsible for presenting a displeasing food might lead to internally experienced aggression toward the parent and to defining the parent, in that moment, as "bad." (See Kernberg, 1976, on early self–other units as important to affect development.) Parallel development might occur with regard to other displeasing stimuli—for example, too binding an embrace. Disgust might then occur when simple displeasure is transformed into a more complex state that includes labeling another as contagiously bad and aggressively conveying one's aversion.

To the extent that eating becomes tightly linked to disgust, the explanation may lie as much in the psychological significance of eating as it does in body-protective instinct.[2] Eating results in a literal internalization of concrete substances, which cross the body and self boundaries and become self. Since the self is strongly identified with the body and can experience vulnerability by way of the body, capacity to enter the body can be equated with violation of the self and can elicit disgust. Ingestibles readily cause disgust because their entry into the body is total. People often admonish, "Don't talk to me about that while I'm eating," because ideas and images, whether food-related or not, more readily disgust us if we are eating. The openness of the body–self is greater while eating, so we must be

---

[2]William Miller (1997) makes the important observation that the English word for disgust, which features *taste,* may incline those of us who speak English to a more food-focused concept of disgust than those who speak, for example, German (p. 1), a language in which the primary word for disgusting—*widerlich*—connotes "an againstness" (per Ben Fortson, personal communication) and the word for disgust, *Ekel,* has no accepted etymology. Even in a language as closely related to English as Spanish, we encounter some surprising departures from English affect language. The Vox Spanish–English dictionary (second edition) translates the English word, *disgusting,* as *asqueroso* or *repugnante.* The English word, *repugnant,* is thought to have evolved from the Latin, *pugnare,* to fight; *repugnant* and *repugnante,* then, derive from *repugn,* to fight back. Note that no sensory emphasis exists in this lineage. The Spanish word *disgusto,* with its roots in "not taste" translates as "displeasure, annoyance," which lacks the idea of infective, contagious awfulness that distinguishes the English, *disgusting,* or the French, *dégoûtant.*

Analyses of relationships between words and categories are complicated by the fact that the category-word a language privileges may incline us to focus our investigatory attention on a slightly different segment of experience than would be suggested by another word. If, for example, Darwin and other English-speaking affect-theorists had settled on *repugnance,* not disgust, as the word best representing one of the basic emotions, that word might impact our conclusions about early roots and core content of the emotion state.

A portion of disgust's power in English comes from the aggressive, spitting way in which the second syllable of the word can be spoken. Cognate words can be enunciated so that their meaning is very close to disgust's meaning, or they can be spoken in a fashion that separates them from disgust. Take, for example, the word *sickening.* Pronounced aggressively—perhaps as a descriptor of fiscal irresponsibility—it is equivalent to disgust. Pronounced reflectively and with inward attention, it converges with *nauseating* in placing emphasis on the ill state of the self and the vileness of the stimulus.

careful of the thoughts we entertain while thus engaged. (See Rozin et al., 1999, for a discussion of two laws of sympathetic magic—contagion and similarity—and disgust.)

Other areas in which such boundary transgression may occur are sexual intrusion and bodily infringements associated with medical care, parenting, or abuse. But even in these circumstances (which may, indeed, bring disgust), what is outside seldom becomes self, except when substances are left behind by the intrusion (semen, for example, or material injected through the skin). Semen often disgusts, but injected material rarely does—perhaps because the content is seen as sterile, not brimming with life.

Humans obviously are engineered with a readiness to develop disgust as one of the affect-maturational trajectories of childhood. The disgust category we develop over time remains, however, a roughly boundaried denomination of emotional response, the edges of which are imperfect and challenging to map (Miller, 1986, 1993). This complexity is evident in the large variety of words the English language offers us for what elicits disgust-like experience: revolting, repulsive, offensive, vile, gross, gruesome, sickening, nauseating, and putrid, among others.

Having posited that disgust aims to protect the self, we can enumerate additional defining features of this self-protective reaction. Disgust responds to an encounter with something experienced as outside the self. That "Other" is felt to be noxious and ready to transfer noxiousness to the self. Therefore, one wants distance from the bad "Other." Disgust thus involves jeopardy to the self, which responds to that danger by devaluing—even despising—something outside, and determining to keep free of it.

Another aspect of disgust important to consider is its interpersonal communication value. We have already noted that in the early months of life—the distaste period—the facial expressions that look like disgust have important caretaker-signaling functions. The disgust-face will directly impact the sensitive caregiver's behavior around biologically and emotionally important activities such as feeding. When true disgust develops, the option will exist to use it in communicating aggressively to a caretaker. However, such communication is neither inevitable nor essential to disgust. Disgust can occur without visible or audible evidence and thus cannot be said to be fundamentally a communication device.

Many disgust responses develop later in childhood and are influenced by learning, especially of the symbolic meanings of food items or other substances. Some of the food aversions we experience after our earliest months rest as heavily on symbolism, social learning, association, and psychological defense as on genuine nutritional concerns. Consider, for example, all the children unable to eat their soggy spinach—despite Popeye's assertion that bulging muscles will erupt instantly—and willing to sit glumly for hours staring at the offending glop rather than acquiescing to a parent's demands to put fork to mouth. For me, as a child, cooked oatmeal was a substance that was simply inedible. Whenever I attempted to eat it, disgust and gagging followed inevitably. Probably, the unfamiliarity of the food (we did not eat it at home) together with its texture supported the feelings of disgust. Conceivably, a meaning-laden aspect to the response was also present in that I had—by report—enjoyed oatmeal as a baby. Was oatmeal, then, a gummy baby food in my mind and not something an older child could eat safely, without risk of regression? To this day, cooked oatmeal would be my choice only if no other food were available and my hunger was pressing.

Though disgust often responds to sensory input, it does not require it. Moral disgust, one of the subjects of chapter 4, is a prevalent form of the emotion that seldom depends on the senses, nor does it manifest with much bodily involvement or sense imagery (e.g., wrinkled nose, averted face, or images of bad smells or tastes). Though relatively unaccompanied by body content, moral disgust has considerable force and is no weak sister to disgust that calls attention to the body and its senses. Moral disgust raises further questions about the body's relevance to disgust and supports the assertion that disgust is fundamentally about the self.

Whether responding to sensory data or to moral or aesthetic concerns, disgust speaks to the sense of identity. It declares what I am willing to accept as me and mine and what I want to assert is outside and alien, what I will embrace with delight and what smells bad to me—whether literally, when held to the nose, or figuratively, when proffered to the spirit. By specifying what I will not accept as related to me, disgust indicates my values but also my anxiety lest some contact leave me contaminated or diminished, brought from high to low, rolled in the mud and muck of experience.

All of us establish self boundaries by determining what will be allowed to pass easily into the self-space, to become intimate with the self, or even to be incorporated into "myself" as I conceive of it. We see these boundary-protective activities at the personal level, both in the bodily reactions and ideationally focused reactions, and we see them at the group level as collective disgust, which specifies what we, as a group, think of those outside our group. Disgust within the intimate family group is examined in chapter 7. Disgust and the psychology of larger groups are the subject of chapter 9, in which disgust and ethnic, religious, and class groups are explored. We will see that disgust imagery is ubiquitous in the language of degradation that feeds intergroup atrocities, whether spoken by the Nazi demeaning the Jew as rat or bacillus or the Rwandan Hutu inflaming hatred for the Tutsi as *inyenzi,* cockroaches. The determination to eradicate all traces of the Tutsi lest some remaining trace revive the group was so great that "foetuses were routinely ripped from the wombs of pregnant women and butchered" (Channel4.com, August 15, 2000). Here, again, is the powerful idea that whatever or whoever is disgusting can contaminate others.

Maintaining a sense of boundaried self is of vital interest to human beings, especially those from certain Western cultures, including the United States. The boundaried state says, "This is me, this is who I am," and challenges to it bring distress. Thomas Merton (1988) states the case well in discussing the modern consciousness:

> In our evaluation of the modern consciousness, we have to take into account the still overwhelming importance of the Cartesian *cogito*. Modern man, in so far as he is still Cartesian ... is a subject for whom his self-awareness as a thinking, observing, measuring and estimating "self" is absolutely primary. It is for him the one indubitable "reality," and all truth starts here. The more he is able to develop his consciousness as a subject over against objects, the more he can understand things in their relations to him and one another, the more he can manipulate these objects for his own interests [p. 22].

We live our lives as gatekeepers, turning away the undesirable and bidding the auspicious to enter, continually evaluating access in the light of what we desire in security and self-enhancement. Disgust effectively banishes unwanted visitors, saying, no thank you, you'll not enter my house, track mud on my carpet, bring your suspect ideas to the ears of my children.

Though we value profoundly the experience of "my self," the boundaried state is not the only state of being humans enjoy and value, nor the only state we seek. We look as well for moments in which boundaries are blurred or abandoned, moments that bring the outside in and cast doubt on the salience of the demarcated self. This urge may be underappreciated by those biological theorists who view disgust only as a means to gain protective distance, but psychologists and poets know that the longing for conjoinment runs as deep as the desire for self-definition. The tension between wishes to abandon boundary and desires for delimitation is a precondition for disgust. Chapter 6 will examine human strivings to allow intimacy, including sexual intimacy, without being flooded by disgust.

What determines when we welcome contact and when we eschew it? A key determinant is our need to feel sound and solid. We want to be capable of holding together as reasonably unitary beings and of maintaining the ability to function in the world. In order to feel sound, we need to feel substantial, not flimsy or friable. We manage our boundaries in relation to that need, which may dictate a variety of attitudes toward boundary. Often, we choose to hold fast to the idea of a fixed and boundaried self that is not too changing. When we are frightened and feeling fragile, we may be especially zealous about the self-boundary and intolerant of acknowledging its illusory aspects. We should keep in mind here that the human condition always involves a good deal of fearfulness and vulnerability, so the anxious insistence on boundary need not indicate a special aberration or weakness. An alternative, equally anxious stance is to admire and absorb indiscriminately from the outside, as if the self were empty, a delineated void waiting to be enhanced by whatever one can incorporate. When we feel relatively secure and can allow things to come and go within the self-space, we are still choosy about what gets access. What adheres to self must augment the sense of solidity, not lessen it, so we allow intake and affiliation but do so discriminately. An even more confident (some would say foolhardy) stance is to venture into affiliations and incorporations of all sorts with an attitude that the self is strong enough to launch effective cleanup operations if need be.

While the primary source of disgust is our need to feel sound, the desire to believe we are good inside also is important (though less so, being a desire and not an absolute need). The desire for goodness likely derives from the need for soundness. Soundness promotes boundary (how can you be solid if you are not separate?) and once we draw a boundary we create two parts, which means we have interacting dyads of high–low, fast–sluggish, substantial–diminutive. Once we have pairings, we have decisions to make regarding affiliation. Should we stand with the high? With the low? With the capable? With the diminished? We thus need judgment: one pole becomes good, the other bad. We label "good" the set of characteristics we think will bring more rewards from the outside, specifically from our human society, so if we are choosing to be good or bad (or to see ourselves as such), we prefer to affiliate with the values we believe will yield interpersonal reward.

A notable paradox is associated with disgust: we use disgust to stay pure and good so that we may attract outer resources to the self to enrich it, but in order to partake of such resources we must allow a self-boundary that is permeable and not too fiercely guarded. Hair-trigger disgust will protect the self from contamination but wizen it to physical and psychological skin and bones by allowing nothing in. An absence of disgust will degrade the self and end our access to resources reserved for the "good," or so we fear. These are the challenges of intimacy and boundary. They parallel the human food-selection quandary that Rozin (1976) calls "the omnivore's dilemma," which describes our need to consider the value of many potential foods but to do so with caution, lest we poison ourselves.

We have considered primarily the universals of disgust development and occurrence, but we also need to ask whether the constitution of disgust is such that particular character types, perhaps particular pathologies, are associated with a high incidence of disgust. In chapter 5, we will look at eating disorders, narcissistic conditions, and obsessive-compulsive characters in order to assess any special relationship between disgust and these psychological states.

The chapters ahead will bring detailed consideration of the diverse realms into which disgust comes crawling, but some quick and impressionistic sketching here will anticipate certain of disgust's varied haunts:

Disgust is about skin. We squash a bug and are disgusted as the insides explode through the bug's tough crust in our direction, perhaps splattering our skin, our own more pervious, less crusty integument. Skin is container, barrier, and demarcater of inside and outside. Disgust is about leakage and escape through skin, about permeation and penetration and soaking and about fears (coupled with wishes) that skin simply dissolve and the barrier between inside and outside—always unreliable—collapse.

Disgust is about dark interiors and moist depths. Anne Michaels's (1996) remarkable Holocaust story, *Fugitive Pieces,* is rich in imagery of disgust's stomping ground: the bowels of it, the womb of it, the mother–father earth of it. Her boy-narrator begins his story by telling us what he's learned of life and we hear about relationships with the elemental earth: "No one is born just once. If you're lucky, you'll emerge again in someone's arms; or unlucky, wake when the long tail of terror brushes the inside of your skull. . . . I squirmed from the marshy ground like Tollund Man, Grauballe Man. . . . Dripping with the prune-coloured juices of the peat-sweating bog. Afterbirth of earth" (p. 5).

This boy is of the earth; he is the earth. In the earth, he is fed and nourished, he is suffocated and dissolved. Both ends of the polarity present themselves, always both, since the engulfing earth is simultaneously holy and unchaste; it knits the cut ends of experience. The boy continues: "I saw a man kneeling in the acid-steeped ground. He was digging. My sudden appearance unnerved him. For a moment he thought I was one of Biskupin's lost souls, or perhaps the boy in the story, who digs a hole so deep he emerges on the other side of the world" (pp. 5–6).

The story of the boy who digs to the other side of the world is exactly right to convey the sphere in which disgust operates. Inside and outside threaten to blur or change place if disgust does not step in and thrust them apart. Outside may seem right and good, untethered and sublime, while inside is breathless and horrid; then the values flip so that inside becomes secure and warm, outside lost and barren. Consider the boy and the man, whose encounter begins the story. The boy emerges from the muck of the earth's interior. He is born into the air, drying off, shedding the muck, escaping the dark wall-space that first confined him and preserved him from the storming Nazis. The man, an archeologist, finds air too thin and vacant; he digs within the earth, seeking his treasures there, a pig with a snout for truffles.

So what is the earth? Tomb? Estuary? Ah, both, always both: source of life and life's replenishment but menacing to individuality and therefore a realm of great ambivalence—we need it, we fear it, it ushers us into the realm of disgust where we draw our lines carefully to try and include just enough earthiness to refresh life, not so much that the individual—always insignificant in relation to nature, always frail—cannot stand defined against a background but becomes absorbed. Chapter 3 continues this look at disgust and nature.

Anne Michaels's earth image is especially interesting because her burying ground is marsh one minute and bog the next, yet in nature marsh and bog are dissimilar. Marsh is organically rich and alive with decay; it soon returns the individual life to the collective. Bog is organically depleted, rich only in acid; it entombs the individual and leaves him awaiting excavation. Bog is a metaphor for the unconscious mind, which sequesters and preserves its contents.

Let us leave aside the human body and skip to another domain of human experience. Disgust relates to empathy, but how? The human mind believes: If I can know it, if I can understand it, then perhaps I can be it, perhaps I already am it. So an anxious stance is adopted that says: I can't understand that violent behavior, I can't relate to that depressive pain ... it is other, it is not me, it is revolting, disgusting, abhorrent ... my sphere may be small but it is good and it is safe. But we pay a price in isolation and exclusion when important things are not-me. Consider the woman whose husband does not know she is sleeping with another man. What is so awful, so devastating to the husband when he comes to know about this occurrence? Part of the devastation is his ignorance. If his wife can do something pivotal and he does not know, if she can do something that says he is ignorant of a major inclination of her heart, then she is not-me, not self, and the idea of their union is disturbed, which leaves him as shaken as he would be if he could not control his own body or being or did not know what he was doing after dark.

Now he will have to make her disgusting. He has to thicken the skin that separates them and say she is entirely outside and Other and he is well encased and well defined (as himself alone) and whole again. Otherwise, his is a partial skin, a skin ripped, with stuff leaking in and out.

His troubles are not over. If he wants the marriage to heal, then he has to open his disgust-thickened skin and let her inside again and try to sew up the skin with both of them inside. That task is difficult; it involves believing again that she is known to him which means he may be surprised once again with a cancer—a growth that is within but is not self.

Let us skip again, to the material objects and the concepts in our worlds and their relation to disgust. Fluidity disturbs us if it appears in the things around us that hold physical and conceptual form. Things should be what they have been in the past: they should hold steady and eschew multidimensionality. New definitions or points of view, as well as blurred or compound definitions all offend. Here we have a conservative mind-set, which leads to firm boundaries and high levels of disgust. What is a Bible? The more conservative thinker might say, "It is the good book, the book of the Lord, a revered text, which we pass respectfully from one generation to the next." Perhaps one says, as counterpoint: "A Bible is also a heavy object, it is an object useful for holding shut my potato chip bag so the chips don't get stale; only its words need be venerated, not its physicality." The conservative may consider this mind-set morally disgusting. The Bible can be only one thing, otherwise it may become meaningless and leave us lost. If I am not religious, I may say, "What is all the fuss about the potato chip remark?" But perhaps I, the irreverent one, am a devotee of fine wine and when you say, "All wine is the same, it gives you a nice buzz," now I am disgusted and think you are gross and uncouth; please do not come to my house for dinner.

The human mind strives to divide and master, not only to divide self from nonself but to categorize all the phenomena we encounter. Mary Douglas (1966) addresses the profound human need to divide the encountered world into identifiable things and "dirt," which is leftover or excluded matter. She discusses the role of dirt, saying, "All through the process of differentiating its role was to threaten the distinctions made" (p. 161) and thus—as threats do—to reinforce the boundaries. Disgust is a primary mechanism for reinforcing the boundaries to which Douglas refers, and dirt, in its various guises, stimulates disgust.

Disgust responds to the tiny squashed bug that spurts its insides on our skin but also to the large events of our world. So we say it is disgusting, morally, that Richard Nixon ordered his "plumbers" to rifle through the papers in Daniel Ellsberg's psychiatrist's office. The President disregards a less powerful man's right to privacy; he chooses to intrude in the man's private sphere and make it public, humiliating him. He makes the man into a squashed bug whose insides spurt out. That is not right. If we are like the man, we want our insides contained, not spilling out, mortifying us. Ellsberg is us, stripped of our privacy; we fight back with revulsion, trying to say to the Nixons, "Get out of my space. You are the disgusting one. You have power, but morally you are a snake."

Many found President Clinton disgusting in his sexual self-indulgence with a young intern. His behavior was so unacceptable to the

Christian, marriage-sanctifying conscience, and the idea of his exposure and fall from grace so frightening (what if it were they falling so? making such a dizzying display?) that many took their mental ink pens and emphatically retraced the line separating his behavior from their own. But for another person, perhaps not so engaged with issues of lust and marital infidelity and their exposure, it might be the President's bald-faced lying that disgusted, his finger shaken in the faces of the American people while the lie was delivered. For that person, it is deeply disturbing to have trusted and believed in this father figure, even as he suffered attack for his morals to have extended oneself to say, "I still believe in him; he's still family; he and I remain a 'we,'" only to learn he had no such loyalty to you and could lie shamelessly and make you look the fool. Out comes the disgust, the reinforcement of boundary saying, "He and I are no longer we, no longer family."

We find certain regularity with respect to the matters that disgust us. When Freud and his students talk of reaction-formation and disgust, they look at a corner of the phenomenon but neglect the gestalt. If I say, "Not only do I not desire X, I tell you I cannot abide X—it disgusts me," the Freudian says I defend myself against the feeling, "I deeply desire X but ought not to desire it because my conscience prohibits that desire." But the conscience is only one component of a larger sorting mechanism that dictates the things with which I can associate safely. And that larger mechanism operates in areas of desire but not exclusively there. The Freudian view addresses instances of libidinal desire and the response of conscience against those, but misses the larger human conflict between isolation and openness to contact. The Freudian view is not apsychological, but it is limited in its psychological scope.

William Miller (1997), echoing Kolnai (1929), says that what disgusts us is what is too alive. We will look more closely at this intriguing and important notion and relate it to Mary Douglas's seminal work on purity and danger and her notions relating disgust and dirt to matter out of place. Matter out of place disturbs the categories we use to order our worlds. Discussion of breached categories will constitute a bridge to creativity, the subject of chapter 8 and a terrain where matter that lies at the outer fringe of acceptability, that has heightened power for emotional arousal, can be integrated—not extruded as dirt—though often in an unstable manner.

In the chapters to follow, I will use case examples, where available, and personal examples. I will also draw on fictional characters. Some may raise questions about the use of the emotions and emotional dynamics of fictive characters as demonstrations of coherent thought and feeling. In my view, such portraits are informed by the psychology of the author, thus they are fully human productions evincing human psychological functioning. A literature has evolved that examines case history as a form of narrative (see Spence, 1982); even the psychotherapeutic process, as it unfolds, has been convincingly portrayed as a constructed, tendentious narrative. Narratives that are admittedly fictional suffer no greater problems as psychological data than those offered by clinicians documenting their psychotherapeutic sessions.

Chapter 2
The Body and Mind of Disgust

> Some days were ghastly from the outset; the breakfast oatmeal was studded with chunks of date like chopped-up cockroach; bluish swirls of inhomogeneity in his milk; a doctor's appointment after breakfast. Other days, like this one, did not reveal their full ghastliness till they were nearly over.
>
> He reeled through the house repeating: "Ugh, horrible, ugh, horrible, ugh, horrible, ugh, horrible . . ."
>
> "Dinner in five minutes, wash your hands," Enid called.
>
> Cauterized liver had the odor of fingers that had handled dirty coins.
>
> —Jonathan Franzen, *The Corrections*

Disgust and the Senses

In its intimate tie to the senses, disgust stands apart from other basic emotions. Most people, thinking of disgust, likely focus first on contacts that stimulate the senses: smells that bunch the nostrils, tastes that draw the tongue from the mouth, sights that squint the eyes. But what specifically is it about sense experience that causes disgust? An example drawn from a clinical setting will raise an essential question and suggest an answer.

A teenage girl, talking about her health, says with characteristic cheerfulness that she used to drink several glasses of milk a day (with gusto, we are led to believe, from her affect). She goes on to say, with unmistakable disgust, that she has slashed her intake of milk since she learned from a friend that milk is three percent blood (yuck! she makes a disgust face). She explains that farmers do not milk their cows the old-fashioned way (she pantomimes pulling teats) but use machines, which are rough on the cows' udders, which then bleed into the milk. Her disgust centers on the image of milk adulterated with blood, which she cannot bear to consume.

The girl's disgust is about taste, which is sense experience. But is it about *actual* taste? Likely not. The milk in her glass is the same as it always has been and should taste the same, if taste depends on composition. Any difference in taste is not owed to the milk's actual content, but to her *idea* of what the milk contains. The idea of bloody milk leads to rejection, with an implication of vileness if the contaminated milk touches the lips. The disgust may not even be mediated by specific taste *imagery;* asked about the taste of the milk, the girl might recognize that it actually tastes the same and that it really is the *idea* of tasting something made of milk and blood that disgusts her. For some, though, there may be much blurring of the distinction between what blood-laced milk is and how it tastes, such that they would insist the milk tastes different (and perhaps, then, it actually does—taste being ultimately subjective, but this is a philosophical question for another time).

The young woman who shared this reaction with me was not prone to disgust. It did not seem to be a prominent organizer of her experience or a character bent, so why did she choose to present this disgust image when she did? What came into my thoughts at the time was the brutality that then characterized her relationship with her mother. Though her conscious concern was entirely on her mother's aggression toward her, the battered cow image suggested to me the possibility she felt some guilt over her frequent assertions that she hated her mother and would like nothing better than to have mother and father divorce or have mother disappear by some other means; she even talked of killing her mother. I knew for a fact that her father had recently spoken to her about how hurt he felt by her attitude toward him. Though she claimed she could not "care less" about either parent's feelings, she was sensitive to images of injured animals and babies and other living things, and that tenderness suggested some latent empathy for her suffering parents.

This young girl's disgust at milk mixed with blood is interesting as an historically suggestive reaction. The symbolization of life through blood is a theme in early Hebraic religion and a basis for koshering meat, which involves draining the blood, which must not be consumed.[1] Also, flesh—even drained of its blood—must not be mixed with milk, because such mixing signifies the cooking of the mother's young in the mother's own milk.[2] These various prohibitions exhort the honoring of life (symbolized both by blood and by the fruit of the mother's womb—the offspring) and the avoidance of destructive acts toward symbols of life. Disgust that results from violations of dietary proscriptions presumably has nothing to do with taste or smell except to the extent that such sensory processing is emotionally laden secondary to the meaning of the food dish.[3] The conditioning process resembles the conditioning that occurs when food causes actual physical discomfort. A food that produces food poisoning accompanied by nausea and vomiting (or a food incorrectly held responsible for such illness) may be regarded as disgusting over many years. My own experience includes an aversion developed to a previously enjoyed fruit juice after a daylong colonoscopy preparation that required consuming little else. Overconsumption of the single sweet food was probably wedded with apprehension about the procedure; the pairing produced an enduring aversion.

In the example of the girl who was disgusted by milk, there is something specious about disgust's tie to information from the taste buds. The same holds true for the relationship between disgust and our other senses. Disgust does not primarily contemn the taste itself, the skin sensation itself, the visual image itself. It shares with other emotions the habit of responding primarily to the meanings of things, yet it is unique in its heightened tendency to clothe those meanings in sense imagery, which suggests physical contact in the encounter between self and Other. Comparing disgust with anger, for example, we see the heightened role of sense impressions in disgust, which tells us that central to disgust, in many cases, is the idea of the self-boundary (and its bodily equivalent) breached concretely by something material. The major exception to this rule of bodily and sensory imagery comes from moral disgust. Disgust's unique emphasis on the material world also accounts

---

[1] "But flesh with the life thereof which is the blood thereof shall ye not eat" (Gen. 9).

[2] "Thou shall not seethe a kid in its mother's milk" (Exod. 33:19, 34:26; Deut. 14:21).

[3] Haidt et al. (1997) researched disgust elicitors in a number of cultures and found both commonality and important differences.

for its defensive utility in that it diverts our attention from a core disturbing idea to a material event.

Exceptions may exist to the insistence on meaning before response, but they are small in number. Unusually strong sensation likely stimulates emotional response in the absence of meaning, but preexisting meaning, or the meaning that rapidly accrues to strong stimuli, may dictate the pole of the emotional response. For example, fecal odors may be inherently interesting, but not disgusting. They may become disgusting to many at a certain point in development due to the weight of societal negativity. Haidt et al. (1997) cite Malson's (1964) study of feral humans in whom no evidence of disgust was found. Yet studies of socialized adults across cultures uniformly find disgust toward feces. A similar interplay of nature and nurture may hold for a number of other substances, for example, vomit and slime, which probably would make the short list of finalists for things likely to disgust universally. But is such disgust innate or is it interest alone that is inborn, with disgust appearing as a negatively judging overlay on the natural interest? A possible developmental pathway features interest as the earliest, innate response, with some further elaboration of that interest (moving toward disgust in some cases) as a genetic predisposition that is likely to express itself in the presence of particular social experiences. Genetic predisposition, maturation, and social learning all may converge.

A brief example of olfactory disgust and its dependence on ideas comes by way of a woman client who had told me many times of her sensitivity to odors and of her tendency to become ill following exposure to scents and chemicals. She was unable generally to use my small, windowless waiting room due to the poor air quality she noted. She sometimes needed to leave work or other settings if painting had been done recently or someone entered wearing perfume. Her response to bothersome odors was disgust complicated by affront at being assaulted by these odors. She prompted me and others to affirm this sense of injury and outrage.

On one occasion, she had an unusual crossing of paths with a male client—a friendly, extroverted man—who was exiting through the waiting room. When she entered the office, she exclaimed, "Whoa, was your last client a doctor?" (paraphrased, based on my memory). "Why that?" I asked, not understanding her inference. "Some pretty heavy chemical odors in here!" she said, then backed off from her inquiry by indicating she knew I could not tell her about another

The Body and Mind of Disgust

client's profession. I had not perceived any odor during my previous session, and still could not.

My client seemed startled by her encounter with the scents filling the air, and curious—almost amazed—as well as a bit annoyed. My overall sense was that she felt both excited and unsettled by the pressure to integrate the idea of a friendly male client leaving the office, but she acknowledged only the man's scent, not the man himself. She seemed on the cusp of adopting a rejecting, hostile, affronted stance by labeling him a repulsive-smelling doctor (she had very ambivalent feelings toward medical doctors, and perhaps toward psychologists this day as well), yet her curiosity and interest also were attendant and influential, so she walked the line between responses.

This example portrays a complex amalgamation of responses to odor, not a simple, unambiguous disgust. I cannot speak to what my client actually was smelling, but I was reminded, through this incident, of my overall sense that she used sensitivity to odor at times to communicate a discomfort over being part of the rough and tumble of intimate human society (see Fima's disgust at his father's odors in chapter 6). Earlier in the treatment, she had chosen to portray herself as a victim of human society, one who had been battered and rejected until she retreated to the fringes of sociability. Later in the work, it became clear how strong her wishes to enter fully into social and academic life remained. The smelly-man encounter occurred well into the treatment, when she was much less inclined reflexively to render herself a victim of any stimulating experience, including that of a person-generated odor.

Another olfactory disgust example comes from my own experience of noting in my house the acrid odor of spraying cats associated with the presence around the house and increasingly inside the house (by way of an open cat door) of a stray male cat interacting with my own two cats. I found myself disgusted by the odor, very attentive to it, and busy sniffing out its perimeter: "Were they spraying in the house or just in the garage and the scent carried into the house on my cats or the air? Wasn't that same smell in my car now, after I'd parked it in the garage?" Because the odor was beginning to bother me so, I stopped to consider why it disgusted me. Was it the smell itself or something in the associational network? The smell I found unpleasant. It was strong and sharp. When present, it filled the air. The associations, though, seemed to account for a good portion of the disgust. I associated the smell with the type of bad-smelling house that people visit, then later comment to their friends about its disagreeable odor, presumably indicative of poor housekeeping or hygiene. I connected the smell particularly with old peoples' houses, looked on with contempt by the young, and saw it as emblematic of a person growing older who is oblivious to the odors in which time and use have steeped her home. Clearly, a person whose house exuded such an odor would impress no one. I also knew the tenacity of such feline smells, so that one might be stuck with them indefinitely and against one's wishes, despite efforts to combat them. It would be a losing battle: me against nature, age, and complacency.

This example, like those preceding, suggests that the sensory richness of disgust experiences does its work primarily by stirring meaningful associations, which tend to carry us into a finite number of content areas, some of which are examined in this book. For instance, my disgust association to an ambivalently regarded environment of grandmotherly odors easily links with innumerable other disgust images people generate associated with someone's body being too close and sensorily present. Underlying the anxiety and disgust about the too smelly, too loud, too decrepit, or too blemished body often is a concern about being overly intimate emotionally with the other person, or too identified with her or him with respect to human frailties.

Haidt et al. (1997) conclude, "Disgust is triggered not primarily by the sensory properties of an object, but by ideational concerns about *what it is,* or *where it has been*" (p. 2). I agree with this statement; my agreement, however, does not contradict the idea that disgust is more closely tied to the senses than are other emotions. Even when disgust is ultimately about the identity and history of something we encounter, our encounter occurs through the senses, or at least we believe that it does. An example of a belief that misconstrues the nature of the encounter would be the young woman's idea that the bloody milk disgusts her. She likely would have some sense of the milk having a vile taste even though she had previously consumed the same type of milk with gusto. Whatever the "objective reality" of the taste (a slippery concept when discussing sense experience), the experience is of disgusting sensation.

One young woman talked at length of feeling "grossed out" by a number of images of body damage or disturbance. The long chain of associations began with a recollection of witnessing people at a Red Cross blood draw. Seeing the blood leaving the body disgusted her because of the "idea of your blood going out of your body" and also the sight of it. The image and the idea were inextricable. The idea would have lost power without the image, but the image would have meant nothing without the attendant meanings. Her associations led on to childbirth (another body boundary violation) and to bodily aberrations such as removing ovaries from a cancer patient before radiation, then reimplanting them but in the patient's arm where they would escape treatment damage. The young woman's conversation continued to images of infinite space and alien life-forms and to existential questions, for example, who created God? These existential considerations troubled her, too, but rather than disgusting her, like the bodily frailties, these dwarfing realities "creeped her out." Thus, the ideas and sensory input centering on immediate, physical vulnerability and images of disturbed body function led to disgust while ideas about the small place humans hold in the cosmic scheme led to a patently fearful state that seemed closest to terror.

We move now to touch and to another disgust incident that was entirely dependent on meaning and context. A friend walking with me in the woods, far from houses and other walkers, encountered a small tassel of fluffy, bright white material hanging from a shrub at about eye level. She responded to it with pleasure, reaching out to touch it and trying in her conversation to decipher its origin and identity. She thought for a moment that it was a rabbit's foot and believed someone had hung it there as a marker of some sort. When I said the wind might have wrapped it around the branch because it had been extremely windy for several days, she rejected that supposition, seeming not to like it, and said a person surely had hung it there. Again, she seemed to like the sensory quality of the item and her fantasy that it signified something—perhaps some communication from one person to others, something auspicious suspended there so bright and white and unexpected in the drab winter woods. Suddenly—her hand still stroking the fluff—her eyes widened and her hand recoiled and she exclaimed, "Do you know what this is? Oh, yuck, it's a tampon. Look. Look. It's like a ..." She became tongue-tied, started to shake in the air the fingers that had touched the thing, then wiped them off on her clothes—though her fingers were dry—and muttered about getting some awful disease as if the awfulness of the revelation of what a personal, bodily thing she'd touched (something intimate to another's body) made the thing literally sickening.

As with the previous example, the complete shift in this woman's attitude toward an object when the object itself had not changed—only her conception of it—demonstrates that the disgust follows not from the sense experience itself but from the person's conception of what is being encountered by way of the senses. In this case sight, too, played a role in the person's experience of the object. She had in fact been drawn to it by sight. But touch mediated her experience of its value and touch limned her sense of vulnerability.

The following example of disgust elicited mainly by sight lacks the feature of sudden reinterpretation of a familiar sense experience that characterized the tampon incident and the bloody milk rejection. Instead, it shows disgust as a response to a change in the sensory data available to process, which leads to turmoil in the observer. In this example, it appears that the visual event—the picture before the eyes—is judged disgusting because of its departure from the experience of what is familiar and healthy.

An adolescent girl reacted during a session to a "cracking" in her shoulder, and to the thought that her shoulder had slipped out of place, by immediately associating to a childhood experience on the playground. She had seen a young friend dislocate her arm when she grabbed the pole supporting the swing set as she swung past. My client made a disgust face while describing the memory and tried in words and expression to convey her sharp, youthful disgust at the image of the arm hanging lifeless at the playmate's side. When I asked if the sight scared her, she said firmly it was disgusting, not scary, because these dislocations happened to the friend from time to time and the friend had reportedly become matter-of-fact about them, thus stirring little anxiety in those around her. My client stressed that her response was disgust at the weirdness and awfulness of the sight. As in the tampon story, there are elements here of sudden change (but this time, in the stimulus itself) and of something odd, unexpected, and out of place. Despite her disclaimer, my young client might have reacted with flagrant anxiety on the playground and in the consulting room had her character style not discouraged that. She chose to emphasize elements of her experience that promoted disgust. Her disgust was an expression of her struggle with regard to integrating an unfamiliar body form.

The client's childhood experience reminded me of my own experience, on a number of occasions, of stopping circulation to an arm by sleeping on it, then waking to touch a completely numbed limb (which had no proprioception whatsoever) and experience it as an alien thing—most akin to a dead body—lying in the bed where my arm should be. I remember the experience of disgust touching the limb, which seemed rubbery and lifeless. Anxiety arose as well—mostly centered on the pain to come—but clearly disgust at encountering this odd, misplaced "thing" (like the tampon in the woods or the dislocated, limp arm of the little girl) that I could not integrate as ordinary experience. This challenge to integration is important in many instances of disgust. Often the person is torn between a need or desire to integrate something surprising and an instinct to reject it via emphatic disgust.

The tampon incident illustrates a struggle to make sense of something "out of place." The words of the tampon-toucher help to make this point (used with permission from and with thanks to the source):

> As for the Tampax [tampon] episode ... had I known from the outset that the object hanging from the tree was a Tampax, I think I would still have been put off by it, but also maybe perversely amused. However, it was totally unexpected and out of context. There we were having a nice walk through the woods on a crisp, nearly-spring afternoon, we noticed what appeared to be a tag hanging from a tree and went to check it out. Then I thought it was a rabbit's foot, and I reached up and stroked *the thing* [italics added] with my BARE HAND and suddenly I knew what it really was. EEEWWWWWW (or however you spell that sound we make when something is really yucky)! The Tampax turned out to be clean, but my initial reaction reflected the notion that it might have been used and that I'd touched it. Dirty? Diseased? Something like that, I guess. When I was growing up, menstrual things were, if not shameful, then at least very private. Never even mentioned with men or boys around. (How things have changed, eh?) I remember as a freshman in college that one poor girl was ostracized for a whole semester because her dorm roommate told all the rest of us that she had left a used Tampax out on the dresser. That was considered an unpardonably gross social/hygienic sin. So, surprise + physical contact + "dirty" connotations (two kinds of dirty?) led to the disgust, perhaps.

The woman's wish to dissociate from the tampon by way of disgust rests on her experience of the contact as threatening to her sense of social acceptability (which depends in part on cleanliness and health). The struggle is evident even in linguistic structures: for example, the tampon suddenly becomes "the thing" (a distancing locution) when she gets wind of what it might be. By way of her story of the girl ostracized for a full semester at a vulnerable time in life, she lets us know that she understands the social risks of not taking distance from such a thing. Her efforts to integrate her regrettable tampon-touch show in her representing of the girl in the dorm as a "poor girl" (a hapless victim, not a fundamentally disgusting person), and in her calming herself enough to examine the tampon further and establish its cleanliness.

The example also illustrates Rozin and Fallon's (1987) concept of contagion, which makes the history of an object important because an object whose history involves touching something disgusting (a stranger's private parts, in this case) becomes a purveyor of disgustingness to anyone who touches it. In a therapy session, discussing a hated, patronizing parent figure of whom he could not rid himself (the person seemed clinging and omnipresent), a man commented on his nemesis' willingness to come to work ill with stomach flu and risk giving the bug to unsuspecting clients during psychological testing sessions. He made a comment about all the objects handed back and forth during a testing and said, "He touches the stuff . . . they touch it . . . yuck!" I noted the quick disgust reference because it managed to convey so succinctly and well the unpleasantness and threat contained in the image of touching another whose essence offends. Such uneasiness resides in the thought that the Other's awfulness could convey itself to the self via touch. Though my client stressed his general hatred of stomach flu (as the worst kind of sickness), I suspected that the germs of this particular man were especially vile because of who he was in my client's eyes.

A flurry of disgust responses in the *Ann Arbor News* (2003) regarding a "naturist" group's use of the local recreation center illustrated well the principle of contagion of the disgusting. A local columnist's (Mathis, 2003) story about the subject was entitled, "Nude rec has a certain 'ick' factor." She went on to share her fantasy of using "equipment that hours earlier had been sat upon by a naked rump." She turned her attention directly to the part of the body most associated with dirtiness in order to convey her anxiety about contagion. Some of the letters to the editor in the days following the story emphasized less the grossness of body contact than the contagious moral disgustingness of the nudists' behavior. One person predicted a plague of moral sickness, characterized by such depravities as incest and rape.

Returning to the notion of a disgusting, alienated "thing," we see in the arm dislocation story that the arm is treated as "the thing" to be

The Body and Mind of Disgust

rejected or integrated. The arm is an aberration—something limp, dead, and dysfunctional. The girl's disgust is not centered entirely on the arm itself in the way that the tampon-toucher's disgust centers on the tampon; that is because the girl's visual comfort would not be restored simply by removing the awful arm (as would be the case with the tampon). The dislocation situation is inherently more complex because the limp condition of the arm also disturbs the gestalt of the body, therefore, both armless body and bodiless arm would have to be removed or corrected in order to set things right. The young woman's discussion of her early experience evinces less inclination toward integration than the older woman's does. She presents instead a steady determination to reject the disgusting image and to use her rejection to communicate powerfully to me the depth of her uneasiness about something. I say "something" because the associational field was not clear in this case. It did not seem likely that the point of the story began and ended with the dislocated arm.

These thoughts are conjectural, but I wondered if part of the broader associative network stimulating the younger woman's recall of the odd and troubling arm might have been her adolescent struggle with images of boys' penises in different states and the link between that whole arena and imagery of her own body's vulnerabilities (suggested by the "cracking" in her shoulder that set off the chain of associations). The older woman simply encountered the tampon in the woods—she didn't imagine it—and she gives us part of her associational fabric by way of her dormitory memory. The younger woman seemed to use the occasion of a momentary body sensation in her shoulder, during the treatment hour, to transport herself and me back to the playground event, which she presented without blatant clues to "why now?" or to associative links. My notion about the possible link to sexuality came in part from observing her shy approach to sexuality over a long period of time, and to observing similarly masked approaches to the male body in other girls.

Adolescents' approaches to sexual content are often juxtaposed with soliloquies about minor events of their own bodies (a broken fingernail, a scratch, noise from a moving joint, a mosquito bite). These soliloquies occur with great frequency in adolescent treatment and seem to require of the therapist a sympathetic, engaged response that helps the girl to experience her body as valuable and sound and seems also to help the girl see that the therapist is attuned to her sense of body vulnerability, yet not alarmed about it. In my experience, double jointedness—connoting perhaps the tension between flexibility and falling apart—is frequently commented on by adolescent girls. I make these points, however speculative, mainly to convey that some kind of associational network usually plays a part in our determination that a stimulus is disgusting, and certain webs of associations characterize particular developmental periods.

The element of surprise appears in a number of the disgust incidents cited. Surprise is not essential to disgust but occurs frequently because it adds to the challenge in comfortably integrating an occurrence into one's self-experience. The walker in the woods accommodated herself to the pleasant idea of a rabbit's foot someone had hung as a token of some sort. She approached the item seeking more than visual contact with it, because it seemed pleasing. Suddenly, while fingering it and feeling its texture, she had to accommodate to the idea of something intimate to a stranger's body, linked with that person's flesh, her insides, and her sexuality. She needed to make a radical reversal in her attunement to the experience. The same can be said of the child whose companion's arm suddenly changes into something odd and dysfunctional. Had these people known in advance what they would be experiencing, they might have adjusted to the reality without needing the radical rejection disgust signifies.

Themes of things that surprise and things that are out of place (often the reason for surprise) paint pictures of occurrences robbed of their usual contexts. An ovary implanted in an arm is out of place and was tagged as something disgusting by the young woman mentioned earlier. A passage from Franzen's (2001) novel, *The Corrections,* conveys the importance of context beautifully:

> Like a toothbrush in the toilet bowl, like a dead cricket in the salad, like a diaper on the dinner table, this sickening conundrum confronted Enid: that it might actually have been preferable for Denise to go ahead and commit adultery, better to sully herself with a momentary selfish pleasure, better to waste a purity that every decent young man had the right to expect from a prospective bride, than to marry Emile [p. 121].

Vulnerability to disgust when things are out of place appears to depend on a number of factors. To the extent that the item itself (the ovary, the cricket) has unsettling features, placing it in a familiar context under a reasonable rubric (the abdomen or the backyard) has desensitizing power. Removing it from such context heightens sensitivity to its discomfiting aspects.

Another way that odd juxtapositions evoke disgust is by triggering fantasies of contamination, simply because something in the wrong place is a contaminant by definition. If the particular contamination signifies bodily danger, disgust is even more likely. Franzen's triad of toothbrush in toilet bowl, dead cricket in salad, and diaper on dinner table, all fit this model since all involve something germy in contact with something to be placed in the mouth. Peculiar juxtapositions stir various other unsettling fantasies because they force the mind to bridge an unfamiliar gap, therefore the mind becomes active and integrative and in that creative state opens the person to anxiety and thus disgust. Rather than take something for granted as part of a familiar gestalt, the mind has to question, if only for a second, "What does this thing have to do with this other?" Artists use elements out of place to stir integrative, analytic, and emotional response and, in so doing, risk provoking disgust. Picasso's cubist representations of human forms are examples of this kind of artistic reach.

If an odd juxtaposition results from someone's intention, that choice contributes to disgust because it activates feelings about people who choose to offend or to experiment with regard to propriety. Artists and nonartists can stimulate disgust through this mechanism. Differential responses to nudity illustrate the dynamic. A nurse seeing an obese, unfit person who is asked to disrobe in a physician's office will be much less inclined toward disgust than she would be seeing the same person voluntarily show herself in a bikini on the beach. The beach seems an inappropriate context for nudity for an unsightly body and the woman is faulted for choosing it.

We have touched on disgust in response to smell, taste, sight, and touch. Of the five senses, sound least often disgusts. Touch, smell, and taste suggest a stimulus close at hand and thus readily threatening to the self in a variety of ways. Sight connects us with occurrences near and far. Even the sight of something distant can disgust us, likely because vision delivers a great wealth and variety of information, some of which may stimulate the remaining senses, so that the impression made by a visual image can be powerful, invasive, and threatening to the body, thus to the self. Imagine, for example, the sight of a body with odd, warty, discolored growths marking the skin, or a photo of the same. The visual image may elicit a sense impression of peculiar texture—were the growths touched—and an olfactory impression of body odors, as well as a sense of threat to one's own body, self, and social standing posed by the possibility of things going unpredictably awry with one's physiognomy.

Sound does disgust, though less often than the other senses. The lower incidence may reflect the fact that the information carried by sound, though abundant, often is impersonal. Sound gives us tremendous amounts of information about the weather, for example, or the functioning of machinery or traffic flow. Disgust enters the world of sound when the information carried is animal or person-related, or at least organic. If we think of sounds people make when they are ill (sniffs, rattling coughs, passing diarrhea or vomiting), we may find ourselves in the realm of disgust. The same may occur imagining sounds associated with excessive, ill-timed, or ill-considered sexual passions (cooing pigeons delight some people, but disgust others), or sounds considered ill-mannered (belches and farts, the smacking sounds and sniffs of a dog vigorously licking its anus), or imagining certain voices (those linked to "low class" functioning, or to particular people we have found annoying) or to certain physical characteristics of speech (the person spits when speaking, or slurs words that should be distinct, or uses a pretentious accent). In all these examples, we are dealing with personal information communicated through sound, often through sounds made by the human body or some animal body. The sounds are made by the body and carry information about the being and what the being signifies to the listener (he sounds obnoxious; she sounds ill and contagious; her speech is droolly and a mess; he smacks his lips like a pig when he eats).

We see that disgust often is our reaction to another's being (often experienced by way of that Other's bodily presence and received via our senses). This generalization holds true if we turn back to the proximal senses, for example, taste. Upon closer scrutiny we find that many of the tastes people find disgusting (not just distasteful) are associated in their minds with body waste products or specific body parts (pigs' feet), organs (brain, kidney), or types (insect bodies). The body is crucial as the stimulus for disgust, as the means for taking in via sense imagery what seems disgusting, and as the mechanism for expressing the feeling of revulsion that is disgust. Where the body (human or nonhuman) is not involved in generating the sense experience, disgust is less likely.

Disgust as a response to another's bodily presence and functioning is best understood as a subset of the fundamental stimulus for disgust, as introduced in chapter 1: risk to one's experience of being substantial and valuable. The bodily functioning of others can endanger the self in a variety of ways. If the other person's body becomes too much a focus of attention (it is too active, too conspicuous, too smelly), then I may be dwarfed comparatively. If the Other's body seems too gross and animalistic, by association (since we are kin) I may feel demeaned. If the Other's body impinges too much through noises, movements, odors, or appearance, I may feel vulnerable to penetration or permeation, which may be welcome in some respects but always threatens the self with loss of integrity. Another's stimulating physical presence will be highly interesting (we are kin and are drawn by interest to each other). If the body is too stimulating, through its physicality, I may be drawn out of myself, which can bring the pleasure of love and fascination but also the risk of loss of self. If the body of another is too interesting, I may be lured into intimate contact that sometimes brings social disapproval or disapproval from the conscience, society's representative within.

Particularly likely to disgust are body orifices, especially those used actively in exchanging material with the world outside. Thus, the mouth or anus would be more disgusting than the eye or ear. People can feel disgust toward open parts of their own bodies and especially toward others' orifices, which weep and discharge substances that can contact and threaten the body or the self (by way of the body). The disgustingness of these openings seems linked to the flow of material across the body–self boundary and also to the moisture that promotes such flow and promotes concurrently a fertile environment for proliferating microorganisms. Thus the mouth connotes at times a miniature swamp within the self and the anus a sewer. Genital organs introduce special problems because they carry crucial procreative substances (that may violate the self-boundary cataclysmically in creating an altogether new being) and they also sit beside the excretory parts and are easily confused with them, so it is easy to feel (and sometimes quite correct to believe) that the genitals are carrying waste between persons. The mouth also has special problems of multifunctionality: it is the source of speech, the site of intimate exchange through kissing, and the organ of ingestion. Speech seems fairly innocent of eliciting disgust toward the mouth, unless one invokes the idea of "dirty speech." Because the physical mouth is treated as a source of disgusting speech that is more aptly attributed to the mind, many a child has had his or her mouth washed out with soap and water for the dirty words therewith produced.

Sexual contact and eating implicate the physical mouth. In kissing, the sensitivity to touch of the lips, tongue, and mouth combines with the meanings we attribute to such contact to give us pleasure (if the circumstances are right; meaning, as usual, trumps nerve endings). Eating is particularly interesting as a disgust source, especially when witnessed in others, because eating can involve the deliberate pulverization of a specific and recognizable thing (an apple, a sandwich, a nut) so that it becomes a pulp that is both aftermath (of the food item that was) and precursor (of nutrients that supply energy or tissue mass). We like others to keep their mouths shut when chewing so that we are protected visually (and, thus, mentally) from witnessing the moistening and unmaking of familiar forms.

Other aspects of the body that readily evoke disgust include signs of aging—such as sagging or spotted flesh, shapeless bulges, and deformed joints. The decrepitude of old age is especially likely to disgust, but maturation can disgust as well. Young children, or pubertal children, often are disgusted by sexually mature bodies. Pubertal children sprouting their first pubic hairs not infrequently react with disgust. The same disgust can appear toward symbols of the mature body, such as a girl's first adult-style nylon underpants, meant to replace the cotton undergarments of childhood. A later chapter on health and illness will also consider these bodily disgusts.

Subtypes of Disgust

Determining the boundaries of any emotion state is difficult. In life, emotions are not so well delineated as they appear in many formal presentations. Thinking about disgust, I have tried a number of approaches to categorization. One approach defined a prototypical disgust reaction that would include a strong impulse to seek bodily distance from something viewed as unacceptable for bodily contact because it is thought to possess contagious badness. The impulse manifests on the face and in a mixed emotional-ideational state. Other forms of disgust would be deviations or partial manifestations of this core because they exhibit only a portion of the full syndrome.

Problems arose in using this approach, which isolates one relatively circumscribed set of experiences as the core emotion from which other experiences diverge. What would we do with *moral* disgust, which shifts emphasis from body reaction to the social self recoiling? Moral disgust can be as emphatic an emotion as more body-centered disgust and it exists, as a major form of the emotion, across cultures. I would not want to argue that a person disgusted by someone's choice to drive drunk after killing a child while intoxicated was less profound an emotion than the disgust of a person looking at a strand of blood floating on the surface of an egg yolk. Even if moral disgust derives developmentally from more bodily disgust (which is possible), or appears later in development (which is likely), I am uncomfortable viewing bodily disgust as prototypical. Aesthetic disgust also loses its standing as true disgust, using this approach.

My current best effort at delineating the disgust terrain is to identify three elements that must be present for me to label something "full" or "true" disgust. First, the person must identify as a target of emotion something outside the self, or existing as a subset of the self. Second, part of the moment's experience should consist in labeling that "Other" as bad. Third, the badness must motivate a desire to seek distance, which implies that contact is threatening: one element in the threat is the feeling that the badness transfers to the core self through contact. Within this broad tripartite field, experiences will differ along several dimensions. Images of direct bodily contact with the stimulus (through the nose, mouth, or skin) range from negligible to central. Actual body response (vomiting, disgusted facial expression, wiping the skin) varies in occurrence, intensity and particulars. Belief in the moral and/or aesthetic offensiveness of the stimulus ranges from central to absent. Intensity of condemnation as "bad" extends from mild (even amused) to hate-filled, with the most hate-filled condemnations partnering with strong moral emphasis.

This categorizing approach also makes a place for what I will call "partial disgust" in order to denote experiences that contain enough of the above elements to suggest disgust, yet the full complement is not in evidence. In these cases, the context of the response sometimes suggests the probability of disgust and adds to the impression that some disgust-like dynamic is expectable. For example, vomiting in response to a mutilated body or to binge eating raises questions about disgust that are not raised by vomiting when ill with influenza. Partial disgust has a number of incarnations due to the many possible variations regarding which elements of true disgust are present, which absent. I have identified several, but others likely could be defined.

One variety of partial disgust I call "borrowed disgust." The term is meant to suggest that the person who avows disgust is asserting that emotion in order to harmonize with a group to which he or she belongs; however, he does not feel actual disgust. If the person comes into contact with the "Other" whom he or she asserts is disgusting, no revulsion actually occurs. Other emotions might stir, such as anxiety about allowing close contact with someone or something that the group reviles.

In many instances of borrowed disgust, an outside authority representing the larger community and seeking to speak for that community has issued a prohibition against contact. The outside authority—perhaps possessed of the inflamed passions of true disgust, moral type—prescribes aversion. Such a prescription may or may not result in an experience of full disgust in the person whose hand or heart comes into direct contact with the indicted Other, but the pressure for an actual or borrowed response is felt. The greatest threat to the individual may be the fear that whoever engages in reprobate contacts will become vile to the community. The danger is in becoming morally disgusting oneself and therefore ashamed or self-disgusted. To embrace the assigned condemnation brings inclusion in the community.

An Orthodox Jew steeped in the Levitican prohibitions against foods and behaviors deemed unclean and abominable may incorporate this teaching deeply and feel full disgust and the onset of retching at the sight and smell of a plate of pork. Alternatively, he may feel only annoyance that the "traif" has been offered to him. When he says, "take it away, it is disgusting," little of actual disgust may be present; the absence does not suggest psychological defense but indicates an unemotional internalization of the Levitican prohibitions.

"Emblematic disgust" implies the use of disgust words when the potential exists for full disgust, however, that emotion is not occurring in the present moment. For example, a man refers to a political candidate as disgusting in his views, but his condemnation is emotionless. Later he hears a speech by the candidate that arouses him to full disgust.

The final two varieties of partial disgust both represent defensive short-circuiting of intense affect. The potential for strong feeling is evident, but the feeling is bypassed. The question in regard to all the partial disgust displays is whether a fuller experience of the emotion would emerge with a shift to an emotionally less defended position. In some instances, were the person to move toward fuller articulation of feeling, true disgust would emerge. In other instances, another stressful emotion such as anger, anxiety, or dread might develop, however, unlike with borrowed disgust, the potential for true disgust exists. The two defensive varieties of partial disgust I call "body disgust" and "ideational disgust." Ideational disgust is a form of isolation of affect; body disgust exemplifies somatization.

Ideational disgust involves *ideas* about something being disgusting, abhorrent, abominable, vile, and so forth, but some element of full disgust is missing. Either the effort to seek distance from the stimulus is absent or the clear indication of a well defined Other is lacking. A man abandoned by an alcoholic mother as a young child tells his girlfriend her drinking is "kind of disgusting." He smiles and laughs when identifying his disgust and makes no effort to distance himself from the girlfriend; instead, he shares her drink.

Body disgust involves body signifiers of emotion, for example, vomiting, gagging, nausea; these occur in a context suggestive of disgust. For example, faced with a plate of greasy food, an anorexic vomits. Asked what she feels, she says only that she felt like vomiting. Novelist Myla Goldberg (2000) created a subtle portrait of a woman who has constructed a shrine—captivating, complex, and beautiful—that reflects her childhood love for the view through a treasured kaleidoscope. With its depiction of body and heart split off from mind and head, Goldberg's portrayal offers us a route into consideration of the body of disgust.

Goldberg's character, Miriam, has closed herself off from self and family by way of obsessive-compulsive personality traits (cleanliness, industry, isolation of affect), however, her underground life preserves a core of love for self and Other expressed by way of compulsive theft of small items used to build her hidden shrine. Her social personality is constructed around anal defenses that Abraham (1921) sees as protective against anal-eroticism and enforced by disgust at anal messiness and excitement. She prefers, for example, that her underwear be washed twice before returning to her drawer. But by way of her underground life, Miriam enters messy, earthy, tawdry realms that would shock her social self. In these secret realms (including other people's houses, which she enters in secret), she locates the treasures she uses to assemble her shrine, but at times she "wakes" from the altered state in which she sniffs out her treasures. Once awake, she feels the impact of the dirty world into which she has burrowed, and a collision occurs between her compulsive social self and her underground search for a sense of home. In such moments, we see her overcome with vomiting impulses in relation to tawdry domesticity.

Her vomiting impulse is not full disgust in that the emphasis is on bodily separation from things a person might find gross, but she exhibits no awareness of feeling "grossed out." Her impulses exemplify the body of disgust because complex affect is circumvented. They also show us the intricacy and variability of emotional reactions, and the difficulty of fitting them into a scheme, in that her bodily disgust signifier (vomiting) may point less strongly to defense against full disgust than to failed effort to mobilize full disgust in defense against a deep state of vulnerability. We see her moving directly from vomiting to an acute awareness of vulnerability, with no full disgust emotion ever surfacing.

In the passage to follow, Miriam has entered a stranger's home, ignoring its plates of dried, crusted food doubling as ashtrays, its mold-filled refrigerator, its cockroaches and ubiquitous disarray; she is a heat-seeking missile pursuing the warmth of whatever object will reveal itself as her treasure:

> She finds what she has come for in the bedroom. It's the only ashtray without cigarette butts in it, a piece of pressed copper bearing a cameo profile of a woman's face. It feels warm to her touch.
>
> With the object in her possession, the safety of her shell cracks. The staleness of the air, the dust, and the grime seep under her skin. She is just able to make it to the toilet before throwing up. She is suddenly certain that the barest contact with any surface will cancel her out, dissolving her as surely as a snail in salt. . . . The house has become a crude stranger standing too close on a crowded bus. It presses against her, insinuating itself into her most guarded places [p. 137].

Once having found her treasure, Miriam wakes to her usual bodily impulses toward sterile cleanliness, as well as to a great sense of vulnerability of the self should the distancing mechanisms fail. She does not, however, feel disgust, only the need to vomit. We are shown this single moment in time operating emblematically as it expresses her larger dread of human psychological and physical intimacy. This instance of body disgust may be an example of inability to achieve defensive

The Body and Mind of Disgust

disgust, or of inclination to go direct to the deeper feeling, vulnerability, without calling on defensive disgust. Could Miriam muster full disgust, she might feel less afflicted by vulnerability. Whether this particular trajectory would be followed in daily life, or just in the mind of a gifted novelist, remains an open question.

In her novel *Almost,* Elizabeth Benedict (2001) describes a woman seeking her lost dog, Henry, who may hold the key to her husband's sudden death. She finds the dog in the morgue and goes to view its remains. Her response provides another example of the body of disgust:

> Before I knew it, all of him, lying stiffly on his side, like a stuffed dog that has fallen over, appeared before me. His signature ears still pointed like a German shepherd's, and his Florida birthmark floated on his pink-tinted belly the way it always had. But he was lopsided, like a beach toy poorly, unevenly inflated, and his eyes—Jesus God—his eyes were open, shiny and moist, not as if he were alive, but as if they'd been shellacked. The nausea must have been building since Bree first called, churning up my stomach, so within two or three seconds of jerking my head away from the sight of Henry's eyes, blank and glassy, dead and alive, but mostly dead, I felt every part of me convulse, and I did not have a chance to ask where the bathroom was before I vomited all over my hands, which had sprung to my mouth, and began to cry [pp. 207–208].

The woman's body reacts immediately, violently, primitively to a stimulus repellant to her mind. The body reacts before the conscious mind can organize its thoughts yet the mind presumably has made some split-second calculations of the intolerability of the stimulus and the need to be rid of it, symbolically, through disgorging what is in one's body interior. Whether to consider this response defense against full disgust or simply a primitive, almost prepsychological form of disgust is unclear.

In the first of the two fictional passages, Miriam's tandem use of vomiting and of compulsive cleanliness rituals (e.g., handwashing) raises questions about obsessive-compulsive disorder and its possible relationship to disgust. The relationship between disgust and obsessive-compulsive dynamics, as well as disgust and eating disorders will be examined further in a discussion on "disgust syndromes" in chapter 5.

Family, community, or religious values can lead to neurotic conflict when they oppose private impulses. These conflicts may kindle full or partial disgust. Consider the inner experience of a man listening to a preacher articulate the abominable nature of pornography and those who enjoy it. As the listener endorses the preacher's assertions, he allies with the good–bad boundaries the church has established. In doing so, the man—who is at a remove from any actual disgust stimulus—may feel no true revulsion around the images that the preacher presents as sinful. Emblematic disgust may be present, but no genuine disgust, full or partial; perhaps the parishioner's main emotion in the moment is self-satisfaction with his unblemished behavior. The parishioner is building or reinforcing his character by bringing his mind-set into harmony with his preacher's values. If we imagine this man later in the week clicking on an email subject line offering "big girls on horses," then confronting without emotional preparation a visual display of forbidden but engaging erotic images ten inches from his nose, in the privacy of his own study, we may see him plunge into an experience of intense, in-the-moment emotion, possibly pure disgust at the images presented, but perhaps disgust mixed with fascination, or a partial, body-type disgust response such as gagging. The stimulus is in some sense the same as when he was in church, but his relationship to it has changed. Now he is truly tempted and put in conflict between his wish to be the godly individual the preacher would approve and his wish to indulge his sexual curiosity.

To complicate definitional matters, we sometimes see difficult-to-parse blends of the various disgust types. A client discussed a new acquaintance with whom she was considering friendship. She described the woman's excitement about all kinds of touchy-feely group experiences and said, "Is that someone I really want to be friends with? That stuff makes me want to puke." To my mind, this experience comes close to being full disgust, but something is missing. I believe the point of deviation is her isolation of the wish to vomit from the person, the potential friend, about whom she is reacting, because it is the activities, not the friend, that inspire the wish to puke. Another slight shift away from full disgust comes from the client's emphasis on her bodily action-impulse and not her quite evident, palpable emotion. She does not say she feels disgusted or repulsed or sickened, just that she wants to puke. It is as if she is making a move toward partial (body type) disgust but has not quite arrived. Were she to get there, she would just puke; instead, she expresses the wish and her expression speaks openly of the devaluation and condemnation of the Other. Though she is leaning toward body disgust with her emphasis on body reaction, I do not believe she feels actual nausea or retching. She seems to feel the power of the vomiting imagery, which conveys a wish to reject and condemn something. The palpable emotions that accompanied the avowed disgust were anxiety and annoyance, which seemed covered and denied by the stated puking impulse.

Chapter 3
Nature and Its Excesses

miasma—a vaporous exhalation (as of a marshy region or of putrescent matter) formerly believed to contain a substance causing disease) akin to the Greek, *miainein,* to defile.

—*Webster's Third New International Dictionary*

Disgust for natural processes often emerges as an agent in our efforts to separate ourselves from nature. Humankind's ambivalent relationship to nature has been an important concern throughout human history. In analyzing the course of early Christianity, Pagels (1995) contrasts the pagan view that man is part of nature and should regard all that occurs to him as destiny, with the Christian view that man, once baptized, is filled with God's spirit and not subject to the forces that play on the rest of creation. She discusses Tatian, a zealous Christian of the second century, student of Justin, who "adamantly refuses to see himself as merely part of nature" and instead, since his baptism, "identifies with God who stands beyond nature" (p. 132).

Nature routinely challenges us with regard to matters of personal identity and self-boundary. We labor to keep ourselves apart from nature in certain of its forms, to say we are different from this odorous animal, that moldy vegetation, this fetid swampland. But our materials and many of our mechanisms are those of nature's other lifeforms. We, like they, are stuff inside membranes; we, like they, are bags of matter within a skin that is sensitive to penetration and rupture.

The impermanence of our physical form disturbs our efforts to separate ourselves from nature. The particular assemblage of materials that is me or you does not remain constant: our stuff is in motion and undergoes evolution and devolution, mixing with other forms around us. Gravity and age alter body shape and skin surface. Things slip in and out of us and aggravate any notions we may have of fixity or sharp boundary. Even in the prime of life, long before we bother about our eventual return to dust, we simply cannot hold to the notion of a set or constant physical self. And yet we want to believe that each of us is a single, stable being. We set our boundaries and guard energetically those obvious points of entry we can identify. Disgust is the emotional companion to our acts of bodily self-protection. Lewis Thomas (1974) addresses the composition of a human being with the freshness of perspective so characteristic of his work:

> A good case can be made for our nonexistence as entities. We are not made up, as we had always supposed, of successively enriched packets of our own parts. We are shared, rented, occupied. At the interior of our cells, driving them, providing the oxidative energy that sends us out for the improvement of each shining day, are the mitochondria, and in a strict sense they are not ours. They turn out to be little separate creatures, the colonial posterity of migrant prokaryocytes. . . . Mitochondria are stable and responsible lodgers, and I choose to trust them. But what of the other little animals, similarly established in my cells, sorting and balancing me, clustering me together? . . . My cells are no longer the pure line entities I was raised with; they are ecosystems more complex than Jamaica Bay [pp. 3–4].

We must concede we have great difficulty keeping our distance from nature, since (a) we are nature's materials and design and (b) we are neither steady nor firm so we are in no position to know where we begin and where we end.

We have yet another problem in our relationship with nature, one that is psychological. We want to be apart from nature, but then again we do not. We want to draw close and merge and be one with mother earth or father sky but not be threatened with the extinction of our selves. In relation to nature, we experience the fundamental paradox that in order to be enhanced through feeding and nourishment, whether physical or psychic, we must approach closely enough to put our sense of identity at risk.

Our relationship to animal nature brings a special set of difficulties. We attribute a great range of attributes to animals, including some we admire and happily adopt and some we wish not to recognize

Nature and Its Excesses

in ourselves and others. We often feel disgust toward animals when they are portrayed as creatures dominated by their drives, which are seen as base, unruly, and undignified. Thinking from a Darwinian perspective, we can wonder whether differentiating ourselves from other creatures and striving for greater self-discipline than those other species possess offers us some competitive advantage. Surely the human mind provides great competitive advantage and the mind is underminable by the drives. So it would make some sense to think ill of our drives and wish to disidentify with drive-dominated animals, to nurture instead our higher intellectual functioning. But we have to toil, by way of disgust and other emotions, to achieve such disidentification, since we know our own drives to be a force with which to reckon.

In the game of natural selection that all animals play, nature seems to have given us reason to distinguish ourselves from the larger group by forming a conception of ourselves as nonanimal, and that conception then propels behavior that sets us apart from other animals, or so we like to believe. Ironically, Darwinian ideas about adaptation—a concept that absolutely joins us with all other species—can be used to explain our desire to hold ourselves aloof from the animal kingdom. Human alienation from nature is by no means characteristic of all individuals and all cultures, thus we cannot argue that its advantages are great or benefit us more than other adaptations.

Various arguments have been put forth over the years about what types of stimuli disgust us. I approached this topic in the previous chapters from the perspective of body threats versus self-threats and proximal dangers versus distant ones. Those who champion the notion that disgust is fundamentally about ingestion fall into the body-threat camp; they see bad food or its derivatives as the main stuff that disgusts. Darwin (1872) belongs in this group, as do Curtis and Biran (2001), researchers in tropical medicine and biology who tested the hypothesis that disgust operates to motivate taking distance from whatever is dangerously germ-laden, whether it be feces or rotting meat. Psychoanalytic writers have tended to see disgust evolving either from oral ingestive impulses or from anal touching impulses, or both; disgust develops as a counterforce to these impulses and later comes into service to counter sexual impulses. The psychoanalysts thus introduce the notion of active impulses toward contact that must be countered by reactions against such desires.

A psychoanalytic exception to the theory of reaction-formation was Angyal (1941), who argued that animal waste, including our own, is the central offensive aspect of nature and the focus of all disgust reactions. In his view, animal waste threatens not through biological toxicity but because we consider it base and inferior, thus any contact threatens our self-regard. He sees disgust as a mechanism for psychological risk-avoidance that exists independent of any specific attraction to animal waste.

Allan Schore, a psychoanalytic writer who studies self-development, also leaves aside reaction-formation as the central disgust dynamic and examines disgust as a fundamentally *interpersonal* response indicating rejection and devaluation (Schore, 1994, pp. 206–207). The disgusted maternal face is the opposite of the maternal "gleam in the eye" that shows a child love and admiration. It elicits shame, not delight and security, in the child. Schore and other psychoanalytic self psychologists view disgust as part of an affect system that is fundamentally adapted to manage interpersonal engagement. Their interpersonal emphasis promotes attention to parental disgust toward the child and also suggests the importance of intergenerational transmission of disgust through modeling. The primary psychological processes produced by modeling of disgust are likely to be love-based identification and identification with the aggressor, which turns on the fear one will become the object of disgust if one does not share in its display.

Interpersonal transmission of disgust forms a second root, which grows alongside disgust as a direct, unmediated individual response, for example, to frighteningly invasive vitality. Learned and immediate responses will interact over time in modifying disgust experience. Learned disgust may lesson as direct contact with a stimulus reveals its more benign aspect. Or societal pressure to view something with disgust may overcome an early acceptance.

Schore emphasizes disgust learning in his study of the neurobiology of affect. He cites Lewis (1992), who "points out that a disgusted face is widely used in the socialization of children, though parents are often unaware that they are producing it" (p. 206). Repacholi (1998) talks of children learning to regard specific stimuli with disgust by observing indications of the emotion on the mother's face. Children likely learn disgust for feces in this fashion (with a possible contribution from a late-maturing innate response), as suggested by my observation of a toddler imitating her sister's "yuck" response to the younger one's dirty diaper. Children may learn a negative appraisal for the self, the one who produces the disgusting feces, from a loved one's aversive reaction to the child's production, but may also

Nature and Its Excesses 51

learn to control that negative self-evaluation by rejecting what the loved one rejects. That of course becomes a nonsolution if the loved one rejects all of the child's being. Schore emphasizes the link between the disgusted caregiver and the ashamed child. As we will see in a number of cases, a fluid relationship can exist between shame and self-disgust, so that both may characterize the self-appraisal of the child whose parent displays disgust for the child or his or her body products.

At this point, I leave aside the various theories about germ avoidance and those about interpersonal signaling systems in order to consider how our ambivalent relationship to nature factors in determining what disgusts us. I begin with the work of William Miller, professor of law and student of emotion. Miller (1997) noted many of the same features of disgust stimuli that Angyal identified, but did not in the end support the notion that the waste status of organic products ultimately determines their disgustingness. Miller aligns himself instead with those who see disgust as about the self and its security; however, he contributes his own interpretation of what leads to human insecurity in arguing that disgust is regularly elicited when we confront something in our world that displays a superabundance of life or of life-generating capacity. Miller brings to bear a wealth of persuasive examples in support of his surprising contention. Because I would like to build on his argument, I will take some pains to relate it. His own words, from his intriguing chapter, "Thick, Greasy Life," best introduce his thinking:

> What disgusts, startlingly, is the capacity for life, and not just because life implies its correlative death and decay: for it is decay that seems to engender life. Images of decay imperceptibly slide into images of fertility and out again. Death thus horrifies and disgusts not just because it smells revoltingly bad, but because it is not an end to the process of living but part of a cycle of eternal recurrence. The having lived and the living unite to make up the organic world of generative rot—rank, smelling, and upsetting to the touch. The gooey mud, the scummy pond are life soup, fecundity itself: slimy, slippery, wiggling, teeming animal life generating spontaneously from putrefying vegetation [p. 40].... The generator of disgust is generation itself, surfeit, excess of ripeness [p. 42].

Miller's analysis says we are disgusted by too much life, by excess in the area of fertility. Disgust has been paired with the "animal" by Angyal and others, but Miller tells us it is not animalism itself that disgusts (indeed we admire many "animal" features—consider "animal magnetism" or animal strength, agility, or heart) any more than it is excretion or ingestion of rotten foodstuff. What disgusts is abundant, rampant life: "What the animals remind us of, the ones that disgust us—insects, slugs, worms, rats, bats, newts, centipedes—is life, oozy, slimy, viscous, teeming, messy, uncanny life. We needn't have recourse to the animals for that reminder; all we need is a mirror" (p. 50). Since disgust is so often seen as wedded to experiences of food and ingestion, Miller tackles this relationship: "Food again is implicated, not because food is at the core of disgust so much as because it is feeding that prompts rankness and overripeness and the excessive generation of fat, greasy life whose thriving necessarily implies something else's failing and decay" (p. 43).

Here, in Miller's thinking, is a somewhat remarkable proposition: Disgust is the special emotional mechanism our life-form has evolved for rejecting representations of life in its most rampant, creative and procreative forms. We do not winnow out what is base, as Angyal would argue—specifically linking animal waste with baseness—but we label as base what we have winnowed out as overly imbued with life. By viewing as base any excessive physicality and fecundity, we support our preexisting inclination to seek distance from such matter and energy.

Menninghaus (2003) takes Miller to task for not recognizing the extent to which the "too much life" thesis was explored by Kolnai (1929), a German philosopher whose phenomenological paper, "Der Ekel," was published in a journal edited by Husserl. Menninghaus does us the service of translating into English passages from this paper that indeed do demonstrate Kolnai's keen appreciation of the role of abundant life in stimulating disgust. Menninghaus tells us that

> there is no type of disgust that Kolnai has described more obsessively and more originally than disgust with "crude, unrefined, as it were 'sweating' and 'fuming,' thronging life," with the "*danse macabre* of animation that attends the cessation of properly 'personal' life" [p. 554].... Disgust with insects and rats, for Kolnai, [is] essentially disgust with "a teeming conglomerate ('vermin!')" [pp. 540–541], with excessive sexual fecundity and mobility in connection with dirt, refuse, rotting matter and fear of contact [p. 19].

Miller does not tackle directly the notion of disgust as part of a fundamentally interpersonal signaling system (see Schore), but presumably, in positioning "too much life" as foundational for disgust, he implies that a disgust response to another person, like any other disgust response, could be parsed in relation to anxiety that the other person represents something excessive with regard to the life force.

Miller advances the argument, mentioned in the introductory chapter to this book, that if nature cared only to equip us with an instinct to avoid rotten food or nonnutritious waste, *distaste* would have sufficed, as it likely does for nonhuman animals, and disgust would not have been needed; therefore, disgust must implicate the self and its security, not just the body, from its inception. This argument does not quite convince me in that the possibility exists that natural selection has retained for human beings an especially complex and emphatic emotion, disgust, as a *reinforcer* or intensifier of the animal capacity for distaste. Conceivably, through the evolution of such a reinforcer, we acquired a category of emotional response that chances to have great utility beyond the dining area. If we are going to understand disgust as a fundamentally self-securing emotion, we need to establish some other basis for the view. Miller's arguments about the fright we feel toward too much life go a long way toward establishing such a foundation.

The link Miller forges between the disgusting and the prolific is especially well rendered by David Denby in a *New Yorker* essay detailing his reluctant visit to the Galápagos Islands, a trip he made as a metropolite whose roots were firmly fixed in sidewalk cement:

> As the Galápagos Adventure plowed ahead to the next island, I was sitting at night on the open deck in front of the dining room. Life stirred all around me, and I was caught between wonder and dismay. Something was snorting and blowing out in the dark water. Large birds—swallow-tailed gulls—flapped around the ship, even at night, and earlier in the day, when I was on my way back to the cabin to get some suntan lotion, I looked down at the water and saw a hammerhead shark swimming gracefully by. I had recovered from my disorientation on Santa Cruz, but I was not comfortable in the occasional Galápagos plenitude [p. 58].

Denby goes on to say: "As I walked through the sea lions for the first time, I was disgusted by the oily, rolling, and roaring fecundity—a rank and greasy mass, like a vat of sunbaked Crisco" (p. 58). Undoubtedly, Miller and Denby are sailing the same sea.

Miller's life-disgust argument sounds accurate, but needs to be taken a step farther. What is wrong with too much life? How does it trouble us? Using the terms of our earlier argument, we ask, How does too much life jeopardize our sense of security? Or might the notion of too much life be a subset of some other experience that threatens us?

A paragraph from Peter Hoeg's (1995) novel, *Smilla's Sense of Snow*, portrays a protagonist who responds with partial disgust to her mother's portrayal of nature's procreative abundance, but also its abundant destructiveness of life. The ultimate communication in the passage thus concerns the insignificance of the individual life. Throughout the novel, the protagonist engages in an effort to find the killer of a young boy; she seems to believe that finding the killer will rescue her friend's brief life from immateriality and make it worthy of remembrance and respect. She recalls herself as a young child encountering her Icelandic mother's instruction:

> Later [Mother] once tried to explain to me why one month there are 3,000 narwhals gathered in a single fjord seething with life. The next month the ice traps them and they freeze to death. Why there are so many auks in May and June that they color the cliffs black. The next month half a million birds are dead of starvation. In her own way she wanted to point out that behind the life of the Arctic animals there has always been this extreme fluctuation in population. And that in these fluctuations, the number we take means less than nothing.
>
> I understood her, understood every word. Then and later on. But that didn't change a thing. The year after—the year before she disappeared—I began to feel nauseated when I went fishing. I was then about six years old. Not old enough to speculate about the reason. But old enough to understand that it was a feeling of alienation toward nature. That some part of it was no longer accessible to me in the natural way that it had been before [pp. 35–36].

I believe Miller's notion that nature's teeming life disgusts needs to be expanded to include nature's thoughtless wielding of the death club as well, but our problem is not with death per se (as some, e.g., Rozin,

Nature and Its Excesses

have at times argued) or life per se but with the threat to our sense of substance and boundary. When nature wields the death club, what disgusts is the spilling of life that follows destruction, the breaching of familiar boundaries such that blood flows or flesh flattens or gapes, causing the individual to lose definition. Broadly, what worries us is not exactly too much life, or too much death, but scary life, which may mean life rampaging in a fashion with which we could never keep pace, or life uncontained by ordinary integuments, or life gone dead or lacking the form of an intact and familiar organism with which we can comfortably identify, presenting instead in alien or fragmented (yet organic and invasive) forms that threaten our sense that we are sound and safe. In an earlier-quoted passage, Miller (1997) referred to "fat, greasy *life whose thriving necessarily implies something else's failing and decay*" (italics added). When we begin to identify with what is faltering, disgust may be called forth to strengthen us. The self may wobble in the face of too much life, if the implication of our own dwindling seems present, but we may wobble as well with life unbounded, if we feel it is coming our way and threatening our boundaries, or life that clings and worms its way within, whether by way of the physical skin, grabbed by a leech, or the psychic skin, invaded by a parent. And we can falter, and reach for disgust, in the presence of a body whose life has left it.

A fictional presentation of disgust (Pineda, 1986) renders the breach of life-boundaries that often triggers a disgust reaction, as well as disgust when one is the instrument of that disturbance:

> I surprise it on the ledge, almost within handgrasp: a green lizard sunning itself. (It must have been spring for the light to have shifted.) The sun's slant will not betray my shadow. I hurl the mallet with all my might. The lizard tumbles convulsing off the ledge, the mallet rolling after it. It lies twitching in its death throes. A brown substance oozes from its throat. I seize the mallet, administer the final blow, my eyes averted in disgust [p. 171].

The best generalization I can produce with regard to what disgusts us is that disgust is an emotional option when nature, or any other force, acts to dwarf us as individuals—which may mean overwhelming us with a ferment of life close at hand or destroying life willy-nilly as if the individual signifies nothing, or letting life ooze from its packages, again saying that the containment of life in a particular demarcated form, such as we judge ourselves to be, has been rendered vulnerable.

Whatever lacks a containing set of boundaries of its own and yet is like us, in its organicity, would be most able to invade and overtake our boundaries, or to fascinate us and cause us to neglect our boundaries, or to represent a radically altered form of self the mere imagining of which frightens us. Life that is aged and close to death, or diseased, or badly damaged—even socially, as from poverty or interpersonal oafishness—also threatens us with the possibility we could become like that. The more we feel that something dangerous to us has the potential to *enter* us, the more likely disgust will occur. That invasive potential depends on the stimulus and its composition, but also on one's conception of one's vulnerabilities. Our avoidance by way of disgust protects us biologically (from infection by microorganisms and parasites) and psychologically (from identification and incorporation, the psychological forms of contagion).

Nature is the mother who so abounds in fertility that she cares little about the individual scion—whether it be male or female, bearing two arms or five, entering the world alive or dead. Progeny will come and go, in great numbers and endless forms. As individuals we are eclipsed; we utilize disgust to argue for our significance. We will not be provoked to disgust by explosions of stars a billion miles away, but let nature manufacture a bloom of algae that thoughtlessly poisons a dozen fish and sends them stinking onto our beach, we will be retching with the careless disturbance of order in our neighborhood.

Small, primitive life-forms close at hand are especially likely to disgust us. I believe that is because they seem too likely to enter us or at least to latch on. Large, defined life-forms (imagine a whale or elephant) would not do that. Faraway, inorganic forms (mountains, nebulae) might dwarf us if we attend to them, but we are not obligated to do so. The little things seem more like parts or elements than like whole things, so they seem hungry for an affiliation with something more substantial. If they are structurally designed to cling or ooze, the problem worsens. Though nonliving, a thousand bits of glitter can elicit disgust or its precursor in a toddler because they threaten her skin surface with their strangeness, unexpectedness, clinginess, and abundance.

This analysis about small, unaffiliated parts resonates with Mary Douglas's discussion of "dirt" as representing the disintegration of familiar forms. Dirt, according to Douglas, is most unsettling to us when some of the identity of those forms still adheres to it. In that condition, dirt is emblematic of unstable structure; it is also a part looking for a whole. She tells us that when dirt has broken down entirely, we are able to see it as the beginning of new structure—something we might welcome—rather than the remains of old structure, still fighting for its survival. What she does not say (but William Miller might) is that the final phase of dirt, while still matter (and not as pure as energy), strikes us as nonliving and therefore safe. It may contain the nutrients for life, like the screened, sterile, wonderfully rich black dirt we get bagged in plastic for our gardens, but it is not replete with multiplying life-forms each seeking their own expansion. We imagine it to be available to nourish our personal projects (lovely clay for our sculptures, loam for our vegetables) but it is not filled with minute imperialists pursuing their own territorial aims. We are safe and need not refuse it in disgust.

An additional problem with organic stuff is that we find it interesting because of its relatedness to us. We want to examine it, which means we will approach it closely, putting our boundaries more at risk. This is where Freud's reaction-formation concept makes best sense. It is when interest is greatest that the defenses must be on high alert. Commonplace disgust at feces—especially human feces, especially other humans' feces—likely relates to the high degree of interest in what is so odorous, organic, and recently contained within the body.

Disgust analysis also helps us understand why we sometimes affiliate with nature, but at other times approach it violently or with efforts to corral and control. Passionate colloquy about the evils of exotic, invasive species—frequent among nature lovers—highlights universal tensions about loss of control of one's environment and demonstrates human efforts to differentiate good growth from destructive growth. One can sense the political, interpersonal applicability of the thinking about "exotics" and "foreign versus native" and the easy slide from protecting the self (analogous in this case to protecting loved natural communities) to fearing and suspecting outsiders.

In summary, William Miller, following Kolnai, masterfully elaborated our fear of too much aliveness in what surrounds us; we can take that thinking a step further and posit that the actuality of the not-me threatens to dwarf, overwhelm, inundate, or overshadow our own vitality, to leave us feeling that the science instructor who says we are just a ten cent bag of chemicals may have it right. Thus we heave in disgust—physically or psychically—and experience this emotion as our powerful assertion that we can indeed control our boundaries and reject whatever threatens to diminish us.

Chapter 4
Varieties of Disgust

> Thus, as in each instance when an initial disgust is overcome, I ended by enjoying the dissimulation itself, savoring it as I savored the functioning of my unsuspected faculties. And I advanced every day into a richer, fuller life, toward a more delicious happiness.
>
> André Gide, *The Immoralist*

At the moment of its experiencing, disgust always rejects contact, so it is natural to think of disgust as a refusal to integrate something into the body or being. However, disgust experiences vary considerably with regard to their ultimate goal. In some instances, the disgusted person seems initially and ultimately to seek as complete a rejection as possible of the stimulus at hand; the person may also wish to enlist others to the cause of condemning and despising something. Moral disgust falls at this end of the integration–alienation continuum, as does antipathetic disgust, which may or may not have a moral cast. We will examine disgust heavily amalgamated with hatred and violence in a later chapter on racial and ethnic antipathy, but will look at moral disgust in this chapter.

At the opposite end of the integration–alienation spectrum are disgust reactions that from the outset evince an element of play. Fascination sits astride disgust and is not entirely cloaked, and the disgusted person teasingly invites others to sample a frisson of disgust over something rather intriguing and rather amusing, while watching the other's reaction for signs that the sight might in fact be well tolerated. At this end of the spectrum, disgust displays token rejection as a mechanism for incremental integration.

Certain disgust experiences are "developmental" in that they involve an individual's encounter with something representing his or her future. Many of these developmental disgusts appear to be integrative experiences through which a person reveals a mix of aversion and excitement over something that signifies the person's trajectory into the future. Puberty provides abundant example of integrative, developmental disgust, as boys and girls encounter and generate sexual images and ideas they find transiently disgusting. Disgust toward signifiers of old age and illness is also developmental. We become aware early in life that each of us will age and sicken. The child disgusted by the gnarled fingers of an arthritic old man, or the young adult disgusted by an elderly woman's pendulous breasts fights the troubling prospect of the aging self, while simultaneously entertaining it and working toward accommodation. Some developmental disgust reactions appear to be prolonged stalling operations that mark an experience as something to be absorbed much later down the road. Consider an eight-year-old boy's disgust at the idea of kissing a girl. Developmentally unready for such experience, this boy may use his disgust to exclude himself from all pictures of male–female sexual contact for years, during which time he engages in self-development through play, work, and friendship. His disgust may have an anxious quality that betrays his knowledge of where development eventually will take him, but also a quality of histrionic amusement at exaggerating his association between kissing girls and other gross experiences such as eating vomit.

Other instances of developmental disgust suggest a person who has already begun to inch his or her way toward the new territory. The feelings that 12-year-old girls have about sex sometimes turn on a dime, shifting dizzyingly from the most violent, sickened disgust at thoughts of a parent having sex to the most lovesick longing for a boy (suddenly, the parent's sex life holds little interest). One such child, Tanya, was so appalled and nauseated by the idea of intercourse that she was convinced she never in all her life could tolerate the idea of her mother having sex. She did everything she could to stand between her mother and her mother's male friend and worried about how life could continue if such tormentingly revolting mental images would persist. Around this time, she received at school some literature on menstruation that upset her so thoroughly that she determined to burn it, as if destroying all traces of the literature would arrest the phenomenon itself and her own approach to sexual maturity. Yet, a few short months after all this wretchedness, she was fraternizing happily with boys, her cheeks in a perpetual flush, her new earrings and lipstick advertising her attractiveness as she sent a stir of anxiety through the adults hoping now to preserve her virginity. In other cases, contempt or mocking humor, not high drama, colors the sexual disgust of puberty or early adolescence: the child feels above such emotional nonsense and the shift into sexual interest is incremental and hidden from view.

A lot of the "poop" talk of school-age children displays an integrative use of disgust that can be termed, loosely, as regressive rather than developmental. In some cases, the child may be trying to improve on an uneasy early relationship to body functions, but in many cases, the child is sorting through how to *maintain* his or her relationship to the intimate bodily world of its own poop function while moving into the more sanitized worlds of school and society. Unlike the child who reacts with disgust at the sexual contact that lies ahead developmentally, the school-age child engaged in poop talk and joking often is more excited than disgusted. He (or she) is reveling in the anal pleasures of infancy as he makes himself disgusting to older people or occasionally to another child, who may play the part of the adult and show disgust at his peer's poopy jokes and comments (squealing, "oh, gross" or "oh, you stink"), then turn around and be the jokester, upping the ante with something even grosser meant to turn the first child's stomach. Children will collaborate in a variety of ways in enacting disgustingness. I overheard one happy, competent five-year-old girl whispering to another little girl on the telephone, "I'll be pee-pee and you be pooh-pooh but we won't tell anyone." She seemed delighted with keeping this dirty secret, shared only with another youngster. I had been with this child for days and had heard no commentary on excretory life. Only in conspiracy with her friend (in earshot of the adults) did the subject arise, as part of play that defined her generation as apart from the adults, subversive to adult values, and excited by the return to infantile pleasures.

Holding fast to the messiness and uninhibited exploration of infancy, latency children can delight in dirty play (mooning each other, farting, and talking dirty). A friend who raised two boys recalled the joking among parents about the parents' need to pry off the boys' underpants with a crowbar, when they were eight or nine, lest they wear the same garments for weeks. Popular among those children was the book series, *Captain Underpants* (2002), which let the boys laugh at endless silly jokes about bathroom functions. These children appear to be clinging to the past, but also to be securing for themselves an earthiness and comfort with the dirty and the physical that will be important to them as they go forward to greet adult sexual physicality and the messiness of creative work and art.

The child also determines through this passage whether he can or cannot maintain a relationship—though perhaps an increasingly private or humor-bound one—with his own poop function and still survive in the larger social world. Thus the important developmental achievements from evoking disgust in others are: recognizing one can be dirty, even transiently disgusting, yet still remain within the community; learning one can use disgustingness to arouse and annoy another; and accepting that certain behaviors and interests need to be restricted if one wants to maximize social acceptance. One must toe the line ultimately, if one wants to live comfortably in society. The line may shift markedly depending on one's company and setting, but it always exists.

Children in our society seem to leave behind most of the silly bathroom-play of the younger child as they move closer to puberty and the perils of social rejection for retained childishness. But further down the developmental road, in adolescence, there must be some reclaiming of intimacy with the most physical aspects of self as one copes with the physicality of menstruation, erections, emissions, masturbation, and interpersonal sexual intimacy (preparing as well for pregnancy, childbirth, breast-feeding, and physical ministrations to infants). These adolescent and postadolescent physical experiences do not focus on anality per se, as did the earlier childhood moments (the joy of farting and *Captain Underpants* will have lessened), but they likely benefit from the earlier period of playful and obstinate anality. For young people whose early traversal of the potty-talk period yielded a high level of acceptance of the body self, the later adolescent struggles to integrate the sexual body likely will be relatively easier.

The treatment of an adolescent girl showed use of *shared* disgust in a young person whose family struggled a great deal with issues of cleanliness, propriety, and emotional control. This girl spent much of a therapy hour talking about her disgust over the "bird poop" so often found gracing her bike when she returned to claim it from the bike rack after class. Always an ardent storyteller, she provided dozens of details about the disgusting appearance of the bird poop and its stubborn adherence to her bike. Especially of interest was the veritable rainbow of colors present in the poop, her conviction that her bike was regularly singled out for such painterly pooping, and her abundant associations to childhood tales of pooping and peeing, variously associated with embarrassment, illness, interactions with parents, or keen recollection of a child's curiosity about the mysteries of human and pet anatomy. She

Varieties of Disgust

managed to spend most of one hour happily associating to bird poop, wanting her therapist to share in her amused revulsion and in her attention to her own bodily experience of pooping and being pooped on. She watched her audience carefully, seeming to want to inspire disgust that was also engaged and amused. If met with amusement, not true revulsion—she might move a bit toward acceptance of her own messy body and those of boys and might move as well toward the messy interactions that can occur between people sexually.

Both in the earlier poop-talk phase and the later adolescent phases, the young person seems to be questioning, how much of my physical experience can be tolerated within my social world? From the conclusions drawn, the young person will decide how much of matters messy, matters sexual, and matters messily sexual to accept within the self. If the child is repeatedly told—in humorless fashion—that certain behaviors and talk are gross, weird, or disgusting, she likely will restrict her attention to these matters, or give attention in ways that evidence a high degree of conflict.

Developmental conflicts are mastered, not eliminated. Jokes about excremental matters show persistence of tensions over the disgustingly dirty, anal, earthy self throughout life. For example, a friend wants to tell me about her embarrassment and get me to laugh acceptingly at the image of her and a stranger, the carpet cleaner, discovering a thick trail of mouse poop behind the sofa they needed to move for the carpets to be shampooed. In response, to comfort us both, I share the story of unhappily discovering piles of cat feces on the basement floor when I descend there with the furnace inspector. Both stories involve strangers getting a snapshot of one of us as unkempt and unhygienic.

If the developmental disgust experiences tend to be integrative in their intent, then which disgust experiences occupy the opposite end of the integration spectrum, being wholly condemning and rejecting? Observation suggests that moral disgust tends to satisfy this description. A large group of disgust experiences not yet considered are those that respond to what a person considers morally offensive. Indeed, informal observation suggests that moral disgust accounts for a large percentage of disgust reactions. An interesting evolution of the human psyche, it moves disgust away from the physical. In a good percentage of moral disgust reactions, the body does not figure in any way as *stimulus* for the disgust. The body also recedes to a background position in the fabric of the disgust *response*. The body is present to an extent in embedded images of spitting or lifting the nostrils to convey distaste for an occurrence, but such images are part of a broader picture characterized by reproach and rejection directed at a morally unacceptable stimulus

Moral disgust is an aggressive emotion and also a conservative one that attempts to maintain the value of a cherished concept such as "marriage," "God's law," or "pristine wilderness." It works to oppose alterations—experienced as violative—of what is contained within the boundary of the valued abstraction or being. Consider, for example, the moral condemnation in the following disgusted response to an email listserv exchange, among birders, regarding the deliberate killing of house sparrows, a bird often considered an undesirable invasive species alien to North America:

> This whole thing is sick. What kind of people think they can mess up the earth, then take it upon themselves to act as God and "fix" it by killing those who are weaker? Do sparrows not have nerve endings, or fears? Can you feel their little hearts beating quickly as they face the one who has proclaimed himself GOD? I hope that your child is a forgiving one Tom, when she finds out that daddy is murdering the chattery little "bad" birds. Perhaps it will teach her a useful lesson on how to manage things that seem out of control. The tiny little brown birds are here, because of humans.

At the moment of writing her note, this person has no sympathetic regard for the phenomenon she has encountered. She finds it "sick" and she wants others to be disgusted by it, as she is. She also wants people to recognize the relationship she sees between destruction of nonnative sparrows and willingness to eradicate "undesirable" humans. In later correspondence I initiated to clarify this writer's views, she indicated that "disgust" does indeed capture well her response to the sparrow-killers' attitudes, which she sees as on a continuum with Nazi exterminations of Jewish or Gypsy "undesirables."

With respect to violation of body boundaries, most individuals within a particular society have similar ideas about acceptability and unacceptability. With regard to abstract values we wish to preserve and engender, what we venerate varies considerably and may create major divisions among us. It is interesting though, and perhaps unsettling, to note that the core composition of the disgust state is roughly the same whether one is a separatist set on disenfranchising a detested minority, or a pacifist disgusted by a militant government's aggression against its impoverished citizenry, or an environmentalist disgusted by a senator's decision to vote with big oil against the interests of clean air and water. All these partisans may be indistinguishable if we look only at their emotion and its expression, even though the matters that offend them differ.

Our moral disgust reactions reveal some of our vital self-interests and core identifications. The nature lover who cannot bear to see nature ravaged by industrial waste identifies with wildness in the world. The business person feeling bullied and abused by an environmentalist identifies with the business world and wants to see it free and unfettered. Liberals passionately defend verbal freedom, but want handguns and other nonverbal weapons regulated. Those who abhor government intervention in arms-bearing may be less protective of the arsenal of free speech. Perhaps liberals and NRA members tend to differ with respect to the variety of weapon they personally feel most effective wielding, with liberals more often at ease with words (and fearing guns will enter their sphere only if pointed at them) and gun owners uneasy with words (and imagining guns in their own hands, pointed at a threatening outsider).

The aggressiveness of moral disgust reflects the notions of absolute good and bad in which disgust trades, a commerce that sets it apart from the physical disgust experiences that turn on a more personal, less abstract experience of something being discomforting but not essentially and permanently bad. One can inject humor and frivolity into one's response to what is physically "yucky." One can also imagine variability across time in one's response. What was totally yucky one day might become—on further acquaintance—comfortable: sexual practices, for example. But in the sphere of morality, where absolutes of good and bad enter, disgust is serious business and indictment of something as "disgusting" is humorless and rigid.

The majority of religions make heavy use of the concepts of moral goodness and evil. A related duality is that of worthiness and unworthiness of God's grace. Often disgust is used by organized religions as part of the descriptive set that characterizes the simultaneously wicked and unworthy. Humans cast out what is disgusting, and we attribute the same expulsive impulse to our Gods, seen as casting out the wicked and unworthy of mankind whether from the Garden of Eden or from God's sympathy. Humankind's longings to connect with God and to attain a personal state of godliness promote conceptions of purity as the state that facilitates God-contact, whereas pollution and contamination by earthly and animal substances and impulses will hinder contact with God. This world of acceptance and extrusion, of purity and contamination is governed by a number of emotions, but disgust figures prominently among them.

The counterpart to the search for intimacy with God is the fear of being rejected by God and made valueless through such rejection. Affiliating oneself with a community of believers and abjuring the vile infidel who is outside that community can reduce anxiety about extrusion by God. When the believer emphasizes not only his or her own devoted and reciprocally loving relationship with God (to whom the worshipper is obedient and submissive), but also underscores the contrast between such a desirable relationship and other humans' flawed approaches to God, the emotions in play appear to be similar to those in intense family situations dominated by sibling conflict and insecure ties with parents. God, the Father, has many children. The believer strives to warrant that his or her intimacy with God is great, and feels a need to believe his or her attachment is stronger than the attachment between God and his other children. Thus the other children are rendered as unworthy; they disrespect God and fail to deserve his love.

The God of the great monotheisms lovingly bestows the gift of his presence and ragefully withdraws it, alternately warming and terrifying, or chilling, the believer. The believer wants not to be the helpless child of a mystifying, unpredictable parent, but would be instead a child whose parent rewards or punishes rationally, in keeping with the child's merit. Such a God provides hope for man because he is clear about what he rewards and what he punishes. However, his punishments are severe and terrifying, thus one must safeguard his love and acceptance. The more dangerously punitive God's condemnations are conceived as being, the more likely the believer will find comfort dividing mankind sharply into those who are good and those who are evil, with the evil group becoming the target of the believer's condemnation and presumably drawing God's disgust and rage, deflecting it from the struggling believer. What we have then is a belief system in which the believer's attitudes toward his fellow man precisely parallel his God's polarizing posture toward mankind. We might argue as easily that the believer's prior attitudes toward himself and his fellow man have cast their shadow across his conception of God, so that God's radical condemnations and grace reflect the believer's inner world, as does God's finely tuned nose for the vulgar, abominable, and revolting.

Self-disgust is frequently moral in nature. Often, it is guided by rigid religious ideology or other sources of intolerance within the conscience. People often evince self-disgust when their behavior highlights a conflict between multiple sets of values. For example, a man who has filed for divorce lies to his wife about where he will spend the weekend out of fear of provoking her to rage and physical violence should she know his intention to spend time with a woman friend, a potential lover. He is disgusted by his lie and by his infidelity and spends a miserable weekend fighting his self-revulsion. On reflection, he sees that his belief system is full of contradictions. His thoughtful, tolerant adult self believes that the lie and the connection with another woman are reasonable behaviors given the marital circumstances. He would not judge a friend harshly for such behavior, but would see the pursuit of personal happiness as a worthy motive. However, his childhood religious education made lying and infidelity absolute sins to be condemned without regard for circumstances. His self-disgust followed from these earlier elements in his conscience. Awareness of the conflict within his conscience allowed him to mitigate the archaic superego elements.

What should we make of the fact that disgust changes horses from body offenses to behavioral affronts and enters so fully into the realm of the moral? One simple conclusion to draw is that the moral sphere matters greatly to us and stirs deep passions. Disgust is a big gun, a powerhouse, when it comes to ardent expression of emotion and its core structure of rejection makes it convertible to the sphere of moral offenses. A television performance provided an example of the firepower of moral disgust. The script depicted a prosecuting attorney interviewing a potential witness (a degenerate character with whom a deal had been struck) who was describing his experience of watching the fire he'd set consume a building. He described the fire and its impact on the building in grossly sexual terms and sadistically forced the female prosecutor to experience his lecherous pleasure in coaxing the flames until the building convulsed and fell. The attorney was unable to remain composed in the face of her witness's hostilely employed speech; she interrupted him, fuming: "You disgust me. We want the jury to believe you, not to be sickened by you" (*The Practice*, 2002). Clear in this instance of moral disgust was the use of the simple phrase, "You disgust me," as an assault on another person and all he or she represents, and as an attempt to reduce that person's ability to excite distress. I was struck by the power in the simple phrase, "you disgust me";

the power seemed to flow in part from the spitting pronunciation of the word *disgust* which allows the speaker to enact her passion. Power also arose from the image of the whole self directing disgust at the whole person of the Other. She was not somewhat disgusted, or disgusted by some part of the man: his talk or his voice or his smile. She wanted to convey, *you* (all of you) disgust *me* (all of me), as is shown through her spitting out the word *disgust*. We are on the big stage here, witnessing operatic emotion.

An alternate hypothesis about disgust's prominence in the moral sphere is that aggressive impulses to protect the self (from uncertainty, instability, and worthlessness, for example) enlist disgust and morality as tandem forces. Morality does not precede disgust but works concomitantly with it. The woman so responsive to the plight of common birds that are deemed "bad" and expendable might identify with that vulnerable population, feel anxious and angry, and turn instinctively to self-protective aggression that is justified by the moral conviction about the bird-killers' disgustingly "sick" behavior. Most likely, a disgust reaction can develop either way: as a response to morality or yoked to immorality as a two-pronged response to helplessness.

At times, disgust over moral infractions leaves the purely mental sphere and becomes a bodily reaction, so that we have, within the moral realm, true disgust with both bodily and intellectual elements present. On an airplane traveling to Amsterdam, a friendly and extroverted Iranian man seated beside me expressed disgust at a singer (on an entertainment video) whose singing he considered entirely offensive. His words suggested a strong physical response along with a moral response. He said, "This guy disgusted me . . . every time I see him it turns my stomach." When I asked why, he said the man's singing showed nothing new or creative and that he thought the man was singing because he could not act. He explained that he, himself, takes singing seriously because good singing is something he loves deeply. The performer who stirred his disgust degraded something that should have been wonderful.

Since this man had grown up in Iran but lived eight years in the United States, I asked his impression of disgust reactions in the two cultures. He expressed the view that people in the two countries react with disgust to many of the same things, but in Iran disgust is a fuller, more bodily experience. He believed that an American might not feel such a consuming, even bodily disgust for the singer as he, as an Iranian, did.

Some disgust reactions cross categories and combine responses to bodily stimuli, developmental concerns, and moral condemnation. A teenage client gave an example of disgust that had all these elements. He spoke of his intense dislike for the final scene of Steinbeck's *Grapes of Wrath* and his conviction that the image Steinbeck chose—of a bereft nursing mother using her milk to suckle a sick, starving old man—was an inept, poorly chosen image, from a literary perspective. Though he understood Steinbeck's need to convey the wisdom of "passing on the gift of life," he saw the image selected as grossly ill suited to the novelistic task. He went on to condemn all of Steinbeck's writing, apparently influenced in good measure by his rejection of this single image.

Factors in this young critic's own makeup and development appeared to contribute great emotional intensity to his critique. For example, he was facing separation from his parents and also his therapist as he approached college. Separation had always been enraging and frightening for this boy, thus the regressive image of an old man nursing like an infant may have been especially troubling to him. He also seemed offended by the sexual suggestiveness he found (and articulated) in the image and likely by the incestuous sexuality one might glean from the image of an older man, a father figure, sucking on the breast of a young woman who might be his daughter's or granddaughter's age. Even without the added stimulus of the old man's suckling, the image of the nursing mother who was childless, thus overflowing with milk in a messy, boundary-neglectful way, seemed "unpalatable" to this young man; and the image of the infirm old man was repulsive apart from his interaction with the young mother. Weaving the two images together compounded their grossness. In the young man's response to a fictional scene, we see common human reactions amalgamated with the idiosyncrasies of individual development. He responded to many physical elements of the scene (with his own physical and mental revulsion) and he imbued his response with moral condemnation, as if the choice of so inept and so offensive an image was, in itself, a moral offense. The developmental aspects of the disgust concerned his struggles with sexuality and with separation, and integrative effort was apparent in his desire to discuss his reactions in therapy with great attention to their mechanics.

Though many disgust utterances march under the flag of morality—of right and wrong, good and bad, godly and profane—moral passion often disguises or at least coincides with narcissistic concerns. We direct moral disgust toward those we find narcissistically threatening:

because we envy them, because we resemble them (sharing unattractive traits), or because we see them as threatening to our survival. When we perceive our own deficiencies in others and try to destroy the bad self in its externalized form, utilizing projective identification, we can be especially merciless. The young man disgusted by Steinbeck's image of an old man at the breast clearly wrapped issues of self-regard (what kind of worthless baby would he be if needy and hungry?) and self-survival (would he survive away from home?) in the flag of moral umbrage over an irresponsible authorial choice. Haidt et al. (1997) point out that passion often kindles moral disgust, which is rationalized after the fact by moral argument.

Not all self-protective disgusts have a strong moral cast. Neediness in others frequently elicits disgust that has self-preserving elements. Such disgust may display or lack moral coloring. Exemplifying the absence of moral argument is the young woman who found the blood-adulterated cow milk so disgusting. She talked one session of her distress over a clingy male friend who was pestering her in a fashion she found disgusting. He was forever whining and visibly suffering over his need for her to consider him for a boyfriend. She insisted the two of them were "friends, just friends, almost like brother and sister," and she saw his badgering and his ideas as intolerable and "sick." Increasingly, she felt tempted to cut him out of her life altogether. She couldn't stop talking about this friend and how upset she was about his aggravating her. She felt she needed to be left alone, that this friend was driving her nuts with his sick pursuit of her. Her disgust was strictly interpersonal, with little elaboration of sense imagery; it had little moral content either. She needed the comfort of space—she didn't want *any* boyfriend—and this boy interfered with her independence. She was frantic in her need to get free of him, as if he were some awful clinging matter stuck to her skin and sealing off the pores.

I was reminded of her relationships with her parents and of her anxious drive to maintain space between her and them. She found both her parents (but especially mother) repulsive and, when possible, she stayed out of the house if her parents were home. If she had to be home, she spent all her time in her room. Intermittently, she felt so desperate for space and detachment that she determined to move out, even though she was a minor and realistically had no way to support herself. Her dynamics represented an exaggerated form of normal adolescent reactions. Occasionally, she introduced an element of morality into her disgust—for example, the idea that the boy's attentiveness was "sick"

Varieties of Disgust 71

carried the suggestion of immoral incest—but generally, moral emphasis was lacking.

A middle-aged woman talked of her elderly mother's neediness. Her face wrinkled in disgust as her voice emphatically whined the censuring word, "needy." She began to sob (seeming herself very needy) as she protested the burden of her mother's wishes. My knowledge of her from a lengthy period of work suggested that her fury over the mothering she herself had received, which combined tight control and little empathy for her needs, had led her to take great distance from this parent. However, the mother's decline in old age deprived the daughter of the option for such distance and forced her back upon her own unsatisfied needs for love and admiration from a rather formidable and chilly parent. The view of the mother's neediness as disgusting appeared to be an effort to find a simple emotional solution (condemnation and distance) to a complex problem. Evident in a number of examples of interpersonal disgust with self-protective aims is that witnessing behavior in others that is felt to be developmentally inappropriate for oneself often stimulates disgust. The behavior witnessed may seem too infantile for one's age (neediness, for example) or too advanced (sexual behavior, if viewed by a child). The conflict may derive from one's wishes (to be an infant, for example) or one's fears (of being an adult). If disgust arises primarily in response to one's wishes, it protects the person from recognizing the appealing aspect of a behavior or state. If it arises in response to fears, it protects the person from recognizing his or her fear.

Some disgust instances that have no obvious moral element reveal, on closer inspection, a subtle moral aspect that turns on a belief that one person is deliberately exposing another to something unpleasant. The idea of a human *intention to distress or offend* introduces feelings about right and wrong action. I think of telling a friend the story of being disgusted by a lengthy, physically unsettling story of a man's sinus infection, related by a colleague. The friend said she would find the story disturbing but not disgusting. "Why not disgusting?" I asked, remembering that I had in fact felt disgusted. "Because the sick person in the story didn't do anything *on purpose*," she said. She offered a contrasting example of a woman telling her a man vomited on her feet on a bus. She thought that was disgusting because the man had chosen (she assumed) to direct his vomiting in the woman's direction. It strikes me that, in this example, the vomiter's intention gives extra disgust power to an action already liable to elicit disgust. The man didn't step on the woman's shoe; he vomited on it. Vomiting tends to disgust us, but not always. The moral element of one person deliberately exposing another to something often deemed disgusting pushed the incident over some threshold of disgustingness for my friend.

My colleague's story of sinus infection, which I found disgusting, concerned behavior that seemed outside the realm of choice. The patient in the story had not chosen to have infected sinuses or to expose anyone to their output. As I pondered my own disgust reaction, I realized that my position in listening to my colleague and my friend's position in listening to me differed in an important way. The disturbing physical images in the story were the same, but when I heard the story, I was in the presence of someone who chose to tell me a story in great and sustained detail. She was trying to affect me, indeed, to infect me with disgust, as she herself had been infected. So there was in fact an element of choice, not for the man with the sinus infection whose story was related, but for the narrator. My colleague was disgusting me, and the disgust was the result of her intention to present the illness imagery as repulsive. In feeling disgust, I was feeling what I was supposed to feel, whereas my friend, getting the story one more time removed, must not have taken from me a desire to disgust her or to induce her to share my disgust.

The search for subtle moral judgments concerning intentionality of exposure directed my attention more broadly to those who seek an audience in order to influence that audience's emotions. Gary Larson's humor pivots on disgust (as well as horror) that is sadistically evoked in the reader, in relation to images of some person (usually rendered as an animal or a fictive life-form) helpless in the face of violence and cruelty. The common formula is: a big creature stomps on a little creature and takes pleasure in the stomping. The artist entices the reader to watch the vile operation: the reader becomes the victim of the artist's images and his intentions, cunningly blended.

Hundreds of examples of the characteristic admixture could be culled from Larson's body of work. One shows a fortune-telling chicken, kerchief on head, consulting a crystal ball in order to offer fortunes to half a dozen chickens queued in the barnyard (Larson, 2002). To the attentive chicken at the front of the line, she says, "Whoa! Another bad one! . . . I see your severed head lying quietly in the red-stained dirt, a surprised expression still frozen in your lifeless eyes. . . . Next." The central actor—the fortune-telling chicken—is protected from the awful emotion. She sadistically inflicts it on her audience of chickens as Larson inflicts it on his (willing) reader. Larson's

Varieties of Disgust

position and the fortune-telling chicken's are linked in that both take pleasure in exposing their particular audience to the grisly imagery of an utterly defeated, helpless chicken. Another example (Larson, 2002) of the dynamic shows a crocodile reclining, relaxed, on an analyst's couch, saying to the doctor, "You know those teeny tiny little birds that walk around so trustingly inside a crocodile's mouth? Well, I just been eatin' those little guys like popcorn." Here the crocodile has the fortune teller's powerful role. The analyst is the initial shocked, horrified, disgusted audience and, as always, the readers are the ultimate audience, the ultimate "little guys," and Larson is eating us like popcorn. The image of the fondly described birds crunched between the teeth is particularly affecting; its physicality combines with a devastation of form and substance that one being inflicts on another as, gleefully, it demonstrates its power.

We may understand the artist's wish to play with the audience's emotion (he, himself, is part of his own audience and identified with our squeamishness), but why would anyone voluntarily read this stuff (and laugh)? Why do we sometimes avoid those who stimulate our disgust (and view their efforts as morally disgusting) and sometimes laugh with them? There is something captivating in the artistry of this humorist's "got you!" power to disgust and horrify and something irresistible in the images themselves that draws us to process them, but it is probably the artist's cleverness in reaching our emotions and graphically representing their truths, using absurdly unexpected forms, that has us surrendering to his world view. An artist or storyteller will fail to elicit the admiration sought if he or she presents disgusting ideas clumsily, without cleverness, surprise, or some other compensation. A failed joke occurred as a friend and I envisaged my working on this book during our shared, upcoming vacation. "You're *still* working on that?" she asked, with apparent disapproval. She then told me if I wanted a disgust experience while on the trip, I could come to her bathroom when she gets diarrhea from the local food. I made a deliberately mirthless disgust face to reject her offer. Her image was too disgusting for me and felt aggressive, as if she were forcing me into something unpleasant out of some anger I didn't understand. My dramatized disgust said no thanks to her "gift" and rejected the idea her offering was humorous. It challenges me even to relate the exchange because the disgust principle of contagion tells us, intuitively, that associating oneself with such a disgusting image makes one disgusting. Contagion anxiety can cause dramatic disruptions of relationships, as when families extrude members who have a condition that causes them to smell bad or to lose bowel control.

The fascination in disgusting material may lie in our urge to acquaint ourselves fully with all potential threats and to digest the nearly overwhelming emotion they elicit, in order better to prepare ourselves for any real trauma life inflicts. An emergency room nurse offered two examples of experiences she found disgusting, but also fascinating, and her fascination spoke to the desire to confront the traumatic and digest it. One story involved the gangrenous feet and legs of a homeless drug abuser; the other involved a woman's face, which was terribly abraded when she was deliberately dangled by the legs from a car window and dragged over a roadway. In both these cases of degenerated structure and wet, sticky tissue, the nurse encountered the disgusting body parts by unwrapping them layer by layer. When asked whether the gradual unwrapping might have added to apprehension and ultimately disgust, she said yes but added that it also intensified the fascination she felt as she wondered just how gross and anomalous the tissue might be. Danger inheres both in ignoring abnormal body states and in letting fascination fix our attention to them. Nature has provided us with an antagonism of attraction and aversion, rather than allowing either highly motivating force to prevail unopposed. Regarding these two instances, I wondered whether the disgust was somewhat heightened by the element of human causation and responsibility. These elements were pronounced in the case of the woman who had been forcibly suspended from a moving car and were more subtly present for the self-neglectful homeless individual. Human agency can add a second layer to the imagery of biological dysfunction, since it suggests psychological or moral aberration at work in creating the biological disturbance.

A teenage girl in treatment one day launched into a lengthy story that concerned a friend, who had had nasal surgery, who one day began to bleed voluminously from the nose and had to rush to the emergency room. The central, disgusting images of the story concerned the blood pouring out unstoppably and, worse yet, some blood-soaked packing inside the boy's nose and sinuses that had to be pulled out (over and over) so that he felt as if his brains were coming out. The story featured a relentless repetition of disturbing detail, since the treatments failed repeatedly and the boy returned several times to the hospital, gushing blood anew and leaking bloody packing material. I began to feel as if I could not bear to listen to this story much longer.

Especially awful were the images of the boy's tender sinus cavities stuffed with something artificial that shouldn't be there (the packing material), which then is pulled out of them, taking with it some of his tissue. This I found both disgusting and horrid. I noted, though, that my young patient, intent on her story telling, bore a face unmarked by any strain or disgust. When she finally, blessedly, brought the story to its end, I commented on it being an awful story and rather hard to listen to. At that point, her face lit up and she announced that she hadn't even told me the disgusting parts, because when the boy told her the story he included endless gory details (now her face shows disgust), so that at one point she felt (akin to my feeling), "If he doesn't stop right now I'm going to vomit." Her comments seemed to confirm her externalization of the disgust and her need for me and her both to digest these awful images. As audience, I stood for her and occupied the position she'd occupied. She tried to master her distressed disgust by watching me wrestle with similar emotions, or perhaps by giving them over to me for disposal.

After relating to me her own experience as audience to this story, the young woman associated to needing to go to the doctor for several problems, including the desire for birth control pills to regulate normal but unpredictable menstrual bleeding, and the wish for sleeping pills to help put her to sleep at night. The menstrual association seemed responsive to the ideas of unregulated bleeding and awful packing (introduced and pulled free of the body). Even had her associations differed significantly, she as a vulnerable human—as we all are—likely would have felt some need to engage herself and perhaps to engage a listening Other with this disgusting material. This boy's terrible experience spoke to something traumatic that all human bodies can endure; therefore, we are inclined to prepare ourselves emotionally for such tribulation.

Several of the anecdotes used in this and the preceding chapter have pointed to the importance of the anticipatory mind-set in determining whether disgust and related emotions will occur. Preparation for something disturbing reduces the likelihood of disgust. Unguarded interest or fascination increases its incidence. A bird-loving friend told the story of watching a Cooper's hawk perched in her yard. The bird had caught a house sparrow, a species of songbird little cherished by this friend. With fascination, she watched the bird ready its meal. The bird plucked each feather from the dead sparrow as my friend continued to watch, delighted in her opportunity to see this behavior close at hand. Mother of a large brood, much accustomed to food preparation, she had no difficulty watching this operation. Listening to her relate the story, one had a vivid sense of her impatient anticipation as the hawk took care in plucking every feather.

What she expected to witness next was not clear, but what she got was entirely unexpected, and it disgusted her. The hawk grasped with its beak one end of a length of the sparrow's intestine and pulled and pulled, drawing the long, slimy thing from the carcass. This image was deeply disgusting to my friend (who showed the face and body shudder of disgust, perhaps mixed with horror). She related this disturbing image twice, as is typical of storytelling centered around a moment of disgust. Her emphasis was on the unexpected nature of the act and how it followed her long moments of attentive watching and anticipation and also on the insides emerging from the body (akin to the bloody sinus-packing image).

Sudden disruption of an idealization represents a particular form of surprise that may elicit disgust. An example comes from a novel called *The Bee Season* (Goldberg, 2000). It shows the integrative and alienating impulses of disgust wrestling within a single moment. A kindergartner, Eliza, who had idealized her older brother, Aaron, as her all-powerful protector, one day discovers Aaron being beaten and humiliated by other boys in the schoolyard. She reacts to the shocking sight with disgust, pained by the assault on her idealization. Disgust is not an unusual reaction to the destruction of an idealization, since the collapse of the idealized image disrupts the person's world view and requires significant adaptation, which initially may seem beyond the person's capability. The disgust is both an acknowledgment of something bad that has been perceived and an attempt to deny or at least to distance onself from the perception:

> [Eliza's] inaction is spurred by the revulsion that sweeps through her at the sight of the boy [her brother] on the ground: his absolute stillness, his silence, his wide-open eyes. Even a half-blind stray dog would struggle. Even Sucker wouldn't lie there, soundlessly accepting his fate. If Eliza intervenes, she will have to touch her almost-brother. He will need help getting up. And there's no way she'd be able to help this boy who can't possibly be Aaron. Aaron who knows all the secret moves of the Jedi. Aaron, who saves Eliza from bad dreams [pp. 29–30].

Along with Eliza's revulsion comes a determination not to touch the offending Other, which reminds us that defilement is contagious. The wish physically not to touch is fused with the wish to deny kinship. Aaron is, at best, her "almost-brother." When I read this passage, which concerns a Jewish family whose Judaism is of central importance to their story, I hear the reverberations of tormenting Holocaust-era questions regarding the speculation that Jews went (shamefully) like lambs to the slaughter—never protesting, never fighting.

We tend to think of our emotions as following automatically from the nature of the provoking situation. But many situations have complex characteristics that allow us to respond by choosing one of a variety of emotions. Situations that elicit disgust may be open to management through shame, embarrassment, contempt, hatred, horror, or anxiety, all of which suggest a negative attitude toward an occurrence, but a different form of negativity than disgust. In asking "Why disgust?" we need to look at the costs disgust levies and the benefits it confers, as well as looking at what is possible psychically for the particular person at the moment in question. Since disgust is, above all, an effort to dissociate oneself from something, we can look in this realm of distancing or disconnection to find both advantages and disadvantages.

At times, little is lost and much is gained from distancing a negative experience through disgust. For some people, disgust is a favored "first responder" emotion and they will use it if they are able. I think of the young girl who felt disgust at her friend's dislocated arm. She frequently favored disgust responses to complex situations. Many children would have responded to a friend's arm hanging limp with great and lingering anxiety. This young girl may have opted for disgust rather than anxiety (regarding body integrity) in part because she *could;* she had that option because disgust was a well-traveled path for her, and for her parents who modeled for her a particular defensive style. The costs of using disgust had not been well articulated or intuited by her. Another child might have hesitated to use disgust to characterize her response to a friend, even if the disgust focused on the friend's predicament, not the friend herself, but this girl was relatively at ease with disgust and avoidant of anxiety.

To the extent that the occurrence we want to disavow is entirely negative, little cost may be incurred from engaging in the emphatic rejection constituted by disgust. But what if the stimulus is constructed more complexly, having both loved and hated features or aspects to which we are tied by loyalty or duty? Then we cannot respond with emphatic disgust without paying a price in disrupted intimacy. We may pay less dearly by feeling and showing amused contempt, or mild annoyance, which do not disturb our relationship with the Other so radically. Examples of interpersonal pairings in which disgust interferes with relatedness are parents with young children, medical workers with patients, or psychologists with clients. Imagine a psychologist with a low threshold for disgust over neediness attempting empathic response to a depressed person, or a physician disgusted by older or unfit bodies, or a parent of a young baby horribly disgusted by feces. Nature does seem to help parents by supplying strong drives to parent and also by making breast-fed infant feces odorless. Disgust that survives these protections can trouble a parent–child relationship, around toileting, breast-feeding, temper eruptions, or some other aspect of infant life.

Whatever one's personal emotional needs and dynamics, disgust can only be used if the stimulus to which one responds can be construed as something specific of which one can rid oneself. Vague, permeating feelings will seldom disgust; visible, palpable glop on the skin frequently will. Later examination of horror (in chapter 9) shows situations that cannot be interpreted in ways that allow their management through a focused disgust response; the offense is too distributed or amorphous to be well addressed through disgust.

Chapter 5
Disgust Syndromes

> There is something I have observed about skinny men. Some, like Chade, seem so preoccupied with their lives that they either forget to eat, or burn every bit of sustenance they take in the fires of their passionate fascination with life. But there is another type, one who goes about the world cadaverously, cheeks sunken, bones jutting, and one senses that he so disapproves of the whole of the world that he begrudges every bit of it that he takes inside himself. . . . I would have wagered that Galen had never truly enjoyed one bite of food or one swallow of drink in his life.
>
> —Robin Hobb, *Assassin's Apprentice*

Studying shame, I noted shame's special importance in narcissistic disorders. Others exploring shame support this conclusion (see Morrison, 1997). Approaching the study of disgust, I had little preconception regarding what types of people might be especially prone to disgust, except perhaps to wonder about disgust's relationship to the various eating disorders and to obsessive-compulsive fastidiousness. Having attended to disgust reactions for some time now, I still see nothing that equates with the "shame personality" (Mayman, 1974), for whom the avoidance of painful shame states is a central dynamic. Although Freud, Anna Freud, and many other psychoanalytic writers regularly juxtapose shame and disgust in discussions of superego reaction-formations, more recent consideration of shame has highlighted its painfulness more than its protectiveness. The absence of a disgust syndrome likely speaks to disgust's less painful and more successfully self-protective character when compared with shame, which at times operates defensively but is fundamentally the emotion of the vulnerable self in painful self-awareness.

Disgust makes appearances in various character types and neuroses, but our conventional diagnostic categories do not establish any particular group of people for whom disgust-proneness is pathognomonic. Some borderline individuals, but certainly not all, use high levels of aggressive, vituperative disgust. When disgust does appear prominently in borderline personalities, it may be associated with passionate envy that the individual wishes simultaneously to deny and assuage. Rather than admit and express envy toward someone who has something the individual associates with personal worth and good fortune, the individual devalues the envied person—and his or her possession or attribute—by attacking the person as disgusting: in his or her materialism, for example, or social extroversion, or political power. When the self-protective disgust fails or is surrendered, the individual may feel hopelessness, emptiness, and shame. One borderline woman frequently demeaned her second husband's daughter as disgusting, practically spitting the word as she uttered it. The daughter's perceived character flaws (some of which were the woman's projections) could have been characterized in a number of other ways: as pathetic, or pitiable, or infuriating, or as simply human and deserving of compassion. I could see little that made disgust uniquely applicable other than the woman's experience of it as the most satisfyingly demeaning response she could articulate toward someone with whom she appeared to feel massively competitive. She did not seem able to manage competitive feelings in a mature fashion, but resorted to an infantile, no-holds-barred assault on the other woman. Aggressive disgust was prominent in her armamentarium and in her case seemed part of a broadly regressive and "oral" approach to life.

The masochistic need to position oneself as helpless in relation to a powerful Other may bring in its wake resentment over the other person's power. One male client, away from work for months with a psychological disability claim, felt resentful of the insurance agent who had the power to establish or withdraw his disability status. Ashamed of his psychologically based disability, yet clinging to it despite much evidence of his ability to work, he often referred to the claim agent with deep disgust as "the incomparable Miss Frances." Similarly, he referred to a woman friend with whom he had a dependent, highly ambivalent relationship as "the lovely Lorna," his voice dripping with a mix of disgust and contempt as he simultaneously elevated and demeaned this woman. Both these figures had great power in his life, power that he had assigned to them but that he nonetheless resented.

Disgust Syndromes

Diagnostically, this man was also borderline, as indicated by his tendency to split human society into those he idealized and those he abhorred. Like the woman who was disgusted by her stepdaughter, his orientation toward others was "oral" both in its biting aggression and its efforts to secure succor.

Although disgust does at times appear as a vehicle of aggression for borderline individuals, it is not a necessary feature of borderline functioning. Contempt, hatred, or physical aggression may instead dominate an individual's attacks on others. It would be interesting to do a careful study of borderline individuals to determine what additional factors need be present for disgust to dominate the person's aggressive expressions. Might disgust-dominated attacks correlate with pronounced oral imagery in other spheres of functioning? Or with themes of anal dirtiness or degradation? Might disgust-governed vituperation reflect a special need to infect or contaminate the other person, perhaps related to the fantasy that one has been the victim of such activity?

One obvious place to look for disgust is in the eating disorders, yet disgust's operation in these disorders may be less salient than one might assume. True disgust plays an important role in the affective life of some individuals with eating disorders, but again, there may be no inevitable relationship. Consciousness may instead be occupied with images of desirable states of thinness, self-control, and perfection, or with images of vomiting that are free of full disgust. Perhaps in these latter instances, the desire for food has been so successfully defeated that appetite is a remote phenomenon, no longer close enough to require control by true disgust. The vomiting can be evaluated as a possible statement of partial disgust. Whether it is or is not a disgust-group manifestation ultimately depends on the meaning of the vomiting behavior.

The variable relationship between disgust and eating disorders reflects the fact that conflicts are seldom welded to specific emotions in any fixed fashion. A conflict can be expressed through a variety of emotions, which may shift over time, depending on other dynamic factors. Therefore, in a young woman struggling with bulimic symptoms, true disgust may not figure at all or it may figure in one of several places. The woman may at times find food items disgusting—being too fatty or rich. Or she may find her own body disgusting; again, the theme likely will be that of excess fat. Or she may find her eating behavior disgusting, if she has overindulged in food "like a big pig." One bulimic young woman said she ate "until she couldn't move and felt gross." An anorexic talked of wanting to die in order to free herself of disgust toward her body. Disgust also may surface as a commentary on the vomiting behavior that aims to reduce the unacceptable weight.

Encountering a person who finds her body or her eating or vomiting disgusting, we enter the domain of self-disgust, which involves treating some part of the self as a rejected Other. For one young woman I treated, who had struggled since early adolescence with impulses to binge and feelings of self-disgust regarding uncontrolled eating, the self-disgust around food indulgence was paired with self-disgust around emotional displays and other forms of emphatic self-expression. Her conscious judgments of others showed vastly more tolerance and humanity than her self-assessment; however, exploration of her emotional life led to guilty recognition of a longstanding but often denied attitude of disgust and contempt toward softness, weakness, and emotional indulgence in her mother. The need to deny these critical reactions toward an apparently loving and devoted parent contributed to the torrent of self-disgust over minute lapses in self-control. The logic of the young woman's self-disgust appeared to be: if you can react aversively toward your mother's emotionalism—especially her desire to be close to you, which prompts a disgusted reaction of "peeling her off"—then you had better show the same disgust toward yourself.

Whichever pattern of disgust prevails for those with eating conflicts, the fundamental psychological conflict may be roughly the same. Often, persistent tension exists between the wish for full and free self-expression (symbolized as eating and in other ways as well) and the conviction that such expression is dangerous and must be curtailed. The restriction of self-expression is achieved symbolically by limiting food intake. Disgust—over food, body fat, or bingeing—is one of several affective engines effective in driving the restrictive behavior. The theme of something being gross, because it is in some way excessive, is easily represented by disgust—which often responds to grossness and excess—thus the underlying conflict around self-expression, conceived as surfeit, can be symbolized by eating and driven by disgust. In the case of the young woman cited above, tyranny over self-expression followed in part from guilt over the desire to distance and demean a mother who seemed sweet and loving.

Moses Laufer (1986) discusses an adolescent anorexic, Mary, who "felt that she either had to allow herself to be completely dominated and 'eaten up' by her mother or that by removing herself and becoming

Disgust Syndromes

independent she would cause her mother to collapse and 'to starve'" (p. 274). The girl at times felt active disgust toward her own body, a disgust that Laufer believed was related to her inability to control bodily desires, a need embedded in her conflict over autonomy. She felt that "if she could not control her bodily needs (as in eating), she would have to reject her body altogether, as in killing herself, because of her disgust with it. . . . Mary had already experienced herself as an object of disgust during latency, as was shown in the repeated nightmares she reported of being covered by crawling insects or skin diseases making her feel 'like a leper, untouchable'" (p. 275). Laufer's case illustrates the occurrence of active self-disgust in which the self or body is treated with the kind of revulsion more often reserved for what is nonself. I have seen this type of florid self-disgust in sexual abuse survivors who see the body—tainted by the abuser—as something vile and infected, even infested (with bugs or disease). The person wants to destroy the body, not to feed and sustain it, as an effort to master the helplessness and shame of the abuse. Without the awful body, the abuse cannot exist.

In looking at bulimic vomiting in the absence of any feeling of disgust, it is important—case by case—to consider whether one is viewing the "body of disgust," as discussed in chapter 4. Does the bulimic's vomiting—even when devoid of disgust proper—suggest underlying dynamics of needing to distance oneself from something awful, as in the fictional instance of the woman, Miriam, who modeled a shrine after her childhood kaleidoscope.

My observations on disgust and eating disorders are based in clinical work. Formal research is beginning to appear regarding this relationship. Davey and colleagues (1998) conducted a study that showed a significant correlation between measures of disgust sensitivity and eating disorders, in female subjects only. A second study showed elevated disgust for food, the body, and body products in those with diagnosed eating disorders. Disgust for other stimuli was not significantly elevated. Clinical experience would predict elevated disgust sensitivity around food and body issues in some anorexics, but might not predict such increased sensitivity in every anorexic. Elevated group numbers allow for a variety of affect-patterns within the group.

People suffering from severe depression often show active disgust for food. These responses are dynamically distinct from the reactions of those with primary eating disorders. The refusal of food in association with depression appears to be part of a larger pattern of withdrawal from active, pleasure-based engagement with the world.

Anything representing a requirement for such engagement is met with rejection. Additionally, the depressed person's state of pain can be so acute that the idea of feeding and sustaining that pained being is repulsive.

Disgust can appear prominently in obsessive-compulsive individuals who are preoccupied with the fear of contact with dangerously contaminating elements in the physical world and dangerously corrupting thoughts. Those with anorexic-type eating disorders often show obsessive-compulsive character organization, so that we see, for the anorexic, a general orientation toward living life in an impossibly disciplined fashion. For anorexics, food and appetite-driven impulses may be the overt focus of disgust, while in other obsessive-compulsive individuals, contact with sexually or aggressively suggestive outside objects or inside thoughts may be especially threatening. A fictional portrayal of adolescent anorexia (Krummel, 1985) demonstrates a girl's passion for purity, an interest common to anorexics and others with obsessive-compulsive personality organization. The protagonist, Ariadne, revels in her hospital experience of being cared for "like a lovely fairy princess—pure, ethereal, white" (quoted in Kuznets, 1988, p. 183). Her imagery betrays the association between her personal passion for purity and common societal images of the upper classes as white, clean, and refined, yet Ariadne turns these common image-sets for the upper classes on their head, seeing the upper class as gross in its engagement with food, such that her descriptions remind reviewer Kuznets (1988) of "medieval portrayals of the deadly sin of gluttony." Disgust appears as a prominent reaction to earthy food imagery, while Ariadne herself is removed and elevated to the pristine realm of the anorexic featherweight. Ariadne tells us:

> I had to get out of the kitchen. I couldn't look at all that filthy food—meats greasy and slobbering—dead chickens with yellow skin in plastic bags dripping with fatty blood, dirty brown lettuce heads limp and smelly, hunks of cheese with blue running through it, bread that looked like raw, pasty dough, jars of orange and grapefruit juice with pieces of pulp all around the sides of the jars smelling like day-old urine in a broken toilet. Food—disgusting—filthy, full of maggots and ants and roaches. People fighting wars over it—the wealthy writing articles and books around it—chefs—Cordon Bleu and Provencal and Short Order and Greasy Spoon and men marrying women for "their

cooking" and powerful diplomatic contracts being signed over caviar, pheasant under glass, oysters on the half shell—even Communist China inviting Nixon as guest and then giving the American entourage tons of dinners and feasts and food celebrations and liquid toasts and more gala 12-course meals with special colored foods and decorative Peking ducks and oranges and exotic fruits shaped like flowers. Each course an array of what? The same moldy meats and yucky bananas and stinking mangoes and limp chickens and slimy squid that lie in all sorts of refrigerators around the world [quoted in Kuznets, 1988, p. 183].

In characteristically adolescent fashion, Ariadne has taken one set of images of the upper class (the privileged, the well heeled and well fed) and inverted it, making porcine gluttons of the aristocrats, preferring for herself the alternative image of elevation through purification. She does not, however, acknowledge her debt to society (both state and, indeed, church) in embracing these pristine images as symbols of excellence.

Obsessional individuals often have more than the average need to separate the self from messy, uncontrollable nature through unrealistic insistence on control and order, even though such a quest cannot ever meet with full satisfaction. We see their efforts not to touch (physically or psychically) what is despoiled and see the general character trait of fastidiousness, which is associated with a low threshold for disgust over what is dirty or unkempt. Fastidiousness may coexist with overt anxiety about one's potential descent into disorderliness, should vigilance lapse. If the focus remains on others' disorderliness, not one's own, disgust will likely dominate.

Psychiatrist Mary Phillips at the Institute of Psychiatry in London and neuropsychologist Andy Calder of Cambridge University studied a part of the brain, the insula, that appears to be active during the experience of disgust. Damage to the insula results in insensitivity to experiences generally shunned as disgusting. This research suggests that unusually easy stimulation of disgust contributes to the obsessive-compulsive's preoccupation with contaminants (Phillips et al., 1997); however, research by Sprengelmeyer and colleagues (1997) indicated that obsessive-compulsive individuals are insensitive to differences among disgust, fear, and anger, as represented by photographs of people. Thus, existing data regarding the neurological substrates of obsessionalism are ambiguous. A deficit in recognition of disgust expressions may correlate with an elevated internal experience of disgust, but it is by no means obvious that this should be the case. Quigley, Sherman, and Sherman (1996) did, however, show a positive correlation between "Disgust Scale" scores, obsessive-compulsive personality type, and dependent personality type in undergraduate subjects.

The feeling of disgust may evidence itself more in obsessional and compulsive personalities than in full-blown OCD, where specific symptoms manage conflicts around contact; these symptoms may preoccupy so fully that affective life is exchanged for symptom management. In obsessionally organized "normal" personalities, where frank symptoms do not manifest, much of the work of managing disturbing contacts may be left to aversive affects such as disgust, but these ideas are conjectural.

Psychoanalysts have related disgust to primary conflicts over oral incorporation, but have argued as well that it derives fundamentally from reaction-formation against coprophilic and coprophagic impulses of the anal phase. In support of the anal evolution of disgust, we have, for example, Anthony's (1986) statement: "In dealing with the problem of disgust, Freud (1950) pointed out that direct observation in nurseries could tell us something of the coprophilic phase that preceded the development of disgust" (p. 79). Franz Alexander (1948) states: "Although repression is an unconscious process, it leaves certain emotional phenomena of a defensive nature on the surface of consciousness. In the place of coprophilic tendencies, disgust appears. The desire to play with excrement disappears from consciousness, leaving a feeling of disgust" (p. 98). Ernest Jones (1938) remarks that the "tendency to obtain enjoyment from various manipulations of and interest in excremental functions is opposed by the development of disgust" (p. 22, n.).

The insistence on anal reaction-formation as omnipresent in disgust has at times led analysts to adhere to anally based theorizing in the absence of supporting data. For example, Shapiro, Fraiberg, and Adelson (1976) discuss a young mother, Kathie, unable to breast-feed her infant, Billy, due to "revulsion toward vomiting and messiness" (p. 478). They conclude their case analysis with a consideration of anal and oral determinants, stating, "We were interested to see that none of this [revulsion] had carried over to the toilet training of Billy.... It was, then, specifically an oral revulsion on Kathie's part, in which food and vomit may have had anal determinants, but were curiously not

Disgust Syndromes 87

manifest in connection with anal functions" (p. 478). It seems difficult for the authors to consider the absence of significant anal determinants of the mother's conflict. They find it necessary to assert undetectable anal determinants.

As discussed in chapter 3, a hypothesis that resolves the oral versus anal reaction-formation argument postulates that impulses to eat, touch, or otherwise intimately contact feces are a subset of our larger ambivalent engagement with interestingly organic stuff and not something unique to feces or the anal stage. Interest in one's own feces is increased by the powerful idea of creating this visible, smelly stuff oneself and removing it from inside to outside the body. This way of thinking suggests that orally and anally directed reaction-formations both may take the form of disgust, but neither oral nor anal impulses are foundational. Instead, the fundamental interest is in contacting, through whatever mode, organic matter that can enhance or threaten, nurture or poison.

Also important to the development of disgust, yet underacknowledged in the literature, is the toddler's ambivalent attitude toward interpersonal closeness. The toddler resists envelopment by others. The need to protect the self from intrusive relatedness can be as motivating of affect development as are physical needs. Disgust serves the tandem ambivalences: around interpersonal contact and around feces.

I had the opportunity to make some direct observations of toddlerhood while visiting for several days in a home with two lovely little girls, aged five and 20 months. The 20-month-old often seemed to take pleasure in an emphatic use of the word *yuck*, which she pronounced with a strongly guttural final consonant pair. Her mother said that "yuck" had first appeared about two months before, at the toddler's sight of her own feces. The mother was puzzled initially about the genesis of the response, but after giving the matter some thought soon realized that the five-year-old regularly exclaimed "yuck" when in the room while a dirty diaper was being changed. The mother felt confident the baby was imitating the older girl. The father added that the baby seemed to enjoy saying the word, something I, too, observed, as if the word had considerable expressive power that made her like saying it, even when there was no apparent yucky referent.

The toddler did unquestionably experience the word as having meaning, as demonstrated by the way in which she soon generalized its use to indicate contacts she disliked and/or wanted to convey dislike for, whether that attitude was real or humorously put on. I observed her "yuck" response on a number of occasions, as when she put her hand into a drawer that had sticky glitter particles in it and saw that her hand, withdrawn, was covered in glitter. She exclaimed "yuck" and held her hand away from her body as if to avoid touching any other part of her with it. She welcomed my washing the hand clean of glitter. The second occurrence came when I picked a strongly fragrant flower head from a Korean spicebush and put it to her nose. She withdrew her nose, saying "yuck," but then cautiously brought her face to the flower; however, she did not allow me to touch the flower to her face.

These two examples indicated to me the child's quick learning to use "yuck" to indicate a wish to keep control over how and whether she would contact a discomforting stimulus. Well equipped phylogenetically for this learning, she understood her sister's communication that poop was distasteful and should not be touched or otherwise closely contacted. She learned to use "yuck" to enhance her sense of control over other things contacting her body or senses. Glitter and flowers may seem unlikely sources of disgust to an adult, but the baby's handling of the flower brought to her nose showed her desire to control so strong a stimulus by using what is at least a precursor of disgust. The humor and pleasure this toddler showed in enunciating "yuck" may have come from her feeling of having a distinctive and powerful word at her command and may have derived as well from excitement about identifying with her much-loved big sister. It remains unclear whether the pleasurable identification with her sister's good word also relieves the toddler of discomfort that her adored sister has rejected her feces. In observing this child, I had a sense that the need to modulate overwhelming or intrusive interpersonal contacts was as urgent a matter as controlling what food should go in the mouth or what smells should be tolerated. The impetus to hone disgust as a boundary-managing emotion might then come as much from interpersonal need as from bodily need.

Rozin (1999) argues that the contagion principle necessary for fully formed disgust does not appear until between the ages of four and eight. This view of disgust development would suggest that the baby, while expressing some negativity about her feces (or at least *playing* with such negativity) might nevertheless be untroubled by eating on a plate that had just been washed clean of the yucky poop. She may not have developed the idea of contagious badness in which case Rozin et al. might call her responses "proto-emotion."

Narcissistic individuals who are also compulsive sometimes use an admixture of grandiosity, contempt, and disgust to elevate the self and remove it from what is devalued. An expansive, narcissistic client, Ben, was deeply invested in his ideas being so stunningly brilliant that people who encountered them would fall over in amazement. These images of brilliance often were paired with images of behaviors or work products that were "a pile of crap," "nothing but shit," and the like. Whether these images of the exalted work-product and the worthless one refer historically to a child's bowel movements, as the early analysts certainly would argue, we may not be able to ascertain, but surely they speak to contrary and extreme views of the self and the self's creative output. In this case, as with many narcissistic individuals, a major determinant of disgusted or shameful self-appraisals was the conviction that anything short of brilliance was crap. Ben had little interest in pursuing a middle ground of good performance; instead he clung to the idea he could achieve uniformly scintillating success. The middle ground as an antidote to shittiness represented defeat and disappointment to him (see Miller, 1996, chapter 4). Intriguing in this case with respect to conjecture about infantile sexuality and the symbols often linked to anal preoccupation was a presenting complaint about inability to sustain the kind of focused effort needed to produce genuinely good products, not just fantasies of them. The prominent fear was of being "all noise and no substance."

This case was one in which disgust often seemed more cerebral than viscerally experienced. Ben characterized his work as crap, and could label such crappy output as disgusting, but the felt emotions often were shame or agitation rather than true self-disgust. When the shittiness shifted to his brother and the pigsty that resulted from his torpid housekeeping, disgust emerged as a visceral emotion. Though it seemed clear that the brother was in some ways a selfobject such that disgust toward the brother's mess and disgust regarding Ben's own work were in some ways equivalent, the feeling experience differed depending on whose poor work-products were at issue.

On one occasion, Ben's self-directed negativity moved into true self-disgust. He was talking with real anguish about images of himself as a worthless young person and said, "It wouldn't be an overstatement to say I feel self-disgust." He talked of some of these self-images, then said, flagging his omnipresent ambitions, "Would a person like this grow up to be a president of the Rotary Club? Surely not. Who would want to nominate this piece of shit?" It was not clear that the child-self images that disturbed him were part of early childhood experience. His sense was that they represented a retrospective view of his early years. Exploration led to a raft of negative self-images, but also to a number of images of each parent as frighteningly dysfunctional, for example, his father in a drug-induced stupor and his mother sobbing on the bathroom floor. The self-as-crap ideas and images seemed to integrate some of the imagery of the parents as dysfunctional. Specific crap-self images included being the "fat boy with a big butt who can't keep his mouth shut and everyone in his grade school class would like to smack him." He makes this comment with such hostility that he is largely in the role of the smacker, not the smackee, as if his blood is just boiling to smack this obnoxious kid. Another image that makes Ben cringe is that of being an idiotically eager-to-please kid who runs waving and yelling alongside a television truck that has come into his neighborhood to photograph a burnt-out building. He tries to see himself as a little five-year-old but sees instead a pathetic older kid. He has no empathy—only disgust and contempt—for this child bent on getting recognition from the camera crew. These memories arose soon after his answering my question about what kind of responses he got from his father. He said, "None. Dad never took his nose out of his trade journals." Pressed, he said his father saw him as an idiot he had to put up with. His father was proud of him as his flesh and blood, and even told him gruffly, "I'm proud of you, son," but still Ben had the feeling that his father always thought him a fool. This image of his father's perspective is indistinguishable from his own current images of his child self. One conjecture about Ben's self-image and images of his parents is that his inability to tolerate his own disappointment and confusion about negative images of his parents, especially his father, leads to displacing them onto a self-image that he can attack with less guilt, helplessness, and disruption of his overall world view.

 Ben's self-images contained a mix of shame, embarrassment, and self-disgust. The different emotions suggest the adopting of various stances toward the self. With shame, he is the worthless self and is fully immersed in that being. With embarrassment, a split self exists in which he is parent to a pathetic kid whom others may see. With self-disgust, a split self exists, but the relationship to the pathetic self is aggressive and more fully rejecting, saying, in effect, "You're shit." Self-disgust seemed the least vulnerable of the states but the one requiring the greatest internal split between judge and judged. With self-disgust, the crap-self is compiled with the crap-brother and the crap-parents, and all of them are split off from the brilliant self and heroic father.

One result of Ben's narcissistic vulnerability is a fear that anything he creates at work will be seen as a "piece of crap." He is so focused on how others will see his work that he cannot be alone with a project and immersed in it. He tells a story of a piece of work a coworker had done. Ben looks at it and thinks, "It's nothing, it's so simple, I could never let myself produce something rudimentary like that." Yet he knows the end-users are pleased with the simple solution because it meets their needs. He understands that, had the project gone to him, he would have overcomplicated it in order to make it fancy and impressive and would have ended up making it too difficult to grasp and therefore useless. Despite this insight, he finds it impossible to imagine delivering a simple product that just *anyone* could produce. His stories are suggestive of "anal" conflicts and also of key images of his parents. The interactions between those levels of causation remain conjectural.

Interesting in this case were some addictive dynamics that revealed a second source of disgust similar to that seen in some bulimics when gorging themselves on food. This man at times gorged himself on narcissistically charged fantasies of projects he would complete, promotions and accolades he would reap, gadgets he would invent, and so forth. He would engage in fantasy and in associated small tasks (e.g., outlining a future project, fine-tuning a computer spreadsheet) in lieu of doing more pressing work. As he began down the road of fantasy and play, he felt greatly excited, as a gambler might approaching the craps table or a compulsive shopper entering the mall. But later in his "spree," he would feel an indescribable anxiety linked with his knowledge of neglected quotidian work; he would also feel sickened by the gluttonous quality of his indulgence. Here was self-disgust over surfeit that paralleled what we see with other addictive indulgences.

In his work on anality, Abraham (1921) referred to one narcissistic individual who believed that everything that is "not self is dirt." In other words, if it is me or mine, it is good; if it is not mine, it is worthless. Such an individual might have an interesting history with (and adult relationship to) his own bowel movements, which occupy the space between self and not-self and tend to create in most "civilized" people a somewhat anxious recognition that self and dirt cannot be entirely disjoined, and support an ambivalent, not wholly condemning attitude toward dirt. Abraham's case example differs from the one I have presented in that his client apparently could not tolerate any ideas of an imperfect self, whereas my client admitted to grand lapses from which he expected to rebound to great heights, his life assuming the rhythm of bungee jumping. In my client's life, and those of others I have seen, narcissism produced no steady stream of disgust but instead disgust flared on occasion, as did other emotions instrumental in self-evaluation.

A young woman in treatment had a history of significant depression and an eating disorder, both appearing around puberty, both associated with low self-esteem experienced in the context of disparagement and ostracism by female schoolmates. Later in adolescence, this young woman began to recognize and exploit her attractiveness and vibrant personality to excite and engage boys. Because she adhered to a no-sex-before-marriage standard taught to her by parents she admired, she restricted herself to flirting and took care not to give herself over entirely to boys, lest she be condemned by her conscience. In her 20s, distressed by disappointment in her boyfriend, one night she drank excessively and woke up in bed beside a male friend. Images of herself in this compromised position brought an onslaught of intense emotion, much of it characterizable as self-disgust that was viscerally experienced through impulses to "puke" or "throw up" when thinking about the image of herself in the friend's bed. She said that the thoughts "make me sick" and "make me cringe." Clearly, in this case, self-regard was at issue and her self-regard depended both on attractiveness to men and on maintaining her sexual purity and pride. The fracturing of self-regard was expressed more through self-disgust than shame, perhaps because the violent rejection of a noxious self-image through thoughts of vomiting offered a bit of relief. The links between too much alcohol and vomiting also may have entered the associational net and promoted the specific idea of vomiting at the offending self-images.

Of her words, the word "cringing" seems least disgusted and most ashamed; it lacks the idea of ridding oneself of something objectionable and contains imagery of shrinking and cowering that link it to the diminished stature of shame. Shame, disgust, and other negative emotions often work in concert in limning the pain of narcissistic conditions; if I had to dub one emotion as fundamental or as most representative of narcissism, I would choose shame since it is invariably expressive of reduced self-regard, whereas disgust can direct rejection toward self or others or toward nonhumans.

People frequently seek therapy for painful shame feelings. If they seek therapy due to disgust, most likely the concern is self-disgust amalgamated with shame—consider, for example, a contrite pedophile—or it is disgust sharply experienced toward a partner, parent, or child. The latter burdens an intimate relationship with desires to terminate intimacy and often leads to guilt about wishes to hurt and abandon. Individuals who are not broadly disgust-prone nevertheless may be prone to criticize intimate associates as disgusting in their behaviors and traits. Such disgust reactions may suggest narcissistic anxiety about intimacy with an imperfect partner, heightened dependency fears, or neurotic inclinations to become intimately involved with poorly-chosen, perhaps inadequate mates about whom one's ambivalence is then expressed through disgust. Disgust toward intimate others may also reflect projection of unacceptable self-attributes as in the case of one woman, derided as a child for her "stringy hair," who felt disgust for her partner's hair as greasy and stringy. During her bouts of disgust over her partner's hair, she had no awareness of her own history.

Disgust may contribute to presenting complaints in those fastidious, obsessive-compulsive individuals who cannot tolerate close contact with others or with nature without feeling frequent revulsion. Such sensitivity may cause problems in dormitory or barracks living, in parenting or partnering, or in outdoor life. It may suggest an early history of feeling too often invaded and overwhelmed by outside stimuli—sometimes interpersonal, sometimes environmental—or it may suggest a history of childhood *identification* with stimuli seen as grossly excessive and degraded by the child's parent. Rozin, Haidt, and McCauley (2000) conclude from their research that disgust sensitivity varies widely among individuals and that great individual variability is seen across cultures. Their data suggest that, while we may find no defined "disgust syndrome," we are likely to see, clinically, people with great disgust sensitivity—broadly or context-specific—for whom such sensitivity causes life problems and complaints. We may also see people with extreme disgust insensitivity, which in some cases may suggest a crudeness of character that generates complaint from others, however, such low sensitivity to disgust may also signify the achievement of tolerance, whether for nature or the sometimes humbling realities of human nature.

The relationship between age and disgust reactions is another topic worthy of study. One hypothesis would be that such reactions intensify with the self-consciousness of puberty and decline in early to middle adulthood as life experience increasingly demonstrates that all people—not just oneself—have feet of clay. Both self-disgust and disgust for others should rise and fall in tandem, according to this hypothesis, however, evaluating such dynamics can be complex given that disgust for others can defend against self-disgust and vice versa.

Disgust may appear as both defense and affliction in those traumatized by intrusive physical mistreatment, especially sexual intrusion. For these individuals, disgust experienced during an assault represents the registration of a horrid intrusion. It is also an attempt to rescue the self through mental imagery of extrusion, since physical extrusion of the actual bad stimulus cannot be accomplished. In the aftermath of trauma, disgust may continue to appear as a response to the remembered events, and may also be displaced to symbolically related occurrences. The posttraumatic experiences of disgust may feel both protective and tormenting. If the memories of the trauma are themselves fully interlaced with disgust, the recurrences of disgust may seem inseparable from trauma, thus disgust becomes ineffectual as defense and seems more inflicted than employed. The very fact of one's disgust argues that one has been violated.

Disgust displaced onto elements of ordinary life may become a tormenting interference with commonplace activity. I think of one woman—sexually abused for years as a child—for whom many food items seemed disgustingly infested with crawling insects. Her disgust tended to engulf more and more of her life, as sometimes happens with phobias. The disgust became a plague to her as it rendered ordinary life horrific and linked the mundane to the horrific. Another abuse survivor wrote a letter to her abuser and repeatedly talked of her physical disgust toward him. She also talked of his being a morally disgusting person. She concluded her letter saying, "Thinking of you makes me want to vomit." This person was trying to keep her disgust where it belonged—on her assailant, not herself or her daily life—but the intensity of the emotion nevertheless kept alive her victimization.

One of the great complications for abuse survivors is that the self becomes part of the class of disgusting things because of its contact with the perpetrator and its inescapable involvement in awful moments. A simple, physicalistic logic, that of contamination, prevails and says, the disgusting thing (e.g., the penis) has touched one's body,

Disgust Syndromes 95

therefore one's body is disgusting. Unavailable is a more sophisticated analysis that says, what really is disgusting is the misuse of other persons for one's own gratification. The person develops hypertrophied, simplistically placed self-disgust and also acquires the repeated experience of disgust as ineffectual for self-protection. One's heart and head may hurl abuse at the perpetrator (during the moments of abuse, during a million moments of recollection) but nothing relieving or restorative results: no cleansing of the heart, no apology from the perpetrator, no death or humiliation to the perpetrator. One is left choking on a surfeit of miserable emotion. Similar self-disgust, via contamination, can occur in children who feel disgust toward parents of low character.

The young woman abuse survivor's overwhelming disgust toward food items imagined to be infested seems experientially akin to a phobia and suggests that phobic disgust should be considered as an example of painful, highly stressful disgust that stands out from the many instances of the emotion as a relatively comforting defensive response. Phobic disgust strongly motivates avoidance of the phobic objects, which may have symbolic significance and may point to areas of experience (sexuality, for example) the individual cannot integrate. Webb and Davey (1993) divide animal phobias into fear-based and disgust-based phobias, with the latter usually involving animals that are nonpredatory. Their research suggests that phobias of nonpredatory animals correlate with disgust sensitivity, whereas predatory animal phobias do not show such a correlation. Nor do the two phobia types correlate significantly with each other. This research raises intriguing questions and supports the role of disgust in a subgroup of animal phobias. Since disgust is so strongly linked with views of animal characteristics as unbecoming to humans, we should not be surprised to find disgust for animals—especially smaller animals that can, at least in fantasy, enter us—as a common phobic condition. Likely, the disgust-based phobias involve an admixture of fear with disgust, which leads to an emotion some might call horror.

We have considered a number of psychological conditions in which disgust experience is prominent. Some of these conditions are fairly stable balances of forces within the adult that might be called character disturbances, or just character structures (leaving the question of pathology aside). Other "conditions" in which disgust frequently appears include responses to certain stressful situations (abuse, war) and to predictable developmental pressures.

A further mention is needed of the developmental matrix of adolescence, which is consistent with a low threshold for disgust. Typically, the adolescent opens to the world and tries to integrate many new encounters. The high level of anxiety associated with testing fresh ground leads to ready use of disgust to modulate contact and whisk the adolescent back to the safe soil of the peer group or to more conservative, preadolescent preferences. Certain subgroups of adolescents may use disgust more frequently and emphatically than their peers. Informal clinical observation suggests that teenage girls with a high level of hostile dependence on their mothers exhibit frequent disgust. The disgust serves an "indict-and-extrude-mother" command that is central to their psychic lives. The orientation to quick extrusion can generalize and lead to a reflexive, "Just get rid of it" impulse whenever the child encounters anxiety. Some early research evidence supports the idea that disgust sensitivity does decline after the teen years, with a greater decline for women than men (Rozin et al., 2000).

Chapter 6
Sex, Procreation, and Human Intimacy

> The first time Miriam's belly grows, her mind fills with visions of monsters: something premature and malformed, something late and soft-brained. After Aaron is born, Miriam's fear shifts toward herself. Breast-feeding Aaron, Miriam senses some vital part of herself escaping into his tiny, sucking mouth. She resents that her body must continue to give after nine previous months of suckling.
>
> —Myla Goldberg, *The Bee Season*

Intimate Couples

Human intimacy is a battle with our conflicting desires for union and separateness. It survives or falters on this battleground. Nature has designed us to police our personal boundaries, yet we also must form communities for reciprocal advantage and we must mate, reproduce, and nurture our young. Disgust serves our instinct to preserve boundary, while the intensity of sexual hunger and intimacy-seeking ensure for most people that disgust will be overcome sufficiently to serve reproduction and the quest for family ties. Sexual intimacy and family life never stop eliciting disgust, however, as our mixed desires for separateness and sharing interact.

The natural world generally consists of stuff like us but in forms different from our own. Other human beings are the great exception to this pattern; they share our form, therefore intimacy with them involves contact with those who are very much like the self. Societies underscore certain differences among people—always those of gender and age, sometimes race or visible signs of class—but the human-to-human likeness remains impressive. This chapter looks at disgust as a response to psychic dangers humans experience when the desires for sex and community impel one to open the self and perhaps the body to a creature much like the creature one is.

While it is true that humans incline powerfully toward one another through desires for sexual pleasure, generativity, identification, and enlivening experience, human intimacy carries many risks. Another person close at hand may take more than he or she gives, either concretely or spiritually (leaving one hungry, exhausted, or self-doubting). That person may overwhelm the self with his or her certainty or dogmatism, withering one's self-certainty. She may behave recklessly—for instance, establishing a symbiosis in which interdependence becomes requisite, then withdrawing abruptly so that her partner is left teetering. Partnership may encumber one or both individuals with heavy demands of reproduction, child-rearing, and emotional expenditure that may not result in the coveted self-enhancement or self-perpetuation (the offspring may die or become rejecting or otherwise unsatisfactory; a child may come to represent a diminished form of the self rather than one enriched). Thus human intimacy is risky business and often costly. In this arena of high appeal and sizable risk, disgust is on alert, ready to scuttle the rush toward intimacy so as to preserve individuality and relative self-sufficiency.

Closeness often brings threats to separation and autonomy and thus can promote disgust toward the Other: the overly doting grandparent who pinches the child's cheek, the godparent who proclaims "I could eat you up" may evoke revulsion that distances this adult who might consume the child's being. If the adult is well loved and well known, the child may accept envelopment, but whenever identity is precarious or the adult's approach disregards the child's separateness, even a loved adult will quickly become too physical or smelly or gross. A 12-year-old girl complained she could not stand her father breathing on her or passing her in the hall when he was wearing his stinky gardening clothes. An adult patient was "creeped out" by her mother's requests for back rubs. Such feelings can be expressed directly or via displacement, as with a teenage boy—seeking gender definition and separation from his mother—who developed a phobic aversion to soft, fleshy garden slugs one might step on, creating an awful ooze.

In the early, most sexually intense phase of a coupling relationship, a person may complain he or she has "lost myself" in the relationship but may also celebrate that fusion and later grieve its ending. Similar ambivalence appears around the nurture of infants. Nursing mothers complain about being nothing more than milk machines, yet they also talk with delight of the remarkable physicality and intimacy of their tie to the baby and may resist its lessening as the child matures. The passage that introduces this chapter is remarkable for its one-sidedness. The character, Miriam, presents only anxiety and aversion to breastfeeding, not any countervailing desires.

When disgust muscles out desire, as in Miriam's case, the cost to intimacy is high. At times, the disturbing particulars a partner presents are such that fully eliminating disgust could only signify denial. In other instances, exaggerated disgust over small peculiarities or offenses conveys an exceptional need for distance and the extinguishing of intimacy; that need is the main engine driving the disgust, more important than the particulars (of grooming, social behavior, character, and so forth) to which the disgust attaches. It is important, in looking at disgust within intimate relationships, to consider the larger motivational set of the person, whether that be the need to maintain intimacy at all costs, which promotes disgust denial, or the need for distance, which promotes disgust amplification, or a more balanced set of motives.

Common within intimate dyads is some degree of fear that the Other's being will overwhelm one's own being. This fear promotes experiences of disgust toward intimate others, especially when the Other appears urgently to be seeking close contact. So mothers perceived as needy or clinging become like dangerous quicksand one must avoid, or encounter at great peril. If one's own wishes for closeness threaten to fuel some movement toward the needy Other, the danger is even greater, because movement proceeds from both directions. Intense disgust is a likely outcome.

Disgust as a response to the feared power of the partner's, child's, or parent's intrusive being is consistent with the fundamental structure of disgust as an emotion, active interpersonally and elsewhere, that responds to close contacts that threaten to weaken the sense of self. So mothers or children that disgust are "clinging," as are disgusting substances on the skin, and people who are "too much" in their constant verbiage, piercing laughter, or unrelenting dogmatism will disgust as will images or odors that suggest "too much life." The common observation that "absence makes the heart grow fonder" is understandable in part as a result of reduced need to protect the self from the abundant life of the Other. A mother who has lost an adult daughter to death takes comfort in draping herself in the daughter's coat, an action that would not have appealed to her during the daughter's life. An oppositional toddler longs for the embrace of his absent mother or clings to a stuffed bunny, symbol of mother love.

The character Laura Brown in the novel *The Hours* (Cunningham, 1998) illustrates the role of disgust in expressing profound ambivalence about human intimacy. She wants to flee human involvement for something more isolative and ethereal; she, Laura—akin to many an anorexic—sees life as too earthy, imperfect, and embodied, and therefore, at times, revolting. She experiences a "spasm of fury" (p. 205) when her husband blows out the candles on the cake she has made for his birthday. She had invested in the perfection of this cake and felt, in this moment of fury, that "he is coarse, gross, stupid; he has sprayed spit onto the cake. She herself is trapped here forever, posing as a wife" (p. 205). Laura is snared in ambivalence, her love waxing for a time, then eroded suddenly by revulsion, as the next passage—which follows the spasm of fury—illustrates:

> Dan wraps his arm around her hips. Laura feels the meaty, scented solidity of him. She is sorry. She is aware, more than ever, of his goodness.... She strokes the back of his head. His hair is slick with Vitalis, slightly coarse, like an otter's pelt. His face, stubbled now, has a sweaty shine, and his well-tended hair has relaxed enough to produce a single oily forelock, about the width of a blade of grass, that dangles to a point just above his brows. He has removed his tie, unbuttoned his shirt; he exudes a complex essence made up of sweat, Old Spice, the leather of his shoes, and the ineffable, profoundly familiar smell of his flesh—a smell with elements of iron, elements of bleach, and the remotest hint of cooking, as if deep inside him something moist and fatty were being fried [p. 206].

The final phrases of the passage initiate Laura's next descent into the too muchness of the disgusting. *The Hours* does a fine job giving life to the disgust that flowers in ambivalent love. It also portrays the impact of such disgust and torturously ambivalent love on a dependent child.

For one 30-year-old woman, whose separation from her mother had been hard won, considerations of carrying a child brought thoughts of pregnancy as "gross, weird, and scary." She associated this grossness with the parading of her sexual activity; the scariness and weirdness were linked with the idea of an "alien" overtaking her body. Various images of loss of control and loss of separateness surfaced. The idea of deep intimacy appealed to her strongly, but—beyond some critical point—frightened and repelled her.

Birth symbolized that critical point of separation for this woman. Prior to birth, the baby was conceived as somewhat alien and as sapping her own resources, while also exposing her sexuality and her physical, animal nature to the world. After birth, the baby was a bit more Other, a bit more separate, but less alien. The prebirth images were like those that cancers stimulate: something exists that is part self, part alien, which makes for an odd mix that is highly dangerous to the self. The images of a fetus are more complex than those of a cancer in that one must nourish it and devote oneself to it. One cannot try to eliminate it as one does a cancer, yet it may feel alien and dangerous at times, for example, when one is aware that its presence and constant growth changes one's body, being, and world forever. This woman's introduction of the word "gross" is typical of disgust images. Things seen as gross are in some way too much for the person, often because they are excessive in their growth habits and vigor.

Disgust poised to abort intimacy was exemplified well in the later-life dating pattern of a 60-something woman, Patricia, who, after a brief run of excitement, inevitably became viscerally disgusted with new male companions—their tasteless clothing, their poor manners, their breath, laughter, and thinning hair. The intensity of her reactions was such that intimacy became abhorrent even to contemplate. Invariably she concluded after one of these interludes that she was "better off traveling alone." As time passed, loneliness and a sense of unfulfilled potential dimmed her memory of her revulsion and she began searching again, only to repeat the cycle.

In the background for this woman was an unsustaining relationship with her mother, who had been a self-centered person preoccupied with physical complaints and depression. As a girl, the patient indefatigably courted her mother but had little to show for her efforts except feelings of unsatisfied longing. When she tired of her efforts or was lured by the outside world's brighter colors, she traveled far from her mother and lived more contentedly out in the world. These periods were likely experienced as the "traveling alone" periods of her childhood. To enter into partnership as an adult evoked feelings of emotional asphyxiation that honed her awareness of the potential partner's disgusting attributes and moved her to spurn him. In doing so, she partnered with her mother in an alternative, safely abstract way because Mother had rejected Father as "low-class." She also related to the potential partner as a selfobject whose human imperfections of age and endowment were too reminiscent of her own flaws.

Among the important dangers managed through exclusionary and inclusionary matrices that contribute to identity are the paired dangers of being, on the one hand, absorbed by another, if our being is so like theirs or desirable to them that it becomes too easily "digestible" and in no way foreign or "Other" and, on the other hand, unacceptable to crucial others (because we include within ourselves what they choose to exclude, and therefore they must exclude us). At certain points in development, one of the paired dangers may appear more threatening than the other. The infant, for example, may have no concern about the parent who finds her so palatable she wishes to "eat her up." Yet the school child or adolescent may indeed be threatened by this type of engagement and may fend off such intimacy. I think of one of my nieces, who complained to me once, when she was four and irresistibly cute, "Aunt Sue, you pet me like a pigeon." A schoolchild discomforted by an adult's intrusions may take solace in his or her capacity to disgust the parent—with foul language, or farting, or other coarse behavior—thus engendering in the adult a rejecting response that asserts the child's otherness and gives the child needed distance. In contrast, the infant may be deeply disconcerted by precisely the rejecting disgust response the older child courts.

In a third pairing illustrative of disgust's entwinement with intimacy, a girl wrestled with disgust related to a disturbing event that spoiled what had earlier been a satisfying intimacy. The girl had experienced herself and her mother as very close. When she became a teenager, her parents divorced and her mother took a female lover and informed her daughter she was now a lesbian. The girl felt she no longer knew her mother; her sense of their intimacy was shattered. Also shaken was her sense she could rely on identification with her mother to help her with her own developmental struggles with men. She reacted with disgust, organized around images of her mother's sexuality, and wanted to jettison her now-repulsive mother outside the circle of self. But she felt the loss of her mother keenly and soon wanted her back. Thus motivated, she found a way to integrate her mother's lesbianism. She struggled as well to integrate her mother's secrecy (another disrupter of closeness). Finally she began to share information with friends about her mother's change of sexual orientation. Often, she heard from them: "That's awful, I could never accept that; I wouldn't have anything to do with her if it were me." By that point, her identification with her mother had reestablished itself enough that she became offended by her friends' responses. Her friends did not consider what she would lose if she stayed committed to revulsion. In the end, she moved toward lesbianism herself, which eliminated altogether the disturbance in her identification with her mother.

A growing child who largely loves and respects a parent likely will identify with the parent's ideas of what may be included within the circle of self and what must be cast out. If the parent values cleanliness and order, the child will look with positive regard on those characteristics, although the need to individuate may place some limits on the identification. The child will identify with the parent out of love, but also to control the possibility of parental rejection, since associating with things the parent disdains or disallows obviously brings risks.

In some unhappy family groups, the parent will reject the child no matter what choices the child makes. The child is treated as unacceptable, even disgusting. In these situations, a child may opt to identify with various things the parent labels disgusting and embrace them, saying, in effect, "I don't find disgusting what you find disgusting. Your garbage is my treasure." Perhaps the parent detests noise and noisy people at a time in the child's life when the child is naturally noisy; later, the child becomes a band leader, in effect asserting, "this sound is beautiful, not offensive 'noise' but something that merits applause." The implied message is: "You find me disgusting and I will redeem myself by admiring what you find repulsive." For this child, differentiation of self from Other is imbued with a more aggressive insistence on difference than is the case for the loved child, who can differentiate primarily through pride in self rather than rejection of Other.

A child treated with disgust may identify with the parent's rejecting stance and turn against a third party with disgust. So the child becomes quick to label a sibling with the dismissive words, "You're gross." This behavior signifies the commonplace passive-to-active defense described throughout the psychoanalytic literature. Assertions by one sibling that another is disgusting are common, not only as one child's way to dispose of self-revulsion, but also as a way to surmount envy of a sibling by heaping revilement on that child and hoping the parent will follow suit. The child who tells another, "You're disgusting," also hopes to elicit mortification or self-disgust in that child, as if the sibling's pain will relieve his or her own.

Children of mentally ill or otherwise dysfunctional parents often use disgust to fend off frightening identifications with a parent who has failed to thrive in life. These reactions complicate development as the child endeavors to disown anything shared with the parent and, in doing so, disallows behaviors and characteristics that are valuable and in no way suggestive of illness or abnormality. Unfortunately, the fear of identification often leads the child to wholesale disgust toward the parent and rejection of all his or her qualities. Efforts to eliminate anything that could conceivably link self and parent can lead the child to put large swaths of behavior off-limits, leaving little to utilize in day-to-day life. The result is that the child is crippled, not by illness shared with the parents but by an overly circumscribed set of allowable actions and attributes. Efforts at disidentification often exhaust time and energy in wasteful tasks. For example, a woman with a schizophrenic mother spent endless hours cleaning and organizing her own house, as if her mother's poor housekeeping were a cardinal feature of her psychosis that the daughter could not afford to share. It is helpful, in psychotherapy, to stress that an ill parent has many good and normal qualities that the child can safely embody. Not everything about a mentally ill or otherwise challenged parent defines that person's dysfunction. Many strengths remain, as well as shortcomings that are benign and not suggestive of dangerous dysfunction.

These situations are further complicated by the fact that rejection of all identification with an ill parent may impel the child to disown the vestiges of early, deep love for the parent, an effort that may leave the child feeling depleted or feeling cold and inhuman. One woman, raised by a mentally ill parent, dreamed of guiltily catching a beautiful, vibrant bird and forcing it into a freezer while her mother stood by, watching. The bird seemed to represent the woman's love for her mother, toward whom she consciously felt only disgust and anger.

Disgust, Desire, and the Human Body

Sexual intimacy and general emotional intimacy are seldom sharply divided in the human psyche. Sexual intimacy is somewhat special, however, in that it involves softening emotional boundaries and body boundaries simultaneously. For medical doctors we relax our body

Sex, Procreation, and Human Intimacy

boundaries, for friends our emotional boundaries, but for lovers, both must yield.

The body has many apertures, some permanently agape, some ever shut, some good for one direction of passage only, others swinging both ways, or conditionally ajar or occluded. Eyes, for example, must seal against dust, pollutants and projectiles but open to cool moist air or to pleasant sights (yet shut in the face of scandalizing, blinding, or horrifying sights). Mouths open greedily to food when food is needed, but shut when the belly is full or too ill to digest. They open to explore surfaces when we are infants and later to offer and receive kisses, but they shut against intruding objects or unwanted kisses. Vaginas are sheltered by crossed legs, protective clothing, and cautious attitudes but they widen at times in desire and gape unimaginably to give birth. And so on: with ears, noses, minds. As bags of stuff, we are dotted with portals to be managed according to complex codes and readings of inner and outer circumstance. So for the human being to decide to open emotionally and physically to another in a sustained fashion is a momentous determination. Its success depends on the individual's management of his or her own being, on the selection of a partner who has equally good resources, and on elements of fate over which neither can exercise much command (the occurrence of a car accident, a child's death, a disease).

One consequential aspect of intimacy is the likely identification with the intimate Other. Because sexual interaction entails such close association with another person, identification with that person flourishes and can be either delightful or disturbing. The extreme of disturbing identification occurs in cases of rape or child molestation where the victim cannot free herself or himself from the sense of being dirtied by contagion from the awful partner and his awful acts and intentions. A simpler, more benign example comes from an adolescent boy told by a female friend that another girl—one viewed with contempt in their peer group—had been telling people she and he were "hooking up." The boy's response to this information was "eeew, gross." Here, there is only an image of intimacy but it is enough to conjure disgust. The disgust presumably reflects the boy's concern about being identified with this disliked and denigrated girl—either internally or within the peer group or both. The extreme of felicitous identification occurs when partners are deeply in love, and each believes the other is wonderful.

Between these extremes of welcome and unwelcome association, we find calmly ambivalent relatedness, but also frantically ambivalent relatedness as may occur, for instance, when a young person is extremely uneasy with sexual attraction and intimacy. Good representations of these states of mind can be found in fiction. In *The Poisonwood Bible,* Barbara Kingsolver (1998) describes 17-year-old Rachel's attempt to cope with the notion that a Congolese village chief, Tata Ndu, desires to have her (a white girl from the American South) as a wife. Kingsolver conveys her character's anxiety-laden disgust: "The very thought of being married to Tata Ndu seemed to contaminate Rachel's frame of mind, so that every ten minutes or so she'd stop whatever she was doing and scream with disgust" (p. 266). Soon after Rachel's reaction against Tata Ndu, a rapid evolution from sexual revulsion to excitement, so common in adolescence, brings her to approach quite differently a symbolic kiss from an equally unsavory suitor. In this case, excitement competes even more obviously with her dread of a disgusting association: "Then, ever so gently, he put the lit cigarette back in my lips. It seemed almost like we had kissed. Chills ran down my back, but I couldn't tell for sure if it was thrill chills or the creeps. Sometimes it is very hard to know the difference" (p. 290).

Normal adolescent development—in the sexual sphere and beyond—is an evolution with respect to boundaries. Early adolescent disgust reactions to sexual ideas are not just superego-powered flights from something desired (psychoanalytically speaking, "reaction-formations"). They also represent an instinct toward self-boundary preservation, which needs to be challenged by sexual excitement and yearnings for intimacy and novelty before it will be surrendered. It is too simple to say that the fictional Rachel's disgust for an older black man from a vastly different culture—Tata Ndu—is nothing but the flight from desire. Her fear of desire constitutes one component of her disgust, but the disgust also signifies the threat of difference, novelty, and self-reformation and the need to hold onto what is known to be safe. Real dangers inhere in running headlong into what is strange and poorly understood. Disgust serves our natural caution.

Relationships alter the self by introducing identifications and by introducing new self-images resulting from novel experience, including sexual experience. For the heterosexual female child or the homosexual male child first confronted with images of bodily penetration by the penis—a body part that has a distinct and emotionally laden identity—the threat of loss of self or modification of self through sexual activity can be acute. The young male may feel similarly threatened when

Sex, Procreation, and Human Intimacy

dealing with images of introducing a valued part of his body into another body, likely a female body whose vagina threatens either to take and keep what is his or to dilute its identity with what is hers. Presumably, femininity that can kill is in part a creation of the male psyche fearful that the woman will destroy the male's sense of distinct being: she will do so through the strength of her own sexual identity and the wet, warm, interior physicality of her body. Dangerous femininity can be rejected and diminished through disgust.

A novel, *My Own Ground* (Nissenson, 1976), reveals the association a Jewish woman, Hannele, is led to make between menstruation and evil power, while also pairing menstruation and the life force of springtime. Hannele tells the reader: "One time, I remember, in the spring, when he [her father] knew I was having my period, I was watering some lilacs that grew in our little garden just behind the house. His window was open and he saw me. He leaned out and yelled, 'Don't. Do you want to poison them? You'll kill them'" (p. 124). Similar notions about the female body are found in Jamaican culture, where it is said that money stashed in the vagina can kill and where menstrual flow is believed to cleanse the body but be very unclean itself (Cooper, 1995).

Notions about the destructive power of menstrual bleeding have a long history, as shown in Elliott's (1999) discussion of medieval notions of pollution, sexuality, and demonology. The identification of feminine sexuality with pollution and defilement assign a role for disgust as the emotional component of the urge to keep one's distance from such sexual dangers:

> Myths surrounding menstruation were ancient and ubiquitous. According to classical tradition, the blood itself was believed to possess uncanny powers that could alternately destroy or heal—an association that automatically linked woman's body with supernatural forces. Moreover, as Mary Douglas and others have suggested, a state of defilement was fundamentally linked with the sacred, since both conditions were contagious, dangerous, and circumscribed by numerous prohibitions. . . . In the Hebraic tradition, the Levitican isolation of the menstruating woman was grounded on the conviction that the woman was unclean. She required purification when the danger she presented subsided, but until that time her uncleanness was a source of contamination that could be easily communicated to others (Lev. 15:19–24) [pp. 2–3].

The age-old anxiety about periodic bleeding likely relates to the disturbance of body boundary when inside matter flows out. Loss of blood is especially threatening because blood is known to be essential to life and in the Old Testament was viewed as life itself (see Lev. 7:26, Gen. 9:4). Other powerful emotional dynamics surely contribute to the blend of anxiety, revulsion, and awe in response to menstruation, not least of which might be the fact that menstruation separates woman from man and highlights those functions of woman that man cannot perform, thus leaving the man vulnerable to anxiety about possible incompleteness and inclined to isolate the bleeding female and ritually cleanse her of her femininity before resuming association with her. Though bleeding is associated with body injury and the imminent possibility of death, women regularly withstand bleeding without loss of health, which may contribute to a primitive mixture of awe and fear in connection with their periodic bleeding.

Other matter that leaves the body and disturbs its boundaries—especially when linked with emotional events such as sexual climax or childbirth—brings its own pollution fears. In the Middle Ages, such fears strongly attached to the release of semen through masturbation, also to waste products of parturition. Elliott characterizes the afterbirth as "a material of unrivaled powers for pollution, inspiring unparalleled horror" (p. 29). Given its association with birth—signifying the creation of one being from another, a Godlike act elevating woman over man, and at the same time an act that disturbs the sense of individual boundary (for both genders)—the link between the afterbirth and dangerous and revolting filth should not surprise us. The afterbirth is integral to procreation—the most powerful, awesome, and divine of human acts—yet it is refuse and must be discarded. It must be removed from the sphere of sanctity and value to the sphere of waste. Disgust serves well the transposition of powerful material from positive to negative power. In the footnote to the passage above, Elliott tells us that "one of the women of Montaillou, examined in Jacques Fournier's inquisition, had a crisis of faith inducing her to doubt the doctrine of transubstantiation precisely because the thought that Christ may have been implicated in the filth of afterbirth presented itself to her" (p. 179, n. 76). Though most people routinely tolerate the juxtaposition of precious child with an afterbirth that must be discarded, and is therefore likely to be seen as disgusting, this woman of Montaillou could not accept the idea of divinity contacting filth.

A more contemporary example of disgust toward material that embodies both sex and garbage would be disgust toward a used condom, a sexually linked object that is trash itself and contains leftover sexual material, also garbage. In our society, the used condom discarded in a public park is likely more disgusting than a stranger spitting on the sidewalk. The garbage disgusts in proportion to the excitement and the privacy of the acts from which it derives. Sex trumps eating in both these interrelated regards—interrelated because the excitement of sex promotes its concealment.

The mouth is an interesting aperture in its combination of sexual and nonsexual functions. Humans use their mouths to contact other humans intimately, and associate sexual excitement with such touching, but the mouth is also the organ of ingestion and thus a site of ready disgust lest we take in what could literally sicken us. We are discriminating regarding whom we kiss, our instinctive wariness of germs mixing with a broader psychological discretion about close contact. Caution regarding others' mouths concerns the moist germiness they can convey and also the potential aggressiveness of the mouth, which can suck, bite, and chew up. The mouth is also possessed of a mysterious, active, slimy, and autonomous creature—the tongue—crucial to the aggressive action, speech, which so defines us as a species and defines each individual.

One's own and others' mouths, through chewing, engage in a transformative act that creates "dirt," in Douglas's parlance. Rozin (1999) captures that process in referring to eating as "our moist and messy transformation of identifiable forms into a disgusting wad" (p. 11). Our mouths take familiar, visually appetizing, formed foods and tear, grind, and mash them, mixing them all the while with microbe-laden saliva, to create a slurry like something one might feed to a pig. The open mouth disgusts as it displays this process, so we encourage others to close their mouths while thus engaged.

Sexual intercourse is another variety of close contact that speaks to our wishes and fears regarding loss of the intact individual. For the child of either gender, first imaginings of sexual union likely bring to mind images of intercourse between parents. These mental pictures bring a complex of challenging emotions including the child's fear he or she no longer is special to the mother if Mother is seen as intimately contacting another (an adult partner). The child also may dread absorption into the mother if the child feels identified with the mother's sexual partner who loses himself inside her, or the child may fear the overwhelming excitement of sexual union. Often these dangers are expressed through disgusted rejection of all images of sex until fear is outweighed by sexual desire. Fear is also calmed by accrual of tolerable interpersonal experiences that counterbalance disturbing fantasy. The young woman disgusted by her mother's lesbian sexual activity is no different from countless pubertal children disgusted by ideas of their parents' heterosexual activity. Given the girl's age, she likely had done some integrative work regarding Mother's heterosexuality before being shocked into disequilibrium and a fresh flush of disgust brought on by images of Mother's lesbianism.

The idea of sexual union can bring anxiety over loss of individuality, but this self-based concern is often mediated by disgust reactions to specific bodily encounters. Contacting others' private sexual parts can generate disgust as easily as excitement, and shifts in the quality of the human connection may precipitate sudden moves from one affect to the other. Touching another's genitals with the mouth easily stirs disgust. The genitals are too proximate to the excretory zones for the mouth (and eyes, and nose) to approach without some ambivalence. Oral incorporation, such as that involved in fellatio, is even more susceptible to disgust than simple oral touch or vaginal intake. A number of explanations can be offered. The mouth is imbued with nerve endings deep inside and down into the throat, whereas the vagina is relatively insensitive in the interior, therefore, the sense of taking the penis deep inside can be greater with fellatio. The associations to eating add to the sense of incorporation, as do smells and tastes. Choking sensations elicit feelings that one is being overpowered as well as instinctive rejection in order to clear the airway. For the male who is orally contacting the female genitals or anal region, associations to anal dirtiness or to the messy aspects of femininity, such as bleeding and discharges, may stimulate disgust, as may images of the face smeared by body fluids in a fashion that fuses the sloppy eating of toddlerhood with anality. Procreatively nonfunctional sex acts such as oral and anal sex lack the endorsement of religion and sometimes of society and thus are particularly susceptible to disgust.

Connections between disgust and sharp desire have been noted and analyzed by writers from many disciplines. Attraction (or desire, keen interest, passion, and so forth) is disgust's counterpart and dance partner. We know that Freud understood disgust—along with shame and morality—to be a reaction-formation against desire, meaning it is an expression of aversion that disguises a desire or an appetite. In establishing this concept, he emphasized sexual desire as the relevant variety. Others have noted this relationship of opposites and used a more inclusive concept of desire. Humans create special settings, such as carnival weeks and fairs, that show the constant human engagement with the interplay between the desirable and the revolting, a duality that often associates with other dualities, such as upper class and lower class (Stallybrass and White, 1986). William Miller (1997) addresses this old dilemma concerning whether disgust is always a bulwark against desire or is at times a straightforward revulsion. He concludes: "On the basis of function we can divide disgust into two distinct types. One works in the manner of Freudian reaction formation as a barrier to unconscious desires; its purpose is to prevent indulgence. The other works after the indulgence of very conscious desires; this is the disgust of surfeit" (p. 20). I would add that the disgust of surfeit also does its work in anticipation of indulgence, by consulting past experiences of taking into the envelope of self too much of something (a quantity excess) or absorbing something that in its very nature is too much (a quality excess). Examples of one or the other—or both interwoven—abound. One man finds his father's wealth to be too much; it is ostentatious and gross—even out of control, like gluttony—though at times admittedly appealing. A woman is "grossed out" by the superabundance of clothes in her mother's closet, which brings a sense of gorging oneself on stuff one cannot use. The man discussed in the section on narcissism is disgusted by his own undisciplined indulgence in fantasies of wealth and accolades. The woman discussed earlier regarded pregnancy as "gross." This particular colloquialism, "gross," is especially favored in informal, American language as an expression of disgustingness. It reminds us that disgust generally concerns what has grown excessively and is too large, lively, or vigorous; it thus recalls Miller's hypothesis about "too much life."

With respect to disgust's link to desire, Miller goes on to argue that disgust may actually kindle desire by putting certain things off limits, thus inflaming the human instinct to breach barriers, desiring what we cannot or ought not have. This psychology is what forces the perfectly happy person standing close to the roof edge of a building, absorbing the view, to consider the notion of jumping. It is the aspect of human psychology—perhaps in part a residuum of the child's experience of interacting with parental restrictions—that says, if something is worth proscribing, it must be worth considering and perhaps desirable, like

Eden's forbidden apple, Pandora's box, the breasts the bra conceals, or the lips behind the burka.

A number of writers have shown that disgust and desire battle when complex situations present naturally repugnant elements that have become inextricably intertwined with naturally appealing elements, whether the appeal is sexual or otherwise. The bodily closeness that occurs with sexual exchange, parenting, or lively play often presents such a brew of desirable and disgusting elements. Demonstrating a situation containing massively conflicting impulses, Angyal (1941) discussed certain rites of native peoples that centered on ingesting excrement. He argued that these ceremonies in no way illustrate an absence of ordinary disgust; instead they illustrate the overcoming of disgust, an effort undertaken in order to achieve some highly desirable end, for example, inoculation against the destructive power of a God.

Such an analysis, which involves overcoming disgust to achieve a desired end, would apply in a commonplace situation such as a parent overcoming disgust in order to change the particularly dirty diaper of a loved infant, or a man overcoming disgust over menstrual bleeding, or touching the anus, in order to have intercourse with his female partner. But in the case Angyal presents, it is too simple an analysis to say that such a situation represents an amalgam of the desirable and the undesirable, in which the chaff inevitably must be handled in order to harvest the wheat because the two occur in close association. The analysis is too simple because the juxtaposition of negative and positive elements has been engineered by humans; it is not a natural, ineluctable occurrence such as that faced by an infant's parent. Humans in the tribal example have determined that their security can best be assured through the single form of ingestion that is most disgusting to them (excrement ingestion), which suggests there must be something critical about the power and willingness to overcome revulsion. Perhaps it is a particularly human notion that one needs to suffer or to surmount adversity as a way to show devotion or demonstrate strength to one's God or gods. When disgust toward some stimulus is experienced as one's own natural rejecting response, to defeat that disgust as part of a religious rite may prove devotion to God, or it may demonstrate a strength of will that would impress any god. Some would argue that we first create our gods, then strive to impress them with our devotion.

Sexual Orientation

Sexual pairing potentially threatens us because it involves some loss of individuality. But the societal stamp of approval on certain types of sexual partnering usually helps us overcome the associated risks. We are one with the larger community in attempting approved types of intimate pairings. Correspondingly, socially maligned pairings are higher risk emotionally because they involve all the dangers of other intimate pairings but lack the associated societal sheltering. It follows that disgust is a common response to images of such coupling. Consider, for example, the common homophobic response to images of same sex couples.

Individuals who are themselves gay, lesbian, or otherwise sexually "atypical" sometimes cannot admit their desires or act on them because the danger to self-regard paralyzes them (see Magee and Miller, 1997; Drescher, 2001). The presence of a subculture within which people can feel safely affiliated is a powerful mitigation of the danger of ostracism. Ironically, the danger of ostracism is so intolerable for human beings that we must be safe from ostracism before risking the other great danger, that of intimate union.

A special challenge for gays can be the threat to self-boundary associated with a partner who is too much like the self. Similar dangers are associated with twinship. The ideal of firmly established gender difference and pairings of opposites (or complements) supports the desire for difference as a road to identity. In the 1999 American film *Boys Don't Cry*, we have a story of murderous male rage toward a female who blurs difference by impersonating a male, then engaging another female sexually. The logic of the murderer's fury seems to be that, if a girl can pose as a boy and attract a female, then the specialness and distinctness of the actual, biological male is weakened. Furthermore, the idea of female homosexuality elicits the idea of male homosexuality. In other words, if the female's lover can be a woman dressed as a man, then the man's lover, or the man himself, could be a male dressed as a female, in which case the man loses the sense of masculinity that depends on clear difference. According to this schema, difference secures identity whereas sameness dilutes it. An overweight teenage boy told of stripping off his shirt on a hot day and being told, by another boy, "put those breasts back in your bra." The humiliation so obvious in this example of hearing, "You're not a true guy—you're more of a girl—you're disgusting to look at," can be an omnipresent threat for the gay individual.

Another identity-linked anxiety associated with sexual behavior in general is its underscoring of our membership in the animal kingdom. To the extent we want to lord it over the others in the animal tent, attributing disgusting impulse-domination to them but not us, we like to ignore the essentially animal nature of our own sexuality. One of the offending aspects of homosexuality to some heterosexuals is simply that its difference from their own sexual inclinations draws them to take careful note of animal behavior within their own species. Disgust becomes a last-ditch effort to establish an essential difference between oneself and the disgustingly animal. In other words, the homophobic reaction is not necessarily the response to same-sex body contact per se but may be the response to the animal nature of all sexual passions, seen more clearly when looking at something less familiar and slightly alien. The heterosexual psychological defense against self-disgust is to see the homosexual's behavior as entirely different from one's own and hence unnatural, but the real problem for self-regard may be the "naturalness" of homosexual and heterosexual behavior alike.

Thoughts of male homosexuality are particularly difficult to tolerate for many because images of anal penetration suggest acceptance of anal contact and messiness that we learn to consider disgusting early in development. For many men, the humiliation associated with surrendering adult sensibilities and reverting to infantile anality may be compounded by the humiliation of assuming the passive, stereotypically feminine role of being penetrated. Thus, disgust over male homosexual contact may represent an effort at emphatic rejection of any identification with the humiliated (dirty and feminine) position. Another disgust trigger is the idea of penetration from behind, which connotes for both genders animal sexuality.

Breaches of Intimacy

The high-risk nature of sexual and emotional intimacy creates a readiness quickly to reject a partner who is perceived as unacceptable. We may fight the flowering of such disgust if we are motivated to maintain the flawed relationship, but if the motivational balance shifts toward separation from the partner, disgust can blossom in an instant.

Sex, Procreation, and Human Intimacy

As an example of disgust following a breach of intimacy, consider a man who learns his wife has been sexually unfaithful. He feels intense disgust toward her and reviles her as garbage, trash, a slut, a whore, a piece of filth. One way to understand this fairly common reaction is to think about the shift in self-boundary that accompanied the couple's commitment to partnership. When a couple is formed and formalized, the individuals protect the boundaries of the couple as they otherwise would protect only the self-boundary. The couple becomes a unit and the partner (even if at times hated) is regarded to an extent as self. The investment in the "we unit" is deepened by its inclusion within the self-system.

One of infidelity's agonies is that the disloyal partner has chosen to hold a complex and meaningful secret that belies the idea of oneness. If the couple is unitary, if the partner is self, how can one not know what is happening in the partner's world? Never mind that we do not understand our own psychological workings, the revelation of which may bring self-disgust analogous to our disgust with the dissembling partner. If we learn of secrets that shatter our understanding of our partnership, then the illusion of oneness fractures. Disgust for the partner then serves to extrude that person emphatically from the self-sphere so that the original, unitary self-boundary can be reestablished. So disgust may be an attempt at managing the rent in the sense of self that occurs when the two-are-one experience fails. If the betrayed partner hisses, "You disgust me," he or she is attempting a comforting oversimplification and recasting of the relationship that portrays the partner as easily expendable.

Certain things arise predictably if the deceived person tries to heal the partnership. One is the desire to know everything that transpired between the lovers, even though such knowledge torments. To know what the partner has been doing and feeling can bring that partner back into the realm of self. The pain of such enlightenment mimics the pain of looking at one's own disturbing impulses, for example, toward child abuse or business fraud.

One patient, confronted with her husband's infidelity, used the analogy of being sick and retching to describe the process of mentally confronting what had occurred. She remarked, "When you're sick, you get to a point where you think you're okay but then realize you're not. You need to retch some more." The retching expressed abhorrence of the images of the husband's betrayal. The wife needed to take in all the images and instances in order to contain it all and not feel left outside, but what was taken in kept triggering revulsion. This process typically continues until the person can take in everything without reacting with nausea. Digestion, in a manner of speaking, has occurred.

This woman saw it as a step toward healing when she could tease her partner and expect his tolerance. The good feeling in humor reestablished a bond whereas the pointed quality of the joking sublimated the continuing reality of anger. There is also a sense of, "I can be bad, I can hurt you, as you hurt me, and you will suffer it," which endeavors to even the score a bit; since the hurting occurs as part of a consensual play routine, it is not destructive in the manner of the secret betrayal. There exists a testing quality, too, to the hostile joking, which is akin to the young child's hitting Mother or hurting her feelings in order to see whether she can contain and limit the child's aggression without despising him. The betrayed woman wants to see whether her partner can tolerate her anger and respond to it without repeating the betrayal.

Nonsexual Intimacies and Ambivalent Closeness

Let us look now at some intimate relationships that are not predominantly sexual and consider the role of disgust. Novelist Amos Oz's (1993) title character, Fima, a middle-aged, socially marginal Israeli, illustrates with great humor the role of disgust in ordinary struggles around familial intimacy. Fima has not fashioned much of an adult life for himself, except in his head, which is full of ardent opinions and passions. He lives like a child who cannot pick up after himself, cannot manage his daily schedule, and has no adult relationships. Within this world, his expansive European father looms large and elicits considerable disgust, likely because he does stand so tall, a reality that strengthens Fima's need to stay clear of his shadow and also the gravitational pull of his protective embrace. The disgust keeps Fima from being dwarfed entirely by his father's broad spirit and vivid physicality:

> As the taxi drove off, the old man waved it good-bye with his hat, following his invariable habit. Being a sentimental person, he treated every farewell as final. Fima went out to meet him. He could almost hear him humming a Hasidic folk tune to himself as he climbed the stairs. Whenever he was alone, and even sometimes when he was being spoken to, the old man would be constantly intoning the characteristic ya-ba-bam.

Sex, Procreation, and Human Intimacy

> Fima sometimes wondered whether he did it in his sleep too: like a musical liquid welling up from some invisible hot spring, overflowing his father's shrunken body, or seeping out through the tiny cracks caused by old age. Fima could also almost sniff his father's special smell wafting up the stairs, that smell that he remembered from his infancy and could identify even in a roomful of strangers: the scent of airless rooms, old furniture, steaming fish stew and boiled carrots, feather beds, and sticky liqueur.
>
> As father and son exchanged a perfunctory embrace, this Eastern European aroma aroused in Fima a revulsion mixed with shame at the revulsion, together with the long-standing urge to pick a quarrel with his father [pp. 68–69].

Oz's words delightfully evoke the sensual and emotional brew that is Fima's father (and all his Old World ancestors), the richness of which threatens to engulf Fima's wobbly self unless he picks a fight with Father and engineers some distance. Wrye and Welles (1998) examine this type of connection in their study of "maternal erotic transference," their term for the early physical-emotional bond between mother and infant. They state, "Maternal erotic transferences and countertransferences re-create this primal, preverbal, sensual-erotic contact between mother and infant, and often have a kind of juicy as well as gooey and messy dimension" (p. 35). Fima's erotic bond is to his father, but the definition applies nevertheless. It is in this swamp of sensory impressions of another's body and mental impressions of another's total being that danger (and delight) lurks and disgust stands ready.

The passage also returns us to the humble image of ourselves as "bags of stuff." Fima's image of his old father shows the weakness of Father's failing body, which shrivels and aches, yet his inner "stuff," his spirit, still overwhelms and eclipses Fima. The image of his father's inner stuff is that of the inexhaustible spring of song that flows within the man. An additional passage introduces us to Fima's drive to become disgusting as a way to be as sensually cornucopian and complex as his father:

> When he went into the kitchen to take the towel off its hook, he saw that the sink was full of dirty dishes and that there was a frying pan on the drainboard with pieces of food in it, while on the table the jam had congealed in a jar that had lost its lid. A

rotting apple was attracting swarms of flies on the windowsill. Fima gingerly picked it up between forefinger and thumb, as though it might be contagious, and threw it in the trash can under the overfull sink. But the can was overfull too. The infected apple rolled off the top of the heap and managed to find itself a hiding place among the old canisters and bottles of cleaning fluid.... But when he prostrated himself and started searching behind the trash can for the lost apple, he discovered half a roll, a greasy margarine wrapper, and the burned-out light bulb from yesterday's power cut [pp. 77–78].

Familiar foods become disgusting as time and the elements alter their form and nudge them toward the biologically and psychologically dangerous. The filthy kitchen—symbol of Fima's decadence—disgusts us and him, but lets him compete with his father in being just as vividly alive. We often see people using the power to disgust when they are in a threatened position, for example, the encopretic child desperate to demonstrate separateness or the adolescent impelled to show a parent he or she cannot be controlled. The child produces something it knows the parent would find offensive, whether unwashed hair, foul language, or body piercings. At times, the choice to appear disgusting is a pseudo-choice, a passive-to-active shift in a person whose fear of really being disgusting to others impels him or her to take control of the process, counterfeiting choice. A 10-year-old boy, for example, pours catsup on his ice cream at a birthday party, knowing the kids will say, "You're disgusting." Healthy children often use the power to disgust in order to experience the thrill of having power in relation to adults. Artists use this power as well, as we shall later see.

Fima's father's presence in the organically overrun kitchen becomes unmistakable in the form of the horrible, hated, ineradicable cockroach, a tough, ancient, and graceless denizen of all our hearths who is both Father and Fima, Jew (hunted by Hitler) and Palestinian (hunted by the Jew). Here and elsewhere, disgust is used to resist the attachments that threaten our boundaries and the attractions that bring into focus others who threaten our self-certainty. In this passage, we see Fima moving from disgust at the dirty, refuse-filled, cockroach-infested corner to awe for the tough, six-legged survivor, and we hear him speculating about the root causes of our aversions. His focus has shaded now

Sex, Procreation, and Human Intimacy

from disgust into horror, a related emotion to be considered further in chapter 9. Fima is on hands and knees, searching for his apple, when

> suddenly a cockroach came strolling toward him, looking weary and indifferent.... Still on his knees, he slipped off a shoe and brandished it, then repented as he recalled that it was just like this, with a hammer blow to the head, that Stalin's agents murdered the exiled Trotsky.... The shoe froze in his hand.... He was filled with awe at the precise, minute artistry of this creature, which no longer seemed abhorrent but wonderfully perfect: a representative of a hated race, persecuted and confined to the drains, excelling in the art of stubborn survival, agile and cunning in the dark; a race that had fallen victim to primeval loathing born of fear, of simple cruelty, of inherited prejudices. Could it be that it was precisely the evasiveness of this race, its humility and plainness, its powerful vitality, that aroused horror in us? Horror at the murderous instinct that its very presence excited in us? Horror because of the mysterious longevity of a creature that could neither sting nor bite and always kept its distance? [pp. 77–78].

Fima's speculations about our horror of cockroaches intersect Miller's comments on "too much life" as the primary stimulus for disgust. Fima refers to the cockroach's "powerful vitality" and its "mysterious longevity" despite a lack of aggressiveness.

Tina, a young teen who had entered therapy at age 10, resembled Fima in her outspoken venting of disgust. She treated her mother in a hostile-dependent fashion. She required Mother to tend to her every need and resorted to tantrums if Mother frustrated her. She monotonously portrayed her mother as tyrannical, harsh, hateful, and aggressive. In Tina's case, disgust appeared frequently and seemed linked to a terror of deep and loving attachment.

Throughout the therapy, Tina generated many images of tough hides. She seemed highly ambivalent about toughness. She saw her mother as the ultimate in toughness and was critical of tough-hearted people like Mother. Yet she identified with toughness at times and appeared tough to me in her treatment of her mother. From time to time, she talked about Nazis, the emblem of toughness to the point of brutality. One day, she regarded the office sofa, on which she was seated, and asked, "Is this leather?" followed by, "What is leather? Is it skin?" She reported, wrinkling her nose, that the Nazis made lampshades out of human skin. She wondered if they got the idea from furniture (made out of animal skin) or if the idea of leather furniture came from the Nazis.

The sense I had, on this and other occasions, was that she wanted to *be* a Nazi—tough, squashing others like bugs, reacting to the living world as full of disgusting, degraded creatures she had every right to spurn. Though her conscience could not countenance such cruelty, Nazism nevertheless maintained its appeal, and soon after this session, she talked about wanting a personal "bubble" so she could zap any person, germs, or insects that got too close. That would be cool, she said. Her stance was smug. She wanted to label lots of stuff out there as "gross" and keep it out.

She got specific about what things she considered gross. She thought her science teacher was gross because he took the class for a walk through a swamp where she got dirty (and a boy touched her shirt with a dirty stick). Her uncle was gross because he breathed on her. Public bathrooms were gross because things could touch you, like used sanitary napkins hanging out of wall-mounted receptacles. She herself used only the extra-wide 'handicapped' stalls, where nothing could touch her.

Tina seemed for a while comfortable with her disgust and happy to wield it as a weapon, but then she began to talk about Michael Jackson and his gloves and surgical masks and his device for disinfecting anyone who comes into his house so his air stays pure. Such behavior too could be like a sickness and she thought him "paranoid" and his behavior "gross." Twice she used this disgust word, *gross,* to describe his hypercleanliness. So just when she had committed herself to being the great zapper of disgustingly germy human interactions (the tough-minded Nazi wiping out the earth's vermin), she switched sides in the debate and revealed the part of her that was disturbed by too harsh an attitude toward human contact. Her use of disgust to designate the too finicky or delicate in sensibility was largely unfamiliar to me, and I was interested to find in the work of Menninghaus (2003) a number of references to this variety of disgust in German society. He states, for example, "Since the eighteenth century, the German *eckel sein* not only signifies what is disgusting in the sense of being extremely offensive to the taste; it can likewise be ascribed to persons who are exceedingly delicate, oversensitive, hypertrophically addicted to making refined distinctions" (p. 5).

Over months and years, Tina struggled with her wish to stay in her protective bubble and be the Hitler who vaporized all the vile intruders without feeling any human vulnerability. My sofa seemed to be a particular problem for her because she was drawn to it. She found it restful and she often felt like napping there. She seemed to like talking to me, and she expressed a great deal. She wanted to share and be close, but how could she do all that and still be safely tough? She could not make herself into a Nazi, even if she could let go the wish for closeness, because her conscience would not think well of her for being brutal. One temporary solution was to surround herself with Nazis (her brutal mother, her therapist whose furniture might be made from human skin). Who would want to be close to those people? Not Tina. Their awfulness would abridge Tina's own impulses toward intimacy.

On a later date, Tina spoke of her fear of the germs one might contact in a shared washroom facility. She seemed fearful and ready to react with disgust if the image of touching something contaminating should get very real. Then she started to talk of her fear of Saddam Hussein who had germ weapons and could cause us to get diseases. Then she said she was afraid of Hitler, though he was not a real threat to her, but she would hate to be related to him because people would treat you badly and think you were like him. She implied a belief in a core, genetic self that makes you bad and hated, which is shareable between people, like the diseases transmitted by germs. She has a central idea of a badness that is contagious. You want to stay clear of it, stay pure, but that is hard to do. You try to think of it as someone else's badness or sickness and keep clear of them. Tina seemed trapped by her logic: If you're tough like Hitler or Hussein, you are bad and detestable. If you're not tough, you have no skin at all and are vulnerable to every dangerous condition imaginable.

Tina found closeness even more dangerous than do most of us. The sense I got was that she feared she could want someone badly and if that person were out of reach she would be left in an agony of longing, perhaps also an agony of shame that she wanted someone who did not want her. It was better to be tough and react against others with disgust or, if that failed, to construe those others as awful enough to cancel out your desires. On many occasions, Tina's disgust reactions seemed to operate on a continuum with her Nazi stance. The Nazi is so tough and heartless as to be almost beyond feeling disgust. Living things don't impinge much. The skin has been dried to insentient leather. A disgusted person is still immersed in the stream of life enough to feel endangered and fend off contagions.

Self-disgust is another vehicle for expressing conflicts around intimacy. A middle-aged woman I learned about in peer supervision had major concerns about being disgusting to others. The disgust she imagined others feeling had little moral or sensory content; it was primarily an idea of being personally repulsive. A long string of images of rejection included an image of her daughter ostracizing her from the family, an image of being a poor housekeeper, therefore linked to dirt and disorder, and two powerful images of others looking deep within her and judging her crazy, horrifying, or repulsive. She acknowledged her therapist's comment that she feared his finding her "repulsive," saying, "That's a good word." Ironically, she approved, almost admired, the word that identified her own unacceptability. She went on to tell the therapist that what he thought of her was important to her.

For this woman, disgustingness communicated the fear that her own essence would be rejected by another. The wholesale rejection evidenced in the television prosecutor's pronouncement (see chapter 4), "You disgust me," was, for her, the feared outcome in love relationships. Her personal narrative construed her disgustingness as the result of childhood choices to *be herself* at some cost to closeness with others. Her life story focused on finding herself in a fundamental psychic bind. She longed for a sense of a good and meaningful self but she could not proceed toward the identity she desired because she held a conviction that others would love her only if she dissolved her self and mirrored the other's being. If she were genuinely herself, she would be disgusting to others. One important story centered on her relationship with boarding school teachers from her youth. She recalled feeling pressured to say she wanted to be a teacher herself in order to keep her teachers' interest. She remembered a particular teacher one time looking into her eyes, screaming, and running away. Her associations suggested the teacher saw the girl's true self, which was not the self of an aspiring teacher. On this occasion, the girl was defiant in the face of the teacher's distress and laughed. Recalling this reaction, the woman commented to her therapist that he must see her with disgust. "Why?" he asked. "For certain things I do," she said, apparently referring back to her self-validating defiance of the teacher. This case makes clear disgust's ability to convey core concerns about the worth and acceptability

Sex, Procreation, and Human Intimacy 123

of the self and to do so without much sensory imagery or concern for moral issues.

In the introductory chapter, I commented that disgust protects us from contact that will diminish the self and at times protects us from incorporating what seems "bad." In our interpersonal relations the issue of being good or bad often arises, since goodness is seen as assuring nurturing from outside. Our desire to be good and receive nurturance becomes an important element of conscience, as evident in Tina's desire to be tough, therefore safe, but not bad.

Anxiety about incorporating moral badness can arise in unexpected places. One day, I was watching a scene I found revoltingly violent and gory on television and I shut my eyes. Later, I started to think about why I did that, and I came upon the peculiar idea that, if I could bear to see the vile scene, such toughness suggested I was comfortable with what I saw (therefore a monster of sorts), so shutting my eyes separated me from the production of that kind of awfulness. I also had the thought, which follows from some primitive thinking that may be part of our core, that to see something is to create it: to see is to imagine is to create. The idea is that seeing is not just receiving but is also creating. Conversely, to react with disgust at badness means badness is unimaginable and one is good. So if Tina thinks Nazis are gross, she cannot be a Nazi. If I think violence is abhorrent, I am not inclined to be violent myself. Wurmser (1981) addresses related dynamics in his stimulating study, *The Mask of Shame*. He comments, for example, that "love and power are vested in the gaze.... The eyes are used to create reality and to fix it" (p. 94).

Chapter 7
Disgust Within Family Groups

So Enid tried to be patient, but Chipper sat down to lunch and declared: "This smells like vomit!" You could slap his wrist for saying it, but then he said it with his face, and you could spank him for making faces, but then he said it with his eyes, and there were limits to correction—no way, in the end, to penetrate the blue irises and eradicate a boy's disgust.

—Jonathan Franzen, *The Corrections*

In this chapter, we make a closer approach to the world of the clinician by looking at the nuclear family. Within family groups, we will see disgust contriving to maintain or enhance an individual's power and to solidify subgroup alliances. We also will observe the fear of becoming the object of another's disgust, an important group dynamic and, in certain instances, the desire to elicit another's disgust. Also of interest in what follows are the associations among disgustingness, proliferation, and creativity in living.

Two 40-something parents and a pubertal girl, Virginia, make up the Acre family. Virginia has been brought for treatment by a mother and father who are near desperation because of the girl's frequent outbursts of fury and physical violence, most often directed toward Mother. This family is one in which behavior allowable for the self and tolerable in others is defined very narrowly, especially by the mother, who, though soft and round in appearance and publicly reserved, is viewed within the family as a tyrant. Within this family, much in the world is labeled unacceptable; what is unacceptable in the extreme is seen as disgusting. Power lies in active exclusion, which elevates the status of the purified self, secures the self against disgusted rejection by others, and reduces the standing of the Other. Disgust at times has a weapon-like quality and because the weapon is used within the family, trust among family members is limited.

In the Acre family, great emphasis is placed by all members on cleanliness and order and on their opposites, dirt and disorder. The individuals compete with each other with respect to who can be the most fastidious since that individual can claim the most potent disgust toward the messy or disorderly others. Father is disgusted if his daughter does not replace her toothbrush in the holder or if she leaves hair in the sink. Daughter is disgusted if Father dresses badly or overeats. Father states that his marriage to his wife is one of loyalty, not passion or friendship, and that it is hopeless to cultivate anything warmer between them because, "for one reason, I think my wife's disgusted by me." Mother asserts her disgust toward dirt and disorder in the house and also toward moral failings like lack of effort and industry.

In the parent generation of this family, fears of being nobody and fears of being somebody bad both drive behavior. Mother shows great anxiety about people becoming ethically deviant or unsuccessful and she wants her family to reflect well on her. Father seems primarily concerned with people who are more accomplished and mature than he; thus they are, in his mind, a threat to who he is. Father's fantasy of a good life is a hut in the woods with a few books and other solitary comforts and little intrusion into his seclusion. Father feels so insecure about asserting who he is that he has difficulty buying a pair of pants for himself without asking for another's approval. For Father, loving feelings seem to represent an especially great threat, because love is experienced as something flowing back and forth, which violates his closed experience of self.

In the Acre family, the mother's concerns about "dirt," in the broadest sense of the word, seem to set the disgust train in motion for the group as a whole. In the child's psychotherapy, the theme of disidentification with things dirty and disorderly appeared repeatedly. Her alternatives were to become an arbiter of dirty and clean, like her parents, or to become the dirty, devalued one. Another approach, seen in action in the Berry family next under consideration, is for the child to embrace and "purify" what the parent has designated repulsive. In either case, the parent's inclination to divide the world into things that are disgusting and things that are acceptable represents a threat to the child, who lives in danger of rejection and extrusion. When Virginia's mother is angry with her, she tells her "you have no friends; no one likes you," thus fueling the child's anxiety about being an outcast of no value. Alliances within the threesome form and re-form so that Virginia and Mother will share an openly verbalized view of Father's disgusting habits, then Virginia and Father will turn against Mother for her excessive demands for perfection and order.

Central to Virginia's disgust is the notion of trash or garbage. The pivotal interpersonal fear is to be seen as trash and thrown away. The central narcissistic danger is that one sees oneself as trash and feels shame or self-disgust, as if deserving to be discarded. Safety is sought in fantasies of being pure and superior, thus able to regard others with disgust or contempt, or in externalizations that allow any garbage sniffed out within the self to be the responsibility of another, who put it there, so it really is the other's garbage, not one's own.

A primary fantasy for Virginia appeared to be the notion that her mother, who lost an infant before Virginia's birth, throws away babies and might discard her. When I offered Virginia—at age 11—a reconstruction of what a particular, disquieting experience might have been like for her as a young child, she seemed to ignore me but drew a picture of my trash can with a sign next to it that read, "Throw your trash away." When she entered my office for her sessions, she habitually scrutinized what had been thrown in the trash and speculated—based on the garbage—about my lunch selections for the day. She carefully surveyed the carpet and pointed out bits of lint or food, occasionally picking them up between two fingertips in order to convey them in gingerly fashion to the trash can where she made certain not to touch the trash receptacle. On one occasion, she wrote a story about a baby pig that was found in the trash. She told me she planned to write another one, called "baby," about a human baby similarly discovered.

Rather than risk being the one who disgusts and is thrown away, Virginia became the one disgusted. Rather than be the garbage, she became the chief garbage inspector, or at least part of the inspection team. The price she paid for such a finely tuned olfactory sense was that many experiences out in the world had to be rejected with minimal consideration, as did many aspects (or potential aspects) of herself.

Virginia cautiously experimented with rule-breaking, messy behavior in her therapy, such as spilling water. Once she spent several sessions creating food items out of construction paper, after which she spontaneously acted out a play in which a character named "Small" happened upon a great array of picnic food appetizingly spread across an unattended table. After surveying the scene for anyone who might have a claim to the food and finding no one, Small began to eat. He stuffed himself, then rested, later awakening to find the food magically replenished. Though momentarily daunted by the idea of eating again, he nevertheless ate and enjoyed and again slept, awakened, and ate again, until—like a well-nourished infant—he developed an expectation of a full meal whenever he woke. At that point, he awoke to find the food unrestored and, angered, he acted out his distress by deliberately throwing an empty potato chip bag on the ground instead of putting it in the trash. As he committed this breach of civility, a furious "Litter Bug God" descended onto the stage and berated Small not only for his unmannerly littering, but for eating the picnic food, which the Litter Bug God said was his, and his to eat. Small was frightened and very contrite. He carefully placed his chip bag in the garbage.

In talking about her story, Virginia associated the Litter Bug God with her mother, and associated Small with her father, of whom she derisively said, "he does nothing but eat and sleep." Asked if she herself might in some ways relate to Small, who had some legitimate reason for anger when the picnic food suddenly stopped coming, she abruptly and incontrovertibly changed the subject.

For this family, no acceptable life existed at the border or threshold of self. All that was Other had to be rejected rather than seen as something toward which to reach, even to consider embracing. One had to demonstrate that the self was fixed and perfect as is, and that one desired nothing, inclined toward no one beyond oneself since to do so surely would mark the insufficiency of self. They wanted not to want, desired not to desire. Rather than claiming, as some might, that I am a big enough person to encompass what is new and desirable, the child's and mother's unspoken argument seemed to be, we are perfect as we are and choose not to be tainted. The father's stance was, I am barely making it as I am, I am a speck of dust, a hair's breadth above nothing, and can't afford to embrace anything questionable from outside that might overpower me.

This family demonstrates well the passing of disgusted rejection responses from generation to generation, as the younger generation fears becoming the object of the older one's disgust and chooses to reject rather than be rejected; or fears being the only one with a "weak nose" for ferreting out the disgusting, thus running the risk of accepting contact with it. Since disgustingness operates according to the rule of contagion—touch it and you become it—to accept the things or people others see as disgusting makes you disgusting as well. If society tells us that "cleanliness is next to godliness," we had best react with disgust to a neighbor whose bathroom is festooned with hair and soap scum, unless we choose to be known as accepting such filth, thereby becoming ourselves disgusting. This family brings to mind the comments of sociologists Stallybrass and White (1986), who consider how disgust and exclusion support the self:

> It has been argued that "the demarcating imperative" divides up human and non-human, society and nature, "on the basis of the simple logic of excluding filth." . . . Differentiation, in other words, is dependent upon disgust. The division of the social into high and low, the polite and the vulgar, simultaneously maps out divisions between the civilized and the grotesque body, between author and hack, between social purity and social hybridization. . . . The bourgeois subject continuously defined and redefined itself through the exclusion of what it marked out as "low"—dirty, repulsive, noisy, contaminating [p. 191].

Before moving on to discuss another family, I will introduce some process material from the adolescent phase of Virginia's treatment that shows her longstanding, ambivalent identification with Mother's fastidiousness and seems to demonstrate as well how that tension finds its way into her efforts to integrate her adolescent sexual awareness. She seems especially anxious about boundary violations at this time. Her history of fearing "trashiness" suggests that images of intimacy and penetration will stir anxiety about being contaminated and made worthless. Also operative may be a longstanding anxiety about pregnancy, rooted in part in fantasies of killing Mother's other babies, since she gave birth only to Virginia. The anxiety about her own sadism toward Mother's babies joins forces with her fastidiousness to create some powerful disgust experiences around images that appear to represent monstrous pregnancies. The pregnancy images signify her failure to defeat adolescent sexual curiosity and desire. The partial process note that follows was made during the adolescent period of treatment:

> After one week focusing on disgusting, bloody bandages and a second week focusing on horrible skin penetration, V comes in with a miserably painful headache and proceeds to spend much of the hour articulating a disgust reaction so strong it dwarfs

any previously reported and seemed almost traumatic in magnitude. She complains quickly that she was forced—in her painfully headachy state—to look at the most disgusting fish imaginable while eating in a restaurant over the weekend. This fish was the vilest of colors; it was a yellow that was intolerably awful in a fish. I note that yellow is her favorite color, what she calls her "Virginia color" because she's known for loving it. She acknowledges this but insists the yellow was utterly disgusting on this fish which was crammed alone into a tiny tank and didn't move properly or look right. It didn't do anything at all. She explains that most fish have a "meaningful life" but not this one. She repeatedly imitated how its mouth gaped and its wide eyes blinked and she complained bitterly about its "staring" at her while she tried to eat. The boy next to her noted this and expressed horror, exclaiming "that fish is staring at you." She hated this fish. She seemed overwhelmed by revulsion just talking about it. I found myself laughing some internally at the melodrama and the imagery and ideas, but there wasn't much humor for her in the subject matter. She seemed genuinely quite upset and she seemed genuinely angry she'd been exposed to this vile, upsetting thing, and she seemed somewhat angry with me for not fully grasping the awfulness of this experience.

Virginia had been reacting with disgust to one thing or another for weeks, but the revulsion toward a fish seemed so odd, so new, and so pronounced that it struck me as likely to be a symbolically meaningful displacement and, given recent material, I wondered about sexual meanings. I was puzzled over how to work with this material. I wanted to reflect that it stood out as somehow unusual for her and perhaps had some meaning other than its surface meaning. My process note continues as follows:

> I commented a couple times on her seeming particularly inclined to disgust right now, perhaps even toward things she wouldn't ordinarily react to. She said that in fact this fish-disgust was a new thing. She hadn't felt this way in the past. She continued down the disgust road, going on to talk about snails and fish eggs and people buying and eating that weird stuff, her friend's grandfather loving it and buying it and putting it in his

Disgust Within Family Groups

refrigerator. She hostilely suggests you ought to just scoop the disgusting eggs out of the fish tank—it's all the same, isn't it?—not pay lots of money for them. She can eat some fish but only white fish. Tuna is completely disgusting, and catfish—what could be more disgusting than that. Periodically, she mentions something and visibly shudders with disgust over the image and seems angry that these things exist and enter her mind and torment her. She talks about various other things that are disgusting. She talks some about snakes, discriminating different types. Ultimately, they're okay, not slimy, not in water, though somewhat disgusting because they have no legs. But not intolerable. Fish though aren't normal. They have no legs or arms. Again, she's angry that it's not obvious to me that fish are an abomination and shouldn't have been created. At this point, I think she may be one of the drafters of Leviticus.

I am struck by all the imagery that seems in some way threateningly sexual and reproductive. The note continues:

I am trying to find a way to say something without saying too much. I make some general comments, awkwardly, about how sometimes when people are getting disgusted very easily, it can be they're working something out in their minds, they're in a kind of transition. I say that sometimes it's body kinds of things that people have gotten interested in, but disgusted by, too. I mention that I'd asked her last hour whether she was thinking about sex or periods or something like that.

No, she indicates to all of that and quietly shrugs me off but with no evident hostility and a run of new associations. Finally, I say that one thing I think of with all these fish-in-a-tank images is babies in the uterus, with the water around them. That's *my* association, I tell her, to what she's describing. "Really?" she wants to know. Now she's a little interested and we get into a long, somewhat playful exchange. I comment on how people say fetuses go through a fish stage. She doesn't even want to think about that, she says; she doesn't even want it in her mind, awful as it is. But she's interested in the water connection. She hadn't thought of that. She seems a little surprised and confused by the image as if she knew fetuses lived in water but at the same time didn't know it. She relates seeing a film in health class on a human birth, which includes the waters breaking. She seems pretty overwhelmed by what she's relating.

I derived from this hour a sense that there existed some value in expanding Virginia's field of associations to include something more real, less in displacement than the fish, by bringing in the idea of a pregnancy. The route to achieving this was my claiming the association as my own so as not to threaten her with a bluntly interpretive stance that was perhaps inaccurate or at least premature. From that point forward, we could explore her associations and some real memories and ideas about birth, and we could move beyond her state of near-paralysis by the disgust reaction she had had to the fish.

In the Berry family, the borderland region between the groomed, chemically sterilized lawn and thick, greasy life is terrain that holds some degree of interest for the family members and exhibits more than the occasional sign of habitation. Family members view such borderland regions ambivalently, so that whoever is positioned at or over the border evokes at times the special admiration that goes to the artist or creative thinker and at times elicits revulsion.

In this family of three children, the children took differing courses with respect to disgust, the oldest easily disgusted, the second embracing the earthy things that repulsed the first, and the youngest blending the two older siblings' approaches. Alice, the middle child, was viewed ambivalently within her family; she was seen as creative and talented, and was admired sporadically for those traits, but she also was characterized as a messy individual inclined toward poor housekeeping, sloppy dressing, and oddball social behavior. She ventured further than the other family members into the muck of emotional, social, and intellectual life by working with marginal people as a legal aid professional, choosing boyfriends from various races, ethnicities, and socioeconomic classes, declining to shave her legs, and embracing liberal political and social ideas.

As a young adult, Alice sought therapy for depression. Her history suggested some degree of early rejection by her mother, who characterized the child in derogatory ways that classed her as an inferior, disappointing, rather disgusting outsider (these characterizations alternated with equally distorting idealizations of the child as a fair-haired angel). This immature mother drew on traditional terms of racism, deriding the dark aspects of the child's coloring, glamorizing

Disgust Within Family Groups

the light. Father was less inclined to such bifurcated thinking, but was a fastidious individual whose intolerance for disarray was impressed on Alice, who already had been characterized by her mother as somehow dark and unattractive. This child made efforts to identify with the exacting father, who might yet be pleased, but she did not fully disavow or flee the messy child identity that had been assigned her within the family.

The various forces arrayed in this family produced a complex psychological outcome. Alice struggled with ongoing self-disgust organized around notions of badness, but she also found ways to welcome and integrate the dark-child identity by recognizing its association with her creativity and with her love of nature and her affection for dark-skinned people, who had figured importantly among her school friends. Alice owned, or displayed, what others in the household disavowed. As a result, she warranted mixed regard.

Alice's creative bent remained for her a questionable gift because it maintained its association to the bad, dirty, rejected child, yet it was also deeply valued in that it allowed her to affirm herself lovingly by saying, in effect, "I am not a dirty girl, I am a girl who makes things grow out of the soil; I am not a weird outcast, I am an artist; I am not a mess, I am relaxed and natural, like Mother Nature (who drops her leaves on the forest floor and never cleans up)." Also available to Alice was the hostile power of the disgusting one, which allowed her to achieve revenge against others by forcing them into contact with things that make them anxious. This is the power encopretic children may feel in obliging a parent to tend them when they are disgustingly soiled.

Individuals who love nature, as Alice did, often are deeply identified with it, so that the threat of invasion by a bad Other or inundation by too lively an Other is not readily aroused for them in relation to nature. Natural forces are not experienced as alien to the self or more vigorous than the self. They represent instead a distillation of the essence of self, especially in circumstances where direct self-expression is prohibited but self-expression can be found by making an attachment to external forms that represent one's own vitality. Alice showed an early interest in endangered species that spoke to her identification with nature and the threats to it.

An example of the Berry family's interactions around cleanliness, dirtiness, and nature came from a story Alice told in which her father walked her out to her car, which was parked outside her sister's house, and asked her in a good-natured tone, "Which one is yours? the dirty one?" even though the street was lined with similarly dirty vehicles. Immediately after voicing this jovial insult, he turned toward the brother's garden, on which Alice had done a great deal of work weeding and turning the beds, and said admiringly, "I was looking at what you did in the garden." He then went to her car and offered to clean the windshield, again emphasizing the dirtiness of her vehicle and resurrecting, for Alice, his habit of removing her glasses from her face when she was a child, commenting on their being filthy, and lovingly cleaning them.

In these fragments of behavior appears a parent's need to characterize his child as dirty in part so that he can be important to her as her loving cleaner, in part to dissociate from the dirt and disorder that seem to threaten him. Also evident is the admiration for the gardener who makes dirt her plaything and the source of abundance and beauty. He regularly encouraged Alice's creative activities and not infrequently assigned her to do his own creative work, saying, for example, "I had a great idea for a sculpture you could make," or "I saw a wonderful Van Gogh exhibit. Why don't you take an oil painting class?" Messiness removed to the domain of art was safe.

In their adulthood, when Alice's older sister, Ann, came for a visit, Ann commented on a neighbor's wild but much-loved garden—similar in style to Alice's—saying, "Doesn't she ever tend this garden? It's such a mess." The older sister was somewhat like Virginia in her phobic and obsessional characteristics and her clear identification with the fastidious parent. The younger brother seemed to use both the middle child's creativity and nature-affinity and the oldest sister's neatness to create for himself a hybrid of inclusionist and exclusionist attitudes that allowed for a libertarian fashion sense, considerable intellectual inquisitiveness, but a judgmental attitude toward other people.

Identified as she was with the good and the bad of messy nature, Alice liked and shared a poem entitled, "Cattails: A Marsh in March," by Brad Leithauser (1993) which begins, "It's like the morning-after some outré/ultimate year-end blowout, and clearly whatever cleanup was started was a shall we say halfhearted endeavor.... Most of the loose-strung bunting's been taken down but hasn't yet been swept away, the floor's a mess—a massacre—of broken-limbed furniture." This poem seemed to speak to Alice's wish to elevate messiness to something natural, pleasure-associated (the grand party), and allied with art, and to rescue it from associations to parental rejection and aversion, and the "cleanliness is next to godliness" Judeo-Christian ethic.

People like Alice find pleasure and self-regard in an inclusionist stance toward life's varied experiences. They are reluctant to shut the door to sensual, emotional, or intellectual content and their values may deviate from the societal norm. They tend to have enriched inner lives but risk negative labeling and exclusion from groups, and in some cases they will resort to using their embrace of what others consider unacceptable to wield the power of the leper, which is the power to disgust others. They are apt to elicit a degree of admiration if it is clear that their inclusionism has its limits and does not signify a lack of capacity for disgust. In other words, they are not primitives who lack discernment. They are not urine-drinkers or purveyors of child pornography. They draw lines both in the physical sphere and the moral sphere. Ironically, people like Alice may direct their own disgust feelings to the clean and orderly, for example, they will feel morally disgusted, or outraged, by people who are narrow-minded, who "clean out" their libraries of unacceptable materials or "keep their neighborhoods clean" through elitist, exclusionist tactics. Passages from Denby on his Galápagos trip show a movement from his early discomfort and disgust to the more accepting attitude toward nature's abundance exemplified by Alice:

> The frigate birds were scary and strange, yet they seemed to lift me off the deck with their wings. Fear, disgust slipped away; I felt a small tingling on the back of my neck and a great lightness.... A longing to join something I feared...?
>
> Viewing nature as something composed and static was a way of pretending I didn't belong to it. Like it or not, I was part of the ceaseless flux, which induces crabs, spiders, sea lions, frigate birds, and eco-tourists, all equals in nature, to jostle for food and space, competing and coöperating at the same time [pp. 61–62].

People with more exclusionistically oriented identities find satisfaction in their fine noses, their ability to discern excellence and reject mediocrity or inferiority. They draw their self-boundaries narrowly, excluding more than they include. They run the risk of narrowing their experiences and social circles radically; they also risk self-disgust if their own behavior deviates from the norms they have set, but they are relatively safe from disgust-like rejection by the dominant segment of society, and they have a clearly marked path to self-approval, which brings satisfaction as long as they follow it. They, may, however draw contempt as too prissy, or as controlling and unadaptable.

Chapter 8
The Artistically or Scientifically Creative Individual and Freedom from Disgust

> The swamp is soaked with danger—its insidious, murky, sexual wet nature always about to leak through the tight barriers of morality and hard work of anyone who goes there. For aeons, artists have recognized that state of dissolution, the firm lines of logic, brittle with rust, disintegrating, the mind a sudden blender whirring away, mashing one image against another, the dreaming self rearranging visions into slippery, glittery paradox, surreal montages of the improbable. This is the terror and truth of art, this perception of other realities, of mysteries emerging and shattering.
>
> —Barbara Hurd, *Stirring the Mud*

Humans hunger to generate intellectual and physical forms that are original and identifiably our own creations. At the biological level, we want to procreate, which allows elements from two individuals to combine in order to create a unique life. At the psychological level, we strive for intellectual originality in which familiar ideas and observations are brought into new and surprising relatedness, to amaze and delight. In producing babies, what each couple engenders is predictable in the majority of its characteristics. Joy inheres in knowing the child you have fashioned is one of a kind, but joy exists as well in creating what everyone else creates and celebrates (a human child). Major, visible aberrations bring anguish, even revulsion linked with thoughts of monsters. In the realm of intellectual or artistic creativity, a greater variety of avenues lies open to us because the risks intellectual deviation brings seem less consequential than those associated with disturbed sexual reproduction. What distresses more than producing a child seen as monstrous? In the domain of intellectual creation, familiar forms serve as guide, but considerable choice exists; choice leads to special psychic dangers and rewards and to a role for disgust in containing our creative adventuring. Stories such as Shelley's *Frankenstein* (1831) speak to the intellectual's and also the parent's creative tensions.

Creative people easily find themselves at society's periphery. They are individuals not cut from their era's most popular mold. Perhaps they are admired as leading richer, more inventive, more productive lives than others, advancing intrepidly where others dare not venture, but they will also be reviled as bizarre, maladapted, or outrageous, and as disrespectful to an existing ethos. At the extreme, they become our witches or untouchables, whose perversity of nature is feared as contagious. This subject is an old one, already well examined in print. I will therefore restrict my focus to the role of disgust when the creative act becomes threatening to an existing order.

As noted earlier, disgust is a conservative emotion that attempts to maintain the value of a treasured concept. In 1999, a controversy erupted about public funding of the Brooklyn Museum of Art, after the museum chose to display the work of a British-born artist of Nigerian descent, Chris Ofili, whose 1996 painting *The Holy Virgin Mary* was decorated with a clump of elephant dung and cutouts of genitalia from pornographic magazines. Some, including New York City's mayor, Rudolph Giuliani, found the work so disgusting, so vile and sacrilegious, that they fumed over the government's financial support for the institution that displayed it and thus seemed to honor it. Other citizens found it repugnant to imagine the government extending its controlling hand into the business of an esteemed institution that had made a conscientious decision about what constitutes art. For the museum, the revered principle was free expression, and it felt that the juxtaposition of excrement and Christian images in the context of art had no relationship to desecration of an actual place of worship.

Looking psychologically at the reactions to this work of art, one can conjecture (risking offense) that those most anxiously or angrily disgusted by the conjoining of Christianity and excrement might carry, as part of their personal makeup, a greater vulnerability to self-hatred should they offend a parent figure by embracing the dirty, primal self, as compared to those not excited to disgust (even should the artwork at issue displease them on compositional or semiotic grounds). One might even conjecture that harsher rejection—likely conveyed in part through disgust—might have figured in the stridently offended individuals' upbringing, perhaps in the sphere of toileting, perhaps in some analogous domain. An alternate hypothesis, potentially interactive with the first, would be that idealization of the parent was psychologically more valued by the disgusted group. Such need for idealization might rest on anxiety about becoming the object of disgust, but other explanations are possible. An individual might fear primarily his or her loss of respect for the parent, not the loss of self-regard.

For the group that reveres free expression more than respect for boundary, art is akin to a Winnicottian playspace, where adults are able to function in a childlike "let's pretend" or "let's explore" mode of action. Some in society position themselves to separate art from daily interaction, thus they would allow Robert Mapplethorpe to explore sexual themes visually that they would not want their neighbors to explore with anyone's child. Others make no such distinction and consider certain juxtapositions off limits, whether the context is artistic or not. For the indignant, disgusted group, the sacred is among those subjects unsuitable for play.

Creativity tends to join domains, not divide them, whenever meaningful associations can be found by the artistic mind. Seamus Heaney's poems about the earth are simultaneously poems about his father. He shows us the connection between digging in the rich earth and searching for his father. In doing so, he demonstrates the artist's natural inclination to cross boundaries, blending domains often kept separate and risking aversive reactions from those more comfortable with well-defined, compartmentalized realms. In his poems about swamps, bogs, and other sodden landscapes, he chooses a subject matter that itself denies boundaries and, for many, prompts disgust. But for Heaney, these transitional realms are those he cherishes; they are the birthing grounds of richest life and show us the artist appropriating a freedom to explore domains often blocked by disgust.

Heaney's collection *Opened Ground* (1998) begins with the poem "Digging," of which I include the second half. Digging with the spade and digging with the head and heart are analogized, and the poet conveys his sense that the spade-dug, earthy matter most evocative of inner life, in head and heart, is the matter that teases many over the edge of acceptance and into the world of disgust. For him, that includes "the cold smell of potato mould, the squelch and slap of soggy peat":

> By God, the old man could handle a spade.
> Just like his old man.
>
> My grandfather cut more turf in a day
> Than any other man on Toner's bog.
> Once I carried him milk in a bottle
> Corked sloppily with paper. He straightened up
> To drink it, then fell to right away
> Nicking and slicing neatly, heaving sods
> Over his shoulder, going down and down
> For the good turf. Digging.
>
> The cold smell of potato mould, the squelch and slap
> Of soggy peat, the curt cuts of an edge
> Through living roots awaken in my head.
> But I've no spade to follow men like them.
> Between my finger and my thumb
> The squat pen rests.
> I'll dig with it.

Heaney ends his verse by exposing the central metaphor of this, his keynote poem. His father and father's father used the spade creatively as they dug into the earth, removing peat (itself a compression of generations of living matter), planting potatoes, "living roots," but his own creativity employs the pen and the searching mind and heart. The men of his family are his own living roots, restored and nourished by his creativity.

The hip-hop song "One Mike" offers an interesting comparison with and contrast to Heaney's theme. The song turns on a chain of associations among various tools of self-expression and personal power. At one end of the chain is the rapper's microphone. At the other end is "one bullet." The songwriter's logic both mirrors and reverses Heaney's in that, for him, the art form represents the prosocial form of an expression for which the physical form or tool, the bullet, represents the antisocial. In Heaney's construct the art form, the poem, is imbued with a sense of loss, perhaps compromise, because the hard metal tool, the good spade, is not his to command. The rap invites disgust and outrage for its willingness to entertain antisocial violence as par with art. In that regard, it affiliates with the excremental art mentioned above or—outside art's encampment—with many a child's use of bad smells, bad speech, and bad friends to arouse a parent to response.

Disgust itself and slimy, wet, protean habitats are themselves frequent topics of the artist's exploration, a fact that may speak to the artist's intuition that he or she gravitates to the borderlands of our sensibilities. We see Heaney colonizing that earthy realm in the poem just quoted and showing us the creative power he associates with mucky depths. The title poem, "Death of a Naturalist," is a veritable ode to disgust imagery that shows us both the fascination and the revulsion, even horror, of this sphere. The young naturalist in the poem is delighted with the earth's creatures, "But best of all was the warm thick slobber / Of frogspawn that grew like clotted water / In the shade of the banks." Heaney also shows us that earth's procreative passion and urgency are not child's play. An oedipal theme rings out, as rutting bullfrogs—"the great slime kings"—avenge the invasion of their sexual sphere. We are reminded also, as in earlier chapters, that it is overgrowth that disgusts us more often than scarcity or barrenness. This pattern will emerge again in the consideration of disease and its manifestations.

Anne Michaels's child survivor of the Holocaust emerges physically out of a literal bog and spiritually out of the sludge of death and horror he has experienced. Michaels conveys a place of dark chaos—both physical and spiritual—but the chaos is that of life primeval, of *Genesis,* in which we encounter "the earth being unformed and void, with darkness over the surface of the deep and a wind from God sweeping over the water" (Gen. 1:1). It is the dark chaos—place of disgust and awe—that precedes birth, light, and order and forms the vibrant core of them. Michaels's boy hero tells us: "I squirmed from the marshy ground like Tollund Man, Grauballe Man, like the boy they uprooted in the middle of Franz Josef Street while they were repairing the road, six hundred cockleshell beads around his neck, a helmet of mud. Dripping with the prune-coloured juices of the peat-sweating bog. Afterbirth of earth" (p. 5). In comparison to Michaels's bog boy, we have Heaney's "Grauballe Man," who is one with the earth and indistinguishable from it, "as if he had been poured in tar, he lies a pillow of turf and seems to weep the black river of himself" (p. 110).

In the realms of these two poets, everything is connection. The man is the earth; there is no separation and therefore nothing to grieve in his death or odd preserve. In Michaels's "six hundred cockleshell beads around his neck, a helmet of mud," we may hear *The Tempest:* "Full fathom five thy father lies, / Of his bones are coral made, / Those are pearls that were his eyes. / Nothing of him that doth fade / But doth suffer a sea change / Into something rich and strange. / Sea nymphs hourly ring his knell" (Act I, sc. ii). Death, transformation, rebirth . . . all is connection, and the skittish mind and heart are enriched, appalled, and disgusted by the expansion of our beings to include all that lives and creeps on the earth and within it. For a great many poets, the most evocative realm of connection and breached forms is the earth's domain, where we are entirely of nature.

In nature there is no custom, no decorum, no propriety. Our attention is drawn appreciatively to structural qualities or to those that stimulate the senses. The artist of the borderlands may be spurred by nature to cross boundaries that human societies charge with emotion. A photographer such as Mapplethorpe suggests that the sensuous curves of the nude body are the curves of the luscious pear or the stones in a stream: all are nature working her visual, textural magic. But the conservative emotion of disgust carefully considers what lines of demarcation we have chosen to abandon and considers as well all the societal meanings attached to the mingled realms. An anxious member of our human race, armed with disgust, will want to know whether some offense against our ideas of goodness will be committed if A joins with B and will want also to know whether the joining of A and B will somehow muddy or dwarf his or her sense of self. If any of these dangers obtain to the joining of A and B, disgust—the emotion of our caution—will insist on a separation, saying for example that there is nothing beautiful about two men naked together and that the lovely curves, reminiscent of two pears in a pottery bowl, are immaterial. Another nervous one among us will use disgust to draw a line elsewhere, perhaps welcoming the photo of two men together, but feeling revulsion on viewing a photo of a man and a young girl.

Morally informed and invigorated disgust reactions are useful both in situations in which impassioned repression affronts us and those in which unleashed passions appall. Human society involves a dialectic that moves between a nonjudgmental stance, which expands the circle of what we are able to see, to imagine, and to consider without revulsion, and a judgmental posture that establishes boundaries that assign meaning and determine what is good, what is bad, and what shall not pair with what. A literary agent lavished praise on a female client's freely exploratory and explicit novel about female sexual power, but, when she came to a passage in which oral sex was used by the heroine to save herself following a kidnaping, she reacted with sharp disapproval: "Leave out the cock-sucking scene . . . it is ugly and revolting."

Clinically, we ought to alert ourselves to possible disgust dynamics in cases of artistic inhibition, both in those individuals previously productive and in those whose lives have spawned little creatively. All kinds of internal critics inhibit artwork, but not all utilize disgust. Shame steps forward more frequently and tells the would-be artist his or her work has scant merit and will likely bring ridicule or disregard. Self-disgust, or fear of the disgusted audience, comes to the fore when the artistic spirit wants to move into a terrain the mere consideration of which might be unseemly, or when the artist seeks to convey an opinion that could give offense to others and incite their disgust toward the artist. Some *topics* are disgusting regardless of one's perspective or commentary on them. A book on feces or a history of farting are examples. Other topics disgust only if one's particular stance violates a social, familial, or personal norm. Generally, such violation positions the artist on the side of the too permissive, too liberal, or too embracing. Thus, to write about homosexual behavior in a spirit of acceptance or celebration might bring the threat of self-disgust or others' disgust and, in some instances, self-censorship would proceed by way of inhibition.

The fear of being disgusting is never free from social context, but in many cases of artistic inhibition, it is self-disgust (ultimately rooted in developmentally salient social relations) that acts most powerfully and may act unconsciously so that the artist has no insight into his or her own fear that the creative mind untethered may stray or sprint toward areas of unpleasantness about which decent people do not discourse. The mind unfettered may consider sadism, for example, or forms of barbarism, or curious adventuring into darkly anal spaces or fetid mixtures, or impolitic views on race or sex. The uninhibited may travel anywhere, may be savage or pig, tyrant or slave, nymphomaniac or wet nurse. Many would be arrested by disgust before reaching such realms; others would be apprehended by self-disgust for possessing the inclination to venture there.

Good art will at times expand the range of what we tolerate. One mechanism for such effect is the artist's bridging of the space between the acceptable and the unacceptable. The artist invites the viewer or reader into identification with him or her, and into trust in the artist's voice, by offering familiar and pleasing elements that the active audience affirms. The artist then takes a leap beyond the audience's comfort, but the audience extends itself, trusting the artist as guide or good parent, and establishes increased comfort in visiting whatever new ground the artist has led him to reach and explore. Such processes are largely unplanned and incalculable for the artist, who cannot know the emotional range of his or her various audiences, but operates instead from a personal instinct for exploration. The goodness of fit between artist and audience may rest in part on the chemistry that allows a particular artist enough common ground with a reader or viewer that kinship and communication are established, but enough stretch toward new terrain that excitement stirs. If unfamiliarity is too great (producing inscrutability) or too slight (breeding monotony), then the match will not satisfy.

Emotional manipulation is one basis for distrust in the artist and resistance to following. If an artist is caught presenting symbols calculated to evoke strong emotional response and doing so in the absence of important meaning he or she wishes to convey, the audience will likely feel manipulated and will resist emotional response. The "tearjerker" is common parlance for one such inauthentic device. The audience becomes like the child of a histrionic parent who wants to stir the child into distress or delight for the parent's own gratification. A friend complained that a television show was disgustingly grizzly. When I asked specifically what was disgusting, he claimed it was not the flesh and blood in this crime scene drama—his work inured him to that—but the director's exploitation of needless gore to wring emotional response from the audience. That variety of emotional manipulation was morally disgusting to this man. Though he contended he felt disgust only for the director, not for the subject matter, the gory subject matter likely influenced the choice of emotional response.

Creativity has been understood within the psychoanalytic literature as sublimation of instinctive energies. Disgust may interfere with creativity when the sublimation is incomplete and the unconscious or partially conscious trends stir anxiety. Examples include the fiction writer who perennially generates images of sexual sadism that disgust him consciously or cause him to become bored with the work, sleepy, or depressed; or the visual artist, traumatized by an abortion, whose oil paintings invariably strike her as a disgusting mess, an explosion of formless color, she must tear up or paint over before others see it; or a sculptor whose tactile contact with wet clay at times brings delight, but around holidays or dinners with his controlling mother brings agitation about the constant dirtiness of his fingernails, skin, and clothes, accompanied by loss of pleasure in modeling the clay and sudden eruptions of shame and self-disgust when he notes the dirt under his nails when he is in public. In his case, the love of handling clay and the intermittent need to reject that love through self-disgust may derive from early enjoyment of handling feces, later inhibited in its direct expression through disgust in the manner well explored by psychoanalysts, for example, Jones (1938), who told us that "the tendency to obtain enjoyment from various manipulations of and interest in excremental functions is opposed by the development of disgust" (p. 22, n. 1). It may also be the case that intermittent creative inhibition—associated with self-disgust—follows from a multitude of antimess, antiexpressiveness communications within the family-of-origin such that coprophilic impulses are part of a larger conflict around self-expression and not foundational for that conflict.

One woman was terribly disgusted by friends' messy houses, yet she allowed her own environment to become messy, too, and could not keep company with the clutter in order to clear it. She ended up surrounded by precisely the mess she found revolting. This woman was remarkably unproductive in daily life and school, considering it an accomplishment of major proportions if she cut her fingernails. In a sense, her major production appeared to be her mess, which disgusted her. In this case, the sad result of such ambivalence around creativity was that she mired herself in her own mess rather than create something of intellectual, artistic, or interpersonal value.

Artists are by no means immune to disgust. In fact, many are prone to disgust over what they consider to be violations of aesthetics. A painter may feel disgust at certain combinations of color, or a writer at particular usages of words. For accomplished artists, overly conventional, trite, and trivial expressions may be more likely to disgust than the brash expressions that might disgust others. Aesthetic disgust occurs in less sublime contexts as well, for example when two competitive adolescent sisters shop together for outfits and each vetoes the other's choices as "gross," perhaps even concluding that the other has "bad taste," a phrase that nicely mingles aesthetics and edibles.

People widely tolerant of boundary transgression in art may operate less permissively with respect to science. Science occupies a middle ground between art and ordinary life regarding its reality status. In science, we have the concept of a laboratory, which is a kind of playspace where things can be conceived but not fully rendered because the creations are isolated from the real world by barriers the scientist creates. However, great anxiety may attach to the effectiveness of those isolative strategies, because once they are breached, the scientist's play material enters and acts on society. Thus we have tremendous fears about things leaving the "laboratory stage," whether by design, accident, or deceit. Allowing things to materialize in the laboratory inches us frighteningly close to those things existing in society. The story of Dr. Frankenstein's monster, escaped into the world, is one of many portraying our anxiety about the boundary between laboratory and society. Lewis Thomas (1974) depicts our anxiety, and underscores its irrational aspects, in his portrayal of astronauts returning from space and laboring to maintain laboratory-tight isolation of any contamination they may carry:

> They do not, as one might expect, fall to their knees and kiss the carrier deck; this would violate, intrude upon, contaminate the deck, the vessel, the sea around, the whole earth. Instead, they wear surgical masks. They walk briskly, arms up, untouching, into a sterile box. They wave enigmatically, gnotobiotically, to the President from behind glass panes, so as not to breathe moondust on him. . . . If there should be life on the moon, we must begin by fearing it. We must guard against it, lest we catch something [p. 6].

In science, we also have ideas of veridicality that are not at issue (or they are applied differently) in art. What is established through science must be true to life, because science explores reality, not the imaginative realm. Taking on a moral dimension, disgust can shift from the subject matter explored to volitional failures to maintain proper controls so that the correct relationship between science and natural law is maintained. Since science must, above all, cleave to truth, deceptive or shoddy practice—tending to confuse our images of what is real—often elicits intense moral disgust. The same type of moral disgust appears regarding business practices or dishonest politics.

Work inhibitions of scientists parallel those of artists with respect to venturesomeness and exploration. One difference is in the clearer identification of the scientist's subject matter for others to see. The artist who knows her paintings refer to aborted fetuses may or may not present her theme transparently, for the public to identify. The scientist who studies fetal cord blood has no such refuge. However, this distinction is not absolute in that the matters that disturb a scientist and disrupt his or her creativity may be embedded in the subject matter in a way that makes them inapparent to critics, even to the scientist him or herself. A study of cord blood, for example, may disturb the scientist not because of the link to hot-button political issues, but because of unconscious or unarticulated associations to his mother's second child, lost to strangulation by the cord, or it might link to the blood of maternal menstruation, which evoked curiosity, anxiety, and furtive exploration in the boy who became a scientist. Both moral disgust regarding one's subject matter and direct visceral disgust limit scientific exploration, as does fear of disgusting others either morally (e.g., studying contraceptive hormone preparations) or viscerally (e.g., studying stomach content).

We have both fictional and real-life examples of worst-case scientists who failed to use self-disgust to check dangerous investigatory impulses. Often, these scientists are also physicians whose curiosity and manipulations target the human body; this choice makes them especially threatening figures. Dr. Frankenstein has already been mentioned as a fictional example of one who meddles with reproduction (God's terrain) and creates a monster. I recall my own childhood reactions to a terribly real scientist-physician, Josef Mengele, the Nazi who experimented on Jewish identical twins, among others, in the concentration camps. My reaction was one of moral revulsion and also a direct disgust, mixed with fascination, associated I believe with the sexually sadistic cast of the behavior and my identification with the victims (intensified since my mother was a twin). A keen sense of vulnerability followed the idea that a medical doctor could claim such complete access to one's body and do whatever painful or prurient things he pleased, under cover of scientific interest and curiosity. That entitlement to access made the intrusion more vile. Also operative, most likely, was some feared identification with this doctor whose work suggested "playing doctor," the idiom for those not medically inclined, but sexually curious. The fear of identifying with the wicked doctor would intensify both the physical and moral elements of the revulsion.

Mengele was a monster of a scientist. More ordinary scientists nevertheless may elicit, in themselves and others, some revulsion regarding the intensity of their sensory focus and preoccupation, regardless of what they study. The scientist may be experienced as someone with a hungry eye squinting through the microscope or a greedily gathering ear or mind. Both the mad scientist and the absent-minded professor are obsessive in their intellectual determination—to the exclusion and detriment of quotidian reality. The absent-minded professor may amuse us as he trips over his own feet while his eyes blaze upon his data sheets, but the mad scientist expresses our anxiety and occasional revulsion about the dangerously honed mind and hypertrophied senses of the scientist. In the case of the medical doctor, the person's body is the subject of interest and possibly intrusion. In the case of the psychologist, the mind is similarly vulnerable.

Clinical medicine moves us from laboratory research to societal intervention and introduces emotional controversies around what values a society wishes to establish and honor. One person contemplates the use of fetal tissue for transplant and is appalled. For this person, the sanctity of human life is the prevailing principle, and the notion of using human fetal tissue medically, regardless of gain, is an abhorrent breach of a sacrosanct boundary. For another person evaluating the same circumstance, the possibility of extending the life of a fully formed, suffering human being using tissue that no longer has potential to develop is an entirely ethical act. To refrain from such action would stir greater ethical qualms than to proceed with it. For that person, the fusion of fetal tissue and adult tissue might be imagined as an act of nurture, a comforting, ethically correct transcendence of boundary; whereas, for the person opposed to fetal stem cell transplant, the fusion of tissues signifies the murder of one being to benefit another and is the ultimate act of selfishness and of disregard for the supremely important demarcation of human being from all other tissue or matter. The need to dignify that demarcation is often linked with the concept of mankind as created by God, in his image, as his supreme creation, thus to dishonor the creation is to dishonor the creator. Ideas of good and evil dominate these charged conversations about ethics, but embedded in the subterrain are profound anxieties about self-definition and loss of status for the individual. Disgust, usually with moral focus or overtones, is part of the weaponry of condemnation for those scientific ventures that offend our sensibilities.

Art and science intertwine in science fiction. Science fiction is a playground for exploring common fears and fascinations about the impact on our identity of vigorous life-forms different from our own yet obviously related to and impinging on our own, often overwhelming it. Throughout Greg Bear's (1997) novel *Slant,* the author plays with the association between mental creativity and nature's wildly reproductive states. He portrays the fascination, fear, and disgust that nature's strategy of abundance can elicit. Like many successful artists, Bear ventures

The Creative Individual and Freedom from Disgust

quite freely onto terrain many would find disgusting. Bear knows whereon he treads. He knows he is playing with revulsion. He is resistant enough to it to sustain his exploration unflinchingly, but sensitive enough to recognize the lay of the land.

Bear's novel builds from a story representing a variation on the theme of unrequited love: a woman named Seefa Schnee was once lover to Nathan. Nathan and Seefa are scientists who study artificial intelligence. Rather than wish for an ordinary human child, Seefa deeply desires that she and Nathan join mental forces to create a new variety of being she calls a "bacterial thinker," the mental power of which derives from the reproductive activities of bacterial colonies (a notion not so different from research actually under way). Instead of creating an inorganic form of artificial intelligence, Seefa wants an organically based intelligence.

Nathan rejects Seefa's ingenious "brain child" and Seefa is left a lonely, intellectually frustrated woman. Her pain fuels what follows; Seefa sequesters herself in a futuristic structure called Omphalos, where alone she creates her "recombinant optimized DNA device," nicknamed "Roddy," the brilliant, "microbial neural mind" whose unitary body-mind is constructed of and enlivened by (of all things) mud, which is replete with bacterial activity fueled by the natural processes taking place in pea vines, a most vigorous plant. Bear describes Nathan's first encounter with Roddy, Seefa Schnee's "child," deep in the womb of Omphalos:

> The garden covers a space perhaps a hundred feet on a side, surrounded by waist-high walls.... Nathan steps out into a rich scent of moist dirt and greenery: peas, their tendrils curling up narrow stakes onto row after row of trellises. Bees hum industriously between small blossoms.
>
> Nathan stands on the dirt and stoops. His fingers dig into the rich black loam, encountering a slickness of warm slime, disturbingly like reaching into a woman's genitals. He pulls his hand out quickly.
>
> Nathan can no longer doubt what he is seeing. The soil is thick with bacterial growth, connected with and nurtured in some way by the peas on their trellises.... The bacteria "swap spit," exchange plasmids, recipes, solve the challenges, and in so doing, with immense subtlety and power, though perhaps very slowly, bring to bear on human problems the most fecund

and ancient powers of nature. . . . His feet press into Roddy's core substance, Roddy's flesh, Roddy's mind [pp. 456–457].

Bear makes little direct mention of disgust in his novel. In many ways, his story ventures fearlessly into a portrayal of life at the margin of ordinary experience, yet disgust is implied in Nathan's character—in his rejection of Seefa and her peculiar brain child—and we know we are in the realm of disgust and fascination as we enter the muck and bacterial swarms that are Roddy's body-mind. Nathan's abrupt withdrawal of his hand from Roddy's vaginally slimy lifestuff conveys the anxious revulsion that occurs at the point of contact with a frightening lifeform. The moment signifies female sexuality out of place because the sexuality is unexpected, unanticipated, and oddly confused with an intellectual machine of some sort. A heavy historical load burdens the moment, since Nathan had rejected Seefa's plan to procreate—and thus her vagina—years before.

When Nathan associates the slimy mud to vaginal secretions, he is repulsed. Suddenly, the dirt has, in Mary Douglas's lexicon, "identity clinging to it." We might add that the identity clinging to the matter may be clinging to the mind of the beholder as much as to the matter itself. In Nathan's case, his memories of Seefa invade his present experience and the slime becomes vaginal secretions.

Disgust also enters Bear's story through the theme of Tourette's syndrome, a disease characterized by eruptions of foul utterances. In the story, Tourette's represents a disorder Seefa Schnee chooses to induce in herself and others in order to heighten creativity. Thus the link between a socially marginal, repugnant state and a creative state is underscored. Seefa says, "I messed with my own head to keep out in front. I stimulated all the centers of creativity, the entire Tourette continuum" (p. 470). She describes and also displays, through her disjointed speech, the condition she has produced: "Like Tourette, but different. Subtle imbalances. A tweak to the receptors. Let loose the imp of the perverse. They'll all think a little faster, a little more queerly. Thoughts and impulses they'd usually ignore will suddenly be acted upon. Creative impulses" (p. 473). The human mind seeks order, which is necessary for effective functioning. But order also stultifies, so that human creativity is most alive at the juncture between form and formlessness, a tense, active borderland that is the terrain of dirt, pollution, and danger, even evil, but is also—as the artist and the physicist know—the locus of power and creation. We move now from the subject of individual artistic or

The Creative Individual and Freedom from Disgust 151

scientific creativity to the even more unsettling creative turns an entire society may take. Political scientist Don Herzog (1998) speaks of the 18th-century English and their unease concerning the Reformation, saying, "Once again misgivings surface about the Reformation, about the repulsive innovation giving birth to England's proud tradition of Protestantism" (p. 45). Innovation—the creation of difference—indeed is often regarded as repulsive. We have seen that dynamic in the realms of science and art. In the chapter to follow we will explore disgust toward difference within group settings.

Chapter 9
Group Identities and Hostility Across Borders: Affairs of Ethnicities, Classes, and Sects

> The arousal of disgust, in the full sense of the term, pertains... to the Nazis' anti-Semitic propaganda—the portrayal of Jews as rats or as parasites in the "healthy" body of the Aryan *Volk*—or even to the hygienic regime of the concentration camps.
>
> —Winfried Menninghaus

In his 1984 monograph *Self-Esteem and Meaning,* psychologist Michael R. Jackson sketches the story of John, an East European immigrant to this country, an accomplished precision machinist, who worries that he will be seen and rejected as "the foreign element." Jackson reminds us that, for a machinist, the phrase *foreign element* suggests "a bit of dirt or some other substance which infiltrates a machine and disrupts its functioning. This usage suggests a fear on John's part that his entry into the social mechanism would be regarded as a kind of noxious intrusion by something base or contemptible" (p. 102). The machinist's fears may in fact parallel societal fears that the collective will be contaminated by the entry of someone like him. One party's insecurity about being seen as the invading dirt pairs with the other's fear of being invaded by dirt (thus becoming dirty itself). Both fears depend on a hierarchical society that insists one must be high or low, therefore, anxiety about being or becoming low and degraded flourishes.

Disgust is one of a number of emotions that work in concert to reject and devalue outsiders. It has standing as an important member of the group in that it conveys a totality of rejection and a passion in denigration that relate the outsider to all things physically repulsive or morally debased. The feeling of disgust is not regularly present in every moment of rejecting an outsider, but it predictably journeys in and out of the emotional mix and not infrequently dominates it.

In group psychology, the establishment of self-protective boundaries to exclude "dirt" conveys us quickly into the treacherous realms of extreme nationalism and ethnocentrism, and toward the notion of "cleansing" an ethnic group of elements that are suspected of polluting its purity. There is little to surprise us in a quote from an Albanian refugee, playwright Jeton Budima (quoted in Bearak, 1999), who says, "Suddenly, you are an animal on the run, a refugee, a number in the world's book of statistics. . . . Suddenly, you feel like human garbage." His is the point of view of the outsider, the one considered dirt, who may end up seeing himself as dirt.

A bigot may experience his or her bias without feeling disgust, but in the realms of racial, ethnic, and religious hatred, disgust is very much at home. When disgust is absent from a particular moment's condemnation, the judging party likely has already established so great a protective divide between self and Other—often by use of doctrinaire polemics—that the psychic threat posed by close contact is mitigated. Disgust would probably appear if an individual from the despised group initiated some intimate approach—a physical touch, perhaps, or a personal verbal exchange. In reporting such contact to other members of his group and asserting his solidarity with his group, a racist might describe the other's touch or approach as "disgusting." In some cases, disgust would be the ideational type, which is more an intellectual judgment about an event than a visceral response. If disgust actually were felt, as a full, embodied emotion, that occurrence would suggest that the racist fully incorporated his group's doctrine about the inferiority of the Other, and also that he felt quite vulnerable to contracting that inferiority through association.

Across the centuries, those anxious about having their societies invaded or overtaken have at times been especially expressive in their use of disgust and contempt imagery to describe the gross nature of outsiders from other religions, classes, or races who may flood through the gate and pollute one's own group. Racist speech regularly uses the language and imagery of disgust to separate us from them. In a 1774 text, *The History of Jamaica,* Edward Long enlists "disgust" to demean a native population through a smugly articulate discourse on its offensiveness. He describes Jamaican Jonkonnu festivities in this way:

> These exercises, although very delightful to themselves [the Jamaicans], are not so to the generality of the white spectators, on account of the ill smell which copiously transudes on such occasions; which is rather a complication of stinks, than any one in particular, and so rank and powerful, as totally to overcome those who have any delicacy in the frame of their nostrils [quoted in Cooper, 1995, p. 25].

Long advances the common notion that sensitivity or delicacy indicates superiority. In this case, the sensitivity in question concerns one's discriminating sense of smell and the associated lower threshold for disgust. Southern white supremacists proffer similar characterizations when bent on elevating (and simultaneously demeaning?) their women by noting their constitutional delicacy.

A local and contemporary example of this kind of thinking came at a public hearing about the expansion of a mobile home park during which the neighbors who opposed the expansion described vividly and at great length the sewage odors emanating from the present park's open lagoon treatment system. They evinced a determination to rub the developer's nose in the problem as he stood at the podium, listening with evident discomfort (humiliation? embarrassment? rage?) to one after another description of the abhorrent smells his project was loosing on the neighborhood. The clear message was: We don't want your disgusting development; you are forcing it on us and we will shame you for it, making you identify with your malodorous sewage.

In a historical study, Don Herzog (1998) cites Englishman Edmund Burke's revulsion at the women of the French Revolution, described as "obscene harpies" who "flutter over our heads, and souse down upon our tables, and leave nothing unrent, unrifled, unravaged, or unpolluted with the slime of their filthy offal" (p. 32). Given the revolution then capsizing the French class system, the threat of political instability spreading to England engendered a ferment of disgust prose: "The French Revolution, according to Southey, 'threatened to propagate itself throughout the civilised world.' Or, more picturesquely,

'Dogmatical Atheism struts and crows upon its dunghills,' laying eggs, hatching 'hissing, wriggling, and venomous' cockatrices" (quoted in Herzog, 1998, p. 105). An exuberant fusion of images of monstrous birth and of nature in her most wildly propagative mood marks Southey's diatribe against radical politicians; disgust is part of the emotional mix, which also includes contempt and antipathy.

In discussing the war on terrorism triggered by the September 2001 attacks in New York and Washington, DC, public officials repeatedly employed the imagery of disgust in describing our intended response to the terrorists, saying, for example, we will "drain their swamps" and "we'll get those snakes out of their swamps." Given that the terrorists our government had identified as responsible for the attacks live high in the parched hills of Afghanistan, the lowland swamp imagery was remarkable for geographical inappropriateness; it turned on the characteristic disgust logic that says that warm, moist places of rapid breeding are the sites of disgusting occurrences.

In an intriguing monograph on white racial self-hatred, theologian and psychologist Thandeka (1999) argues that class anxiety and class hatred are more potent than race hatred and undergird it. Thandeka believes that the core motivation of Southern whites was to belong to the elevated and economically powerful class, not the denigrated class. Poor whites were as much despised by wealthy whites as blacks were, but were given token affiliation with prosperous whites through the notion of a superior white race elevated over an inferior black race. This racial categorization modestly expanded the privilege of poor whites and substantially enhanced their pride, but cost them affiliation with the poor black workers with whom they previously had identified. Economically advantaged whites benefited as poor whites sharpened their hatred for poor blacks; the natural alliance of poor with poor could not gel and any potential political power of the working poor was destroyed. Thus, upper-class whites safeguarded themselves from the potential political power of the poor, but did so without surrendering their disdain and disgust for the poor white, the "trash" of Southern society.

Blood mixing is an image that recurs and attracts disgust in discourses on both race and class. Special danger inheres in believing we are all of one blood, which would make such mixing inconsequential. Once again, we see the urgency of underscoring difference and setting apart its exemplars in order to establish one's own worth by asserting superiority to someone lesser. Southerners' aversion to race mixing was reflected in various race laws, for example, the legislation passed by the Virginia assembly in 1691 "to prevent mixed marriages and thus mulatto offspring ('that abominable mixture and spurious issue')" (Thandeka, p. 47).

In a study of the evolving concept of "Satan," Pagels (1995) relates an early Christian creation story that spawned a number of versions over the years. The story portrays blood mixed between angels and humans as the source of defilement to the angels. That defilement engendered deviant and destructive life-forms:

> The Book of the Watchers, a collection of visionary stories ... tells how the "watcher" angels, whom God appointed to supervise ("watch over") the universe, fell from heaven. Starting from the story of Genesis 6, in which the "sons of God" lusted for human women, this author combines two different accounts of how the watchers lost their heavenly glory. The first describes how Semihazah, leader of the watchers, coerced two hundred other angels to join him in a pact to violate divine order by mating with human women. These mismatches produced "a race of bastards, the giants known as the nephilim ['fallen ones'], from whom there were to proceed demonic spirits" [p. 50].

In the story of the watcher angels, the desire of the upper class of beings to commingle with those beneath wreaks havoc on society. The watcher angels defile themselves such that the offspring of their earthly sorties are seen as grotesque bastards.

In texts such as the preceding one, we see a call to followers to view a group in disgust-related terms, for example, as defiled or abhorrent. Whether such a call to label or regard someone as a degraded outsider results in moments of full disgust will depend on a number of factors that influence the degree of personal relatedness and vulnerability the follower feels vis-à-vis the ones to be reviled. The alternative is borrowed disgust that seeks to secure one's group membership.

In talking of broad societal tendencies to cast out what is foreign and to vilify and damn it, Primo Levi (1988) addressed the psychology that holds that "every stranger is an enemy." Discussing Levi, Susan L. Boone (1999) said, "The conviction, loosely or rigorously held, that 'every stranger is an enemy' is, for Levi, at the heart of a logic that led to Auschwitz." She adds, in a footnote that ushers in the language of disgust:

> The treatment of those who fall into the category of "the stranger" has been well documented. From "primitive" to "civilized" societies, the stranger/outsider/other has been recognized as an obdurate problem. Associated with a variety of characteristics—dirty, unreliable, lazy—the stranger denotes an inability to calculate, to trust, to establish firm order in the vicinity of so impenetrable and unpredictable a quantity [p. 82].

Here again we have disgust-relevant language and structures (of exclusion and degradation) but no absolute necessity for a clear-cut moment of disgust for one who would accept the societal urging to regard "the stranger" in the terms advanced.

Another example of a disgust-related characterization of the outsider comes from an editorial piece by Will Warner (2002) in which the writer offers his view of how he and other Americans are perceived by Muslim extremists: "As I understand it, they think that I stink up the place, that I stain the soil just by standing on it." This editorial piece is rather formally and eloquently rendered; the writer makes a deliberate descent into the anal language of disgust in order to describe the characterization of the outsider. The language shift works to engage and arouse the reader, but since the degraded language attaches to the terrorists, not the writer, he is protected from its negative impact. Pagels's history of Satan also concerns itself with "otherness" and concludes with a wish that her research "may illuminate for others, as it has for me, the struggle within Christian tradition between the profoundly human view that 'otherness' is evil and the words of Jesus that reconciliation is divine" (p. 184).

Having seen a wealth of examples, we must inquire further into why human beings tend to reject the touch of the stranger as disgusting, and under what circumstances. Several circumstances stand out in the instances I have considered: we may see others as better than we are and want to diminish and degrade them via disgust, lest we feel eclipsed by their superior capabilities; we may recognize but wish to deny some kinship with a reprehensible quality or gross deficiency the Other exhibits lest the kinship tar and belittle us; we may find in the Other something so alien and inscrutable it may unsettle us in a variety of ways, for example, by altering our view of the world such that we fear we may no longer have a secure place in our community. Thus, in our relationships with others, disgust arises in reaction to unwelcome identification and also to difference that is difficult for us to comprehend and digest and therefore disturbing.

Disgust in relation to other groups of humans interacts with envy and also with shame. An example of envy-based revulsion would be the identification in an outside group of a superior athletic or intellectual competence, after which one reduces that competence to something base and suspect: athletic African Americans are like monkeys in the trees, they are "jungle bunnies;" intelligent Jews are beady-eyed schemers, eggheads, or bizarre wizards preternaturally gifted in amassing money. In these instances, one is choosing to treat difference as peculiar or impenetrable, and ultimately disgusting, as a defense against envy. Thandeka's comments on black–white race relations point to the use of disgust and taboo to disavow one's own shameful qualities, for example, lust:

> The lure of the nonwhite zones of American cities thus gains its power of attraction from repressed desires looking for a way to escape their white confines.
>
> The nonwhite zone must be vigilantly patrolled, then, for along its border lies the terrain of race-mixing. Like any line that seems to distinguish one thing from another, upon careful scrutiny, one discovers the line is porous; it is perforated. That which is ostensibly excluded by the line is in fact included. The line thus marks the place where ostensibly distinct, discrete phenomena meet. It is where the "interplay of differences" occurs. Here, race-mixing takes place in the fantasies of real life. Forbidden desire merges with fear and transforms the nonwhite zone into a red light district that both attracts and barricades the white passerby to her or his own desires [p. 26].

In psychoanalytic terms, the dynamic at issue in Thandeka's red light district is "projective identification," which means that one attributes to another something conflictual of one's own, then one continues to keep a close and critical eye on that other. For example, we take our lust and put it in the hands of the disgusting, "primitive" African American, retardate, or Jew and want to scrutinize that person and talk about him or her. We keep ourselves ignorant about our own association with the execrated trait.

The red light district Thandeka describes is formally equivalent to the dirt—with identity yet clinging—that Douglas examines and to the artist's zone of discovery, which often evokes outrage in the public. It is the place where life-forms emerge dripping from the swamp—signifying birth—or submerge back into it—signifying dissolution. It is the vital but disturbing border between life-forms.

Anthropologists have taken us on journeys to what they call marginal or borderland regions and to the related concepts of liminal or threshold experience (see Turner, 1970) and shown us that these places and ideas have a special relationship to disgust. In discussing the relationship between pigs and human disgust in an earlier century, Stallybrass and White also address the idea of marginality:

> Whereas animals which ate grass or berries could be thought of as part of a different habitat and different food system, the pig overlapped with, and confusingly debased, human habitat and diet alike. Its mode of life was not different from, but alarmingly imbricated with, the forms of life which betokened civility. It is precisely creatures of the threshold which become the object of fear and fascination [p. 47].

Creatures of the threshold bring fascination and fear, and that fear often takes shape as disgust, especially in situations, such as that described by Stallybrass and White, where the party in question is seen as debased and its debasement is understood to be contagious.

Psychoanalyst Theodore Lidz (1973) approaches the topic of disgust and other aversive reactions by talking of the general human discomfort with what lies between categories. He addresses specifically the self-and-other categories fundamental to disgust. Disgust can be a response to what lies between solid and liquid, red and green, high and low, but the more the object of our attention disturbs the self-other category, the more likely it will result in disgust.

Phenomena that confuse our sense of proper boundaries, especially self-other boundaries, frequently diminish the sense of identity. Taboo as well as feelings of disgust toward what lies between categories protect us from the intercategorical realm. If we find nothing *between* categories to anathematize, we may declare—however arbitrarily—that a clear line exists between self and Other and we assign dirtiness, decadence, immorality, or some other badness to whoever or whatever occupies the space beyond the dividing line, who is, psychologically, the stranger. For example, a woman might accept both femininity (self) and masculinity (Other), but feel disgust toward hermaphroditism (part self, part Other). Or she might deny the existence of anything between categories, seeing only male and female, but assign badness and deficiency to males, who become the stranger or outsider. In the interpersonal realm, moral badness often is attributed to the outsider and forms a basis for antipathy. Assigning badness to the outsider may provide more security than aversion to the intercategorical would furnish, since the notion of things between categories suggests some degree of overlap—of shared protoplasm—between oneself and the offending Other, whereas complete otherness denies any commonality.

A commonplace example of assigning disgusting badness to the outsider in response to dangers with respect to identity can be seen with an adolescent girl, Sheila, disgusted by another girl she finds too "girly" and "ditzy" and "always in pink." She delights in ridiculing the ditzy girl through demeaning imitation, which means that she carefully studies the girl in order to "do" her for an audience. For a school dress-up day, she decides to dress as "Barbie," which allows her to go all out in trying on the hated symbols of ultratraditional femininity. At the same time that she is rejecting this "girly-girl," she is making great mental allowances for the "hot," "popular" boys she used to reject as phony and snobbish. She has decided these hot guys, who now look her way, are actually "super nice." She also has decided that they see through the ditzy girls and share her antipathy for them.

It would be wrong in this case to dismiss Sheila's amalgamated disgust and contempt as a simple reaction-formation obscuring her envy. She truly does want to disavow a certain stereotypically feminine way of relating. It is not her and never will be: she is bright, athletic, sharp, dignified, and so forth. She is anxious, though, that her own ways in fact be attractive and acceptable and she is not entirely certain they are. Her behavior suggests she is feeling more and more drawn toward males and sexual activity and so the traditionally male-receptive stance of the girly-girls is in some way speaking for a part of herself she is nervously coming to know.

Sheila brings us back to the idea that the most hated stranger may be close kin to the self. What is actually remote, psychically and physically, is less likely to threaten us and elicit revulsion. With regard to nature's forms and activities, we get disgusted by what is fleshy and close at hand, not by the distant and dramatic. At the interpersonal level, a parent or a classmate will disgust sooner than a denizen of a faraway land, as seen with the young woman with the Barbie conflict. Those who are distant—truly different, truly unfamiliar—will disgust only if their difference threatens us with insecurity.

A way to think of this apparent paradox around near and far is to think of Levi's "stranger" as a brother or cast-off part of the self who has been sent off, toting the family's garbage, who now comes knocking, in stranger's garb but carrying the familiar garbage, refusing to stay out of sight and mind. He is the one we emphatically assert is both bad and entirely strange, whom we hate and revile as disgusting. We cannot allow ourselves to know him through empathy, because we want to make an airtight case for his alienness. So when the stranger who knocks is not truly a stranger, but a relative who shows us aspects of the family legacy we prefer to disavow—or even potentials we might want to approach, but of which we are frightened—we will slam the door with disgust and say, "No, you are not related to me." And, if we happen to have some garbage in the house that we would like to get rid of, we may take this opportunity to thrust it into the stranger's arms and say, "Here, take this. Now... see... you have got the garbage... you smell and I am pure" and slam shut the door (but through the peephole watch the stranger's progress). Later, if we start to smell some hint of garbage remaining in our own house we might say, "My god, look how that stranger has entered my house and brought this garbage in. He is revolting; I will build walls and keep him out (while keeping a close eye on him). If that doesn't work, I'll torture him. I may be forced even to shoot him."

The so-called stranger may also scare us with images of something better or fuller we could become, which would require us to alter and expand the self—a frightening evolution, so disgust is the likely response. Thus the one we wish to disavow and discredit may be the one who looks unimpressive and unappealing, but we can't help see he is kin; or he may be the one who seems better than we, more fully developed, but he draws us into realms of experience that would frighten us if we did not repudiate them with disgust.

The hatred and revulsion focused on the Jews during the Nazi period seems to have been a particularly lethal combination of envy and disowned self-hatred and shame. In Ann Michaels's fictional treatment of Nazi psychology, she shows the Nazi mind at work shrilly asserting the dirt, garbage, or nonliving status of Jews in order to facilitate destruction of their vitality. Within the passage to follow, one can see the easy slide from notions of inanimateness into notions of garbage, debris, and vermin:

> Nazi policy was beyond racism, it was antimatter, for Jews were not considered human. An old trick of language, used often in the course of history. Non-Aryans were never to be referred to as human, but as "figuren," "stucke"—"dolls," "wood," "merchandise," "rags." Humans were not being gassed, only "figuren," so ethics weren't being violated.... Similarly, the Nazis implemented a directive against Jews owning pets; how can one animal own another? How can an insect or an object own anything? Nazi law prohibited Jews from buying soap; what use is soap to vermin? [pp.165–166].

The idea of Jews as wooden dolls would not have supported their frenzied extermination. They needed to offend, to become rank garbage or vermin, the very nature of which called out for its destruction. Only living things, or living ideas, not dolls, offend that powerfully. Perhaps the Nazis had to walk a fine line psychologically by first stirring hatred toward the Jews as intensely offensive, inhuman life, then devaluing them as inanimate "figuren" that could be disposed of without guilt.

Sartre (1948) breathed the air of French anti-Semitism and was able to analyze it astutely and describe individual instances of visceral disgust for the Jew that exemplified the collective attitude of revulsion. He wanted to make clear the extent to which disgust proceeds from the mind to the body and reflects irrational attitudes about contagion:

> The same action carried out by a Jew and by a Christian does not have the same meaning ... for the Jew contaminates all that he touches with an I-know-not-what execrable quality. The first thing the Germans did was to forbid Jews access to swimming pools; it seemed to them that if the body of an Israelite were to plunge into that confined body of water, the water would be completely befouled. Strictly speaking, the Jew contaminates even the air he breathes [p. 34].

Sartre's analysis reminds us that disgust's dependence on the senses is often misleading. Disgust may understand and describe its object in sensory terms, but it is the idea of the object, not its actual sensed characteristics that disgust.

Sartre examines the weak and undefined self that underlies anti-Semitism as he probes the anti-Semite's propensity for flawed or false reasoning in assessing Jews. He wonders how people can embrace the distorted reasoning that undergirds anti-Semitism and concludes that the anti-Semite fears the intellectually "open" state that the search for truth demands. He is "attracted by the durability of a stone" and wishes "to be massive and impenetrable" (p. 18). Through Sartre's words, we revisit the familiar motif of the weakened sense of self and of the dread such uncertainty creates. That dread then motivates rescue strategies: disgust figures among those.

A predictable script for racist or ethnic hatred involves the marginalization of a group such that it has little access to the economic or social life of the community or to adequate housing and other resources. The marginalized group, brought low by poverty, is then reviled for being inhuman, living like animals, or being an untrustworthy pack of thieves. No acknowledgment is made of the larger society's role in depriving the marginalized group of the resources that allow people to live in dignity.

The great paradox at the center of disgust dynamics is that difference is felt to be necessary for the self to feel substantial and defined, but difference opens the self to feelings of inferiority because once there is an Other, a relationship exists between self and Other in which one may be better or worse than the Other. So those who insist on difference often are haters of the specific forms of difference they encounter (and maintain). The insecure man who insists that male and female be defined as utterly different may also hate or suspect the female as a threat to his self-regard, just as the white who wants an absolute racial divide may despise the black.

Often people assume that the racist reinforces the line between races in order to bar what is seen as inferior and capable of polluting the self, but the process is a bit more complex in that it relies on the racist insisting on racial division in order to make himself someone special, then insisting on racial hierarchy in order to make himself someone superior. Sartre fully intuited these dynamics, saying, "If the Jew did not exist, the anti-Semite would invent him" (p. 13).

John Updike's (1996) novel *In the Beauty of the Lilies* offers a vivid fictional rendering of the comfort religious people may find in categorical divisions, and the unease associated with blurred or effaced

Group Identities and Hostility Across Borders

boundaries. Updike examines the piety of a dying man, Mr. Orr, enraged with his pastor, Clarence, for refusing to provide the sharp partition of Heaven and Hell, believer and infidel, that would comfort Orr with the possibility he might attain Heaven. Orr cannot assure himself that he belongs in the rescued flock without first imagining those outside the fold. Updike creates for us an encounter between Orr, the first speaker below, and his pastor, Clarence, seen through the pastor's spiritually weary eyes:

> "The time for soft talk is by. What do you think my chances are, to find myself among the elect?"
> The little face in the pillow emitted an odor of dental rot and stale mucus that afflicted Clarence's nose six feet away, though the ward was perfumed with alcohol and ether [p. 44].
> "I'll take damnation in good stride if that's what's to come."
> "Oh, come now, Mr. Orr!—there can be no question of your damnation" [p. 46].

In responding to his preacher's attempt at reassurance, Mr. Orr shows us just how deeply he grasps the purpose of dividing the beyond into Heaven and Hell.

> The man's suspicions were aroused; he repeated the scrabbling effort of his elbows to raise himself in bed. "Damnation's what my parents brought me up to believe in.... There's the elect and the others, damned. It's in the Bible, over and over, right out of Jesus' mouth. It makes good sense. You can't have light without the dark. How can you be saved, if you can't be damned? Answer me that. It's part of the equation. You can't have good without the bad, that's why the bad exists" [pp. 45–46].

Orr continues:

> "I never heard enough damnation from your pulpit. Many mornings I had to strain to take hold of what you were saying, Reverend.. I couldn't figure it out, and got dizzy listening, the way you were dodging here and there.... Take away damnation, in my opinion, a man might as well be an atheist. A God that can't damn a body to an eternal Hell can't lift a body up out of the grave either" [p. 46].

Orr is an either-or sort of fellow. Clarence wants to soft peddle Hell; Orr wants no part of that. He needs his Christ-killing Jews and his Oriental potentates (who, with "all the jewels and wives" are clearly the same brand of devil Al Qaida finds in America, "the Great Satan"). While Clarence refuses Orr his Heaven and Hell beyond this earth, he cannot help but record the hell of Orr's earthly condition, which is fully disgusting in its odors, sounds, and visage. In contrapuntal rhythm, Updike shows Clarence trying to rescue Orr in the world hereafter, while simultaneously heaping every judgment against his earthly being for its deteriorated condition of rot, stink, withering, crusting, and the like. One senses that his disgust at the man's physical condition is inflated by his unease with the man's simplistic views of good and evil.

Division into the pure and the impure is prominent in all three major Abrahamic religions, and also in a number of Eastern religions, as indicated in Renou's (1962) statement that "purity is perhaps the essential watchword of Hinduism and its religious practices of purification are infinitely diversified" (p. 3). Marty (1992) discusses the gursickh and states that, "in order to practice their faith, the gursickh (pure Sikhs) maintain, they must be separate, uncontaminated by Hindus, Muslims, Jains, and other non-Sikhs; they must, therefore, secede from India and establish a separate Sikh state" (p. 191). Purity is seen as essential for contact with God, thus the idea that "cleanliness is next to godliness," which suggests that one can be close to (i.e., "next to") God through cleansing or purifying one's being (see Haidt et al., 1997).

Societies commonly structure themselves such that radical separations exist between those in touch with the population's "dirt" and those insulated from the base, physical, and defiled, who can approach the deity. The great exception to such social hierarchy is Buddhism, which tells us that division is the source of illusion and ego; division establishes false and distracting ordering. Division does not order chaos; it simply disturbs wholeness and denies the natural transience of all things. In eschewing good–bad judgments, Buddhism moves the practitioner away from cravings and away from disgust.

Some societies that assign status allow a degree of movement between stations or classes, whereas others assign one's placement by birth and allow no migration. The Indian Hindu caste system is a good example of the latter, whereas Christianity exemplifies a more mobile structure. Class systems institutionally separate clean from dirty, but how do they interact with the momentary, emotional experience of disgust—which is the individual's instinctive attempt to associate with the clean and acceptable and take distance from the debased? On the one hand, moments of felt disgust may be greater in those societies that do not structurally separate the classes too radically, since the individual is left to protect himself or herself from gross encounters without much help from societal strictures. On the other hand, more resolutely classist societies may promote disgust because the institutions they create so strongly emphasize and elevate cleanliness and purity. Talking about physical illness in Indian society, Arthur Kleinman (1988) remarks:

> In India the body-self is held to be permeable to substances and symbols in social interaction (Daniel 1984). . . . A child is polluted by the touch of a menstruating mother because menstrual blood can enter the porous body (Shweder 1985), just as food received from someone in a lower caste gets incorporated into the body and pollutes it from within [p. 12].

Kleinman's comments suggest that the great sense of body permeability in the Indian psyche promotes stringent behavioral regulation, including those strictures associated with caste. The society's tight regulation is designed to promote mental and physical purity. Kleinman does not speak to the felt experience of disgust and the question of whether disgust helps maintain the society's fundamental structure by sharply marking momentary lapses of proper physical or mental hygiene or class separation.

Writers can be hasty in equating structures that divide the pure from the impure with fully felt disgust. The fact that a Muslim believes that a dog entering his house will contaminate the house and necessitate its thorough washing need not mean he feels disgust when a dog is allowed to enter. He may feel anger at whoever allowed the dog to enter his residence. We must discover whether he feels disgust, not assume it. A similar lapse in reasoning is seen in discussions of psychopathology—especially obsessive-compulsive disorder—that assume felt disgust must accompany anxiety about things wrongly touching. Knowing that a woman with obsessive-compulsive disorder is determined not to let any part of her body touch a library book because such books are handled by others and may carry germs does not tell us that she will feel disgust over such contact. She may, but she may instead feel anxiety. The situations described are best considered forms of partial disgust, unless full disgust is identified.

I informally interviewed two members of a kosher Jewish household about their understanding and experience of the concept of *traif*. The husband of the couple was raised an Orthodox Jew. The wife adopted Orthodoxy as an adult, out of respect for her husband's observance. The wife defined *traif* as "anything unkosher." Asked about how she would feel were a plate of unkosher food presented to her, she said, "If bacon, shellfish or anything forbidden is put in front of me, I do not find it repulsive." She then spontaneously offered that she believes "the smell of ham, bacon, etc., does repulse Harry [her husband] because he is probably really Kosher, from birth on." Thus the wife has no feeling of disgust for *traif*, but she believes her husband feels true disgust. Harry, however, gives an interesting history of the concept—one that promotes disgust—but goes on to suggest he feels no disgust:

> The Hebrew word *traif* means "to tear off," for example, it was common in biblical days to barbarically tear off a leg from a living animal and eat it. Obviously the bible discouraged it. Secondly, the bible lists clean and unclean animals, meaning those that can be eaten, and those which cannot be eaten . . . *traif*.
>
> My answer to "if you're observant and I put a plate of bacon in front of you, what do you feel" is: I was taught by my rabbi that G-d created all animals and that we should not consider the nonkosher food with disgust. Rather we should just say we're not supposed to eat it. And in reality a plate of bacon has absolutely no appeal to me.

The husband suggests he feels no disgust for *traif*, but never actually says so. He says he is not supposed to feel disgust, but is sufficiently emphatic regarding bacon's lack of appeal that one might suspect the wife's intuition is correct: Harry is repulsed by *traif*. We can see here how nuanced the relationship between experience and construct can be and reiterate the value in noting the nonequivalence of the two.

Haidt et al. (1997) have turned their attention to the relationship between culture and disgust experience and have considered the range of concepts of interindividual permeability across societies. They state that "in India . . . and among the Hua of New Guinea . . ., people are thought to be linked together along blood-lines in a web of shared bodily fluid, such that pollution incurred by one person spreads to close family members, just as a snakebite in the leg quickly spreads throughout the body" (p. 125). The implication of this communal body concept is that any individual represents a port of entry to the whole. Haidt et al. use this tight interweaving of bodies and also selves within one social organization as an argument for why Japanese ideas about the morally disgusting differ in focus from American ideas. Americans emphasize irrational violence or cruelty, especially towards those who are helpless. However, the Japanese feel *ken'o*—their concept of disgust—in "everyday social interactions, in situations where things were not going right" (p. 119). Haidt et al. conjecture that the collective self of the Japanese creates danger that one can be shunned by the collectivity—as too great a threat to its well-being—if one is viewed as likely to admit contamination to the whole. Thus the individual, anxious about ostracism, directs disgust toward everyday situations that give evidence he or she is not fitting in with the collective. Examples suggest that the *ken'o* can be self-directed, because of one's failings, or directed at the rejecting group or institution.

Chapter 10
Disgust and Horror

At the end of the war, I was just a year old, so I can hardly have any impressions of that period of destruction based on personal experience. Yet, to this day, when I see photographs or documentary films dating from the war I feel as if I were its child, so to speak, as if those horrors I did not experience cast a shadow over me, one from which I shall never entirely emerge.

—W. G. Sebald, "A Natural History of Destruction"

Disgust and horror are related emotions that focus attention on self-boundaries. Disgust is more likely to occur when an intrusion is limited and a point of physical or psychic entry can be identified; some resistance to the incursion can be imagined and the metaphor of ingestion and vomiting can be applied. Horror is the likely response when little can be done to resist the invasion of some powerful outsider, an invasion that threatens to supplant the self cell-by-cell, often with a spirit that seems alien rather than kindred and familiar. Horror is a response to what truly is alien and other-than-self and thus could obliterate self, whereas disgust more often bespeaks humanness, and kinship between self and Other; this familiarity coincides with a wish to maintain separation and to assert difference from the other. Disgust may also serve when the sense of threat is massive but the person is trying to limit and contain the danger by treating it as something limited, physical, and extrudable.

Certain modern playwrights have been adept at rendering horror. In Albee's (1973) *A Delicate Balance,* the horror of love's fragility enters the house like plague and overtakes all its inhabitants. The family quarrels over whether they are entitled to protect their tranquility by shutting out the disturbing others whom they had regarded as intimate friends. There is no question of mere disgust in this scenario. We are beyond disgust and well within the realm of horror because the very foundation of family—the concept of love—has been disturbed. Just as the plague bacillus may infect and overtake every cell of the body, uncertainty has entered every corner of every mind within the household.

The popular 1979 movie *Alien* captures all the key features of horror. The alien that enters the humans' spacecraft demonstrates complete disrespect for human spatial boundaries, which symbolize the separation of self from Other. The creature invades human bodies and also installs itself in the inside tracts of the ship's body, by way of the duct system that runs through the craft like blood or lymph vessels. Though many of its forms are slimy and ugly, the alien evokes more horror than disgust because of the totality of its threat to human welfare. The mutability of its form makes the alien especially hard to contain and manage. Once in the spacecraft, it reproduces in rampant and unpredictable ways and constantly changes form, so that there is no way of containing it in intellectual or conceptual terms and no way of restricting its movement through space. Only at the very end of the movie, as the alien finally is expelled into space, does it appear in human-like form, as if the fact of its expulsion made it something limited and boundaried and thus less alien.

The final scene may also tell us that what has been within the ship in so horrid a form symbolizes an aspect of self, of our complex humanness, just as Dorian Gray's horribly aging, ugly, veiled portrait represented the corrupted self. In disgust and horror, things move across the permeable membrane that enwraps "self." What is outside and bad threatens to get in; what is inside and bad is symbolized by something outside in order to deny badness within.

If such a thing as a bit of horror exists, a bit of it surfaced for a woman client who talked one day of the dog hair overtaking her house, invading it, occupying it, so that she longed for the day the dogs (who were bought for the children) would die. She talked with disgust of visiting the dog-addicted friends who had persuaded her and her husband to buy dogs for the children. These dog devotees were wearing sweaters and hats made from dog hair spun and woven by a woman they had hired to "revive a lost art." My client described this dog-infiltrated world as "kind of spooky." I asked her what she meant. Was it "gross" to her? "Disgusting?" She said, "You don't understand," and she re-explained how she and her husband "live with dog hair *everywhere*." I then felt I understood that the spookiness (aka horror) grew from the

Disgust and Horror 173

sense of being invaded and overtaken by something unwanted. I had been slow to grasp her experience, because dog hair seems so organic and nonalien to me that disgust made more sense, especially regarding the dog-hair garments. But in her experience, the dog hair had been rendered alien and—since it was also invasive—horror was apt.

Another woman client produced a dream that explored the terrain where disgust and horror meet. The dream featured her father, who in her experience was an orderly, somewhat dogmatic individual. In it, her father was confronted with a milky white, amorphous, slimy, and unidentifiable life-form that crawled out from under the toaster oven, onto the kitchen counter, then disappeared. In response to this life-form, the father displayed a highly uncharacteristic state of agitated speechlessness. Many elements of the portrayal of the small, creepy life-form were of interest in their contribution to the dream's emotions. The creature was amorphous and changeable in shape. It had no known identity. The creature seemed hidden away in the warm, dark space beneath the oven, possibly in the wall behind the appliance, where it might exist with untold numbers of other such creatures. The creature had no color to give it identity, just as it had no set form and no name. All its uncertainties were apparently capable of (designed for?) unsettling the usually self-certain parent. Horror dominated the dream, except for a moment when someone suggested that the life-form might belong to the maggot family. The intensity of emotion in the dream quieted with the assignment of a familiar form.

The total communion of self and Other that occurs with horror has a certain kinship with sexual surrender. While disgust regulates contact by rejecting what sits at the border (thus reinforcing that demarcation), sexual acquiescence involves a sense of boundarylessness that makes for formal equivalence with horror. The shared lineage of sexual capitulation and horror is exploited in fiction, one example being the eroticized vampire tales, which turn on the kinship between horror and sexual ecstasy. Vampires drink human blood. Importing a nonfood substance such as blood into a human-like body, turning our lifeblood into food on the lips, suggests and indeed may elicit disgust in the reader. But for many, the vampire's blood hunger will arouse horror rather than disgust, because of the complete commingling of life forces it involves. The human's lifeblood feeds and becomes the vampire, as it runs through the vampire's veins and warms and flushes his or her body. The practice of koshering meat (draining the blood from the meat before the meat is consumed) speaks to our disturbance over the image of imbibing blood.

In Anne Rice's (1976) popular book *Interview with the Vampire,* the mechanism for creating a new vampire is for an existing vampire to resurrect and transform one of his own nearly dead, drained human victims by allowing the dying human to drink the immortal vampire's blood, thereby reimbibing the human's own lost blood, mixed with the blood of the vampire's earlier victims. Ordinary disgust should preclude this act, but disgust is disregarded and a total cell-for-cell commingling of beings occurs. Life fluids flow back and forth, defying boundaries in a way akin to sexual connection, or to a mother and infant merging at the breast. Though a link to cannibalism exists in the taking of another's body for one's own nurture, the emphasis here is not on meat but on blood, the fluid form of which is important to the images of movement back and forth between beings. In the film *Alien,* the life-form that enters the spacecraft is invasive not only because of its aggressive intent, but also because its nature is so fluid and so disrespectful of structure and boundary. At one point, the alien even takes the form of acid that burns through walls, floors, and flesh.

If we contrast vampirism and cannibalism, we see that with the latter, the Other becomes meat and permanently ceases to exist as a sentient being. One person exists only as food for another and has no further identity while, in vampirism, the victim comes under the influence of the vampire and is depleted but still lives, albeit in altered form. When we contemplate cannibalism, most of the emotion stirred is about the cannibal (the victim is simply meat). We think of the cannibal's perverse appetite and ability to rob the Other of human identity and consume a human body as mere food. Our emotion about such ingestion (even in desperate situations, where death by starvation is imminent) is overwhelming. I suspect the revulsion is ultimately about the cannibal's ability to strip the Other of human identity and make of him or her meat; of course, our horror and repugnance serve the species by making us extremely loath to murder each other to provide a food source. Hannibal Lechter, renowned among contemporary cannibal images, seems to delight less in his meal or even his power over the victim than in his power to horrify the attendant, still living, breathing Other, the witness to his perverse appetite.

The line between self and Other is not the only boundary implicated in disgust and horror. The line between life and death also comes into play, because the failure to maintain that separation in clear form profoundly threatens the sense of the intact self. A bizarrely formed or oddly functioning life-form frequently is paired with the equally threatening zombie, or undead, a creature half-living, half-dead. The peculiar life-form and the zombie both are aberrant conditions that are sufficiently human-like to raise questions about their relationship to the self, but in some essential and frightening way they are not human. So in *Alien* it does not surprise us that the pseudohuman, Ash, who is actually a robot, is the one to admit the bizarre, destructive alien to the ship. And it is not surprising that people in transitional circumstances (e.g., puberty), especially in simpler societies, undergo rituals "the essential feature of [which] is that the neophytes are neither living nor dead from one aspect, and both living and dead from another. Their condition is one of ambiguity and paradox, a confusion of all the customary categories" (Turner, 1970, pp. 96–97).

In some eras, the leper occupied the horrible station between life and death, the zone of the undead or walking dead. The leper ate and breathed, but, according to Lee (1996), socially was regarded as dead: "In early days too and then only in certain places or countries a leper was regarded as already dead. A ceremony resembling the burial service was sometimes read over him and, beside a freshly-dug pit, a handful of earth was also thrown over him as a final sign that, in the eyes of his fellow men, he was dead" (p. 13). In the state of disgust, a person operates as a defined, physically distinct being who has the power to extrude or evacuate something bad from the self and body. In horror, the self-boundary is already diffused. One is nothing but senses and emotion: no specific body parts, no clear thoughts, no directed actions exist. The self has already been overcome and permeated by the impression, so no boundary-keeping action is possible. Horror has its charms, however, probably as orgasm, fainting, sleep, and speaking in tongues do: the loss of self is the loss of burden to maintain self, as Freud (1905, pp. 57–59) understood through his concept of the death instinct and Gilman (1995) did through his exploration of the senses. In horror, one merges with the impression, often visual. One no longer shuts one's eyes in revulsion, one fixes them open in fascination, enthrallment, and mystification.

While driving through the lush hills of West Virginia on an autumn day, I heard a National Public Radio report (Hochberg, 2000) about the failure of a coal waste containment pond. The pond, positioned like many others over old coal tunnels, was meant to contain millions of gallons of coal waste slurry. The containment structure had failed and released a torrent of the black waste into a river at the West Virginia–Kentucky border. Thirty years earlier, a containment site failure had wiped out much of a small town in the same region. A survivor of that accident spoke of the villagers' horror. Listening to the imagery of waves of black death rolling through a river valley, I myself felt horror. Later, the imagery returned to me when I was thinking of disgust, especially the bog and peat images of Michaels and Heaney. Why did horror, rather than disgust, prevail at the image of the black torrent? Both the magnitude and the implacability of the force likely brought horror. The unstoppable black river was muscling its way down the valley, and, as a response to that power, disgust would have been a spit in the wind. Horror was the right response because the deadly flood of slurry was no mere teeming swamp; it was a force of death, not of abundant, unruly life, and it was targeting an entire community, a world.

Throughout this chapter, I have searched for a boundary between disgust and horror, but I remain aware that emotion words do not simply follow the contours of our experience, but also create edges and contours, thus adding shape and tugging an experience into one dwelling place or another. I commonly find that I have reactions I might call either horror or disgust, or something else (e.g., "awfulness"). No single right word exists because the experience is multidimensional and it is fluid, as well. If I choose one or the other label, that label will shape my experience. Generally, for me, choosing disgust makes the experience less overwhelming than horror, and adds an element of mastery, a pleasure of sorts in imagining myself getting rid of what is troubling. Choosing horror leaves me with a feeling of having been permeated or infused more fully by the experience; it is more awful, but perhaps a bit exciting because of the sheer power the stimulus holds to move me.

Chapter 11
Concepts of Disease and Health

> Though man may be fair and strong in fight, he shall be prepared as food for worms. His fair eyes will sink into his head, his handsome body will give a foul stench. Thus will we, both child and grown man, turn to dust of earth and become nobody.
>
> —Friar John Grimstone

The notion of "body politic" is a linguistic invention that speaks to the ready metaphor linking society and anatomy—one that reminds us that in shifting attention now to the body proper, we do not leave society far behind. The "reviled" lower classes or "devalued" races often are portrayed as invading, boundary-disrupting forces either of swarming vermin or of rampant disease such as plague. Susan Sontag's (1977) work on illness considers the veritable corpus callosum of fibers linking the two spheres of discourse. She explains, for example, that "'blight' (a virtual synonym for slum) is seen as a cancer that spreads insidiously, and the use of the term 'invasion' to describe when the non-white and poor move into a middle-class neighborhood is as much a metaphor borrowed from cancer as from the military: the two discourses overlap" (p. 74, n.). Sontag views totalitarians as especially drawn to disease metaphors, which they use in describing social undesirables. "Modern totalitarian movements," she says, "whether of the right or of the left, have been peculiarly—and revealingly—inclined to use disease imagery. The Nazis declared that someone of mixed 'racial' origin was like a syphilitic. European Jewry was repeatedly analogized to syphilis, and to a cancer that must be excised" (p. 82).

Attitudes about society and about our own and others' bodies all ultimately concern our feelings of personal security and insecurity and our fears of loss or deterioration of self. Disease affects the body directly; it also affects the sense of self profoundly, if indirectly. Self-esteem is compromised by disease, as we begin to identify with dysfunction, ugliness, and lassitude. But disease affects more than self-esteem; it also withers our sense of agency, which constitutes a core aspect of the self.

The psychological principle of contagion is important with respect to illness and infirmity; it creates danger in touching the aged or sick. Even touching with the eyes, which means touching with the mind or the imagination, brings the danger of absorption or identification. Disgust opposes these contacts and incorporations. The powerful anxiety associated with contagious disgustingness is evident in contemporary African societies in which families will reject their own daughters if the daughter suffers an obstetric fistula during a traumatic delivery of an infant. Fistulas result in lasting foul odor and incontinence and families often shun their children rather than risk contagion of their disgustingness (Kristof, 2003). A book entitled *Forever Feminine* (Wilson, 1968) was funded by a pharmaceutical company that marketed hormone replacement products. The book promoted a view of menopause as a catastrophic collapse of femininity that would motivate men to reject women as if they were afflicted with the contagious illness of old age. This bit of cultural history provides an example of disgust for the dry and withered—signs of infirmity and age—whereas disgust is more frequently associated with the moist and germ laden, which connote an excess of life and sexuality. Either end of the spectrum can threaten us with images of a weakened or unworthy self. Too much life dwarfs us through comparison; waning life threatens us through identification.

Though actual disease threatens our sense of control over the form and function of the body and, ultimately, the self, our mental preoccupations with disease follow as much from the imaginative pull of the subject matter as from medical affliction to the body. We observe this pull most clearly in hypochondriacs who cannot stop envisioning illness, so that they suffer its ravages imaginatively even when in excellent health (and may cope well with actual illness). This human need to conjure illness follows from the significance illness has in representing the vulnerable, inconstant, perishable self.

Disgust is a common response to the disturbing but captivating images associated with some illnesses. Sontag talks of cancer as the "disease of the other," because, envisioning cancer, we see foreign, mutant cells overtaking the self (p. 68), but, imagining tuberculosis, the self is

Concepts of Disease and Health 179

altered by weakening and wasting. André Gide's (1970) *The Immoralist* turns on experiences of health and illness, specifically, tuberculosis, and its psychological meanings. When the illness makes its first, indisputable appearance in Gide's narrative, disgust enters mated with that experience. We have the protagonist describing the blood he coughs up, saying, "It wasn't a flow of bright blood now, like the other hemorrhages; it was a thick, hideous clot I spat onto the floor with disgust" (p. 16). The word *hideous* conveys the ill man's need to turn the illness into something condemned as bad and enlivened imaginatively as a vile foe.

Gilman's (1995) discourse on disease and health highlights our active desire to articulate a healthy–ill distinction as a means to elevate and inoculate the vulnerable self. One aspect of vulnerability is impermanence, what Gilman calls "flux." He tells us, "Flux is disturbing, permanence reassuring.... The ultimate flux ... is that flux experienced in our sensing of the transience of our lives and bodies" (p. 175). Gilman examines key cultural distinctions as ways to deny impermanence: He gives as examples beauty and ugliness, truth and fiction, health and disease. All such categorizations are attempts to manage our anxiety about "ever shifting boundaries," our "mutability." He articulates the way in which culturally articulated categories hold firm "precisely because they are arbitrary divisions that need to be constantly reinforced" (p. 176). In other words, these divisions exist largely because they comfort and protect us, therefore, we are diligent in maintaining their existence.

Gilman's argument that human insecurity is a basis for entrenched, dichotomous concepts of sick–well, ugly–beautiful, and the like parallels Sartre's judgment, explored in an earlier chapter, that racism, specifically anti-Semitism, expresses the anti-Semite's need for the concept of a reviled, verminous, subhuman Jew whose existence creates an opposite category meant to contain the elevated individuals with whom the anti-Semite wishes to affiliate. As Gide's "immoralist" moves from sickness into a health-preoccupation so single-minded it operates like an addiction, the character's determination to emblazon the categories *sick* and *healthy* gives rise to a need to make his now-tubercular wife into the emblem of illness, as conveyed in this passage describing her sickness:

> Meanwhile the embolism had been followed by serious complications; the dreadful blood clot, which the heart had rejected,

exhausted and congested her lungs, obstructed her breathing, which was now labored and wheezing. Sickness had entered Marceline, henceforth inhabited her, marked her, soiled her. She was a tainted thing [p. 73].

Abhorrent, foul illness has become a grand theme of the man's imagination. Although he labors to achieve health and vigor for himself, his determined categorizations of the ill and the healthy demonstrate the extent to which life and its uncertainties still terrify him and motivate him to simplify and tame experience through the dichotomy of the sick (and hideous) and the well (and beautiful).

Gilman shows us that the concepts of physical ugliness, disease, and inferior race attract each other magnetically and bond strongly, and all are steeped in the brew of revulsion. To this trio, we can add inferior gender. Gilman highlights this easy amalgamation of core categories as an aspect of anti-Semitism:

> By the nineteenth century, male Jews are seen as feminized, belonging to an "inferior race." The Jew, in his "absence of creative power, of spontaneity and of originality... displays in this respect something of a woman's nature.... He is like, but not identical to, the tubercular woman, specifically the tubercular Jewish woman." The Jew's visage is like "to those lean actresses, the Rachels and Sarahs, who spit blood, and seem to have but the spark of life left.... It is the tubercular Jewish woman that the healthy male Jew looks like" [p. 60].

What a remarkable concluding line: "It is the tubercular Jewish woman that the healthy male Jew looks like." Gilman's source degrades the Jew, the female, and the physically ill through his single bizarre conclusion. All are repulsive to him and deserving of revilement.

Another's illness may make us anxious, since it is infectious and we are vulnerable; we nevertheless dwell on illness in order to emphasize that we are personally outside the borders of disease's miserable kingdom. The logic here is equivalent to the logic of caste. As long as there are "untouchables" to whom we can point and say, "They are the ones who dwell in squalor, dispose of excrement, and disinfect areas of disease and contamination," then we can rest assured we are not such people. We may then reinforce our sense of separation by feeling disgust over what the untouchables do and who they are. We may not need to feel much intensity of disgust, however, if the class system insulates us well from threats to the self. Here, again, we have an important research question concerning the relationship between the presence of socially institutionalized separations of the pure and the contaminated and the need for personal, fully felt disgust to assert one's spiritual cleanliness. An American watching an Indian untouchable emerge naked from a sewer, caked in excrement, likely feels disgust. Does the Brahman feel disgust at that moment, or only the correctness of this other man, not himself, emerging from the filthy sewer? And what if the untouchable wants to lay a hand on the Brahman's arm? Is disgust felt over the contact with something soiled or only rage at the violation of the system?

The notion of continuity between visible surface and invisible depth comforts by supporting simplistic judgments about one's own superiority to another, made through observations of what lies visible. We like to assume we can know the depth or the entirety of a being from the observable surface. The more we can detect hideousness and disease on the surface and assume that surface mirrors depth, the more we can comfort ourselves with notions of being different from that which offends our eyes. Early botanical names demonstrate the common assumption that visible characteristics and deep character are indeed linked. A plant called "boneset" has leaves positioned base to base and joined in a clean line, a feature that convinced earlier peoples that consuming this plant might help repair broken bones.

Since leprosy is a disease that shows on the surface, and shows in a manner people regard as disgusting, assumptions that surface predicts depth are particularly damaging to those so afflicted. Brody entitled his 1974 book on leprosy *Disease of the Soul,* reflecting in his title an absolute fusion between physical and moral disease. Viewing leprosy as divine punishment provided a fantasy that one could control this affliction with correct, godly behavior. Brody tells us that Roman Catholic cardinals often associated particular illnesses with particular sins. However, "Of all the diseases that afflicted medieval man, leprosy especially came to be understood as divine punishment for sinfulness and to be viewed as no other sickness known to man has ever been" (p. 11).

While concepts of sick and well, tainted and unblemished operate protectively when we can use them metaphorically and wield them actively—often assigning ourselves to the "healthy" category and others to the "ill"—when real illness overtakes us or those in our purview, the experience diminishes our sense of security in the world. The world of actual physical illness pushes us beyond disturbing sights into a place of great stimulation by the proximal senses. All the body processes we have labored to take under control in moving from infancy through childhood into adulthood, suddenly may be out of control and demanding our close involvement. We must deal with loose stools, runny noses, bloody or pustulent sores, all of which immerse us in smells, sights, and sensations. These contacts threaten our sense of being self-controlled, invulnerable adults, as does the profound idea that one is ill and may weaken, permanently change, suffer, or perhaps die.

Anticipation of and preparation for the messiness and sensory stimulation of disease offer us some inoculation, but a sudden shift away from the expected can disturb our defenses. The man mentioned earlier, who told me of his experience dealing with his partner's long and complicated recovery from sinus surgery, felt no disgust dealing with the ropes of mucus she continually discharged from her sinuses. But when she once passed something that smelled and looked to him like feces, he was horribly disgusted and complained about how this illness had destroyed the sexual feeling he had had for her. The fecal imagery seemed too unexpected and unanticipated for him to integrate comfortably. Or, possibly, when he got to a point of heightened frustration with her unappealing condition, he imposed the fecal imagery on his partner's nasal discharge as an expression of having reached a new level of disgust with his overall situation as caretaker to this suddenly needy woman.

Our motives in relation to sickness and the sick are complex. Avoidance is by no means the only response. Clearly, people do at times want to be sick, for various reasons but certainly because sickness elicits caretaking in addition to fear and disgust. Sometimes people *want* to touch the diseased, old, or dying out of a fascination with decay or from a humane appreciation of the whole person who is more than his or her illness or decrepitude. In other instances, people do not truly want such contact, but they wish they possessed the mental fortitude to endure it with tranquility. The ability to touch what is disgusting or ghastly and yet preserve one's own form (resisting contagion or envelopment) signifies extraordinary strength and thus can be a badge of honor and social standing. We may esteem as heroes or saints those—such as rescue workers—who have withstood harrowing contacts with the disgusting and horrible. We see them as stronger

Concepts of Disease and Health

than we (therefore, worth touching and seeing, since strength, too, can be contagious) and as steeled in the fires of dreadful experience.

A young girl, Misty, was in treatment with me at the time of Princess Diana's fatal accident. Misty talked with fascination of Diana's relationship to the sick and poor. Misty herself was fastidious and quick to discern things that were repellent, which she would avoid touching. She was impressed by Diana's ability to touch common people, especially the sick. Misty had a fantasy of marrying Prince William and becoming a princess like Diana who would touch her subjects. She contrasted Diana with dignitaries who hold back from the crowd and touch no one.

Misty seemed to believe the exalted position of princess would protect her from contamination, thus allowing her contact without danger. Her attitude toward infections and infestations suggested that she saw them as nature run amok within the body and soul. Such natural profusion seemed associated with her own human condition (of loving and longing, of living with a physical body). Only as princess—officially assured of abiding personal worth and popularity—could she contact the earthiness of the self (in externalized form) and reclaim its full potential.

A caller to a radio show exhibited dynamics similar to this girl's when he extolled Diana's ability to venture out among lepers and AIDS patients, "the sick and the wretched," and to touch them, physically and emotionally, in Christlike fashion. The caller repeatedly avowed that he himself could never do such "distasteful" things, like touching a child "with a stinking tumor," and that he thus particularly admired, even envied, the Princess's ability to do so. One suspected he could not engage with others as Diana had because he saw the threat of contamination (i.e., confrontation with what can grow so wildly within the self) as insurmountable. Diana's ability to wade unsullied into what he saw as filth made her almost godlike for him; it intensified her purity beyond the ordinary because she was impervious to ordinary filth. Similarly, we have images of saints unsullied by contact with lepers. Saint Catherine mingled with the sick and reportedly drank urine, but her body, exhumed in 1933, was described by the Church as "incorrupt" and "fresh as the day it was buried" (Saint Catherine Church, n.d.): "Though she had lived seventy years and was in the ground for fifty-seven years, her eyes remained blue and beautiful; and in death her arms and legs were as supple as if she were asleep."

Images of Christ underscore his ability to touch what others dare not and yet to remain unsullied and unaffected by disgust. Though Leviticus proscribed contact with the menstruating female, who was unclean and would transmit her impurity, Christ rejected this instruction. Christ is reported to have said, "There is nothing from without a man that entering into him can defile him; but the things which come from a man, those are they that defile a man" (Elliott, 1999, p. 3, n. 11). As understood by Elliott, Christ's thinking was revolutionary in its refusal to equate the visible, palpable body surface with the inner depths.

Those who fail to rise in Christlike fashion above distinctions between health and illness, and attendant distinctions such as beautiful and ugly, may feel shame for their ignoble responses. For example, when a teacher of mildly intellectually impaired children was suddenly brought into contact with profoundly impaired children, she reacted with such overwhelming disgust that she could not eat for days. In telling her story, she highlighted her shame—shading into the more aggressive response of "self-disgust"—for failing to be professional as well as humanely compassionate and tolerant. She also illustrated the common response of difficulty consuming food when struggling with disgust over a nonfood stimulus. A person's vulnerability to a disgusting Other, and the wish to keep the Other distant, give rise to a general desire to shut out what is outside, especially food, which is consumed in a more volitional, self-controlled fashion than sounds, sights, or smells, and which likely bears a special relationship to disgust because of the wholesale incorporation implied by eating and perhaps because of our species' adaptation to use disgust to discourage ingestion of toxic foodstuff. Any psychological imagery of toxicity—no matter how remote from rotten food—seems to incline us to refuse food while the troubling images are before us.

Societies vary in their concepts of how the body relates to the larger world, and these varying concepts impact disgust experience. Some societies, including our own, seem to conceive of the human body as quite separate from the surrounding world. That separation is established by way of the skin as a container for the body. Jamaicans are said to think of the body as more permeable, with healthful and polluting substances moving freely from inside to outside and back again. Cooper (1995) explores Jamaican ideas about the body, health, and illness in *The Jamaican Body;* she contends that Jamaicans believe the healthy body must be an "open system." Anything contained too long within (menstrual blood, food, excrement) becomes powerfully bad.

Kleinman (1989) argues that Hindus view the body as an open system and that such a conceptualization promotes great concern about purity and impurity. Impurity precludes contact with the Divine. The impact such concepts have on disgust experience is not clear. Perhaps the sense of permeability promotes a greater need to strive to maintain inner purity, and disgust is utilized in these efforts. But such a hypothesis may well prove too simple. Permeable systems also allow for ready flushing and do not promote imagery of bacteria-like breeding of toxins within a sealed space. Nor might they highlight the skin surface and the need for it to appear unflawed, since the skin has less significance as a barrier.

Impermeable systems, in which the body is container, support ideas of the body brewing a bad inner mix, which can be experienced in a variety of ways. One can have a sense of containing inner poison that sickens, but gives a feeling of destructive power. If anger festers within, it becomes hatred, which has the quality of strong, toxic stuff. In the profoundly affecting Holocaust documentary, *Shoah*, a survivor of Nazi horror said, "If you licked my heart you would be poisoned." Anger that flows is clean and mobile; held within, it breeds pustulant stuff that teems with dangerous life. Consider the lepers who were "forbidden to answer if spoken to until he who spoke was 'to windward of them'" (Lee, 1996, p. 13). Might not anger at such isolation and ostracism mingle with the sense of illness contained within (the leprosy itself) to create a sense that one's inner stuff has astounding power—whether that stuff be the pustulance or the fury?

The ultimate danger implied by illness and death is the complete disintegration of the body's form and function so that the boundary between inner and outer collapses. In their book *Gig*, Bowe, Bowe, and Streeter (2001) examine people's relationships to their occupations. They feature, among others, Neal Smithers, a worker who removes decomposed cadavers and cleans the places where they are found. Smithers recalled what happened when he and his sister, a coworker, attempted to remove a liquefying body whose original form had long since collapsed: when they touched the body, the contents broke loose and flooded the two workers, whereupon his sister raced from the house and vomited, presumably desperate to rid herself of what had just touched her both physically and psychically. Ultimately, the family business purchased an extractor to vacuum up and contain such materials. Though the story of the Smithers' occupation is reboant with disgust, a National Public Radio reporter discussing the book addressed the opposite side of the aversion–attraction phenomenon, concluding, "What could be more fascinating than a melted human body?" As always, what disturbs us also captivates us, and the liquefaction of the human body to a formless state is no exception.

Joseph Heller's (1961) *Catch-22* renders the disgustingness and horror of the dissolved human form, not its fascination. His imagery is interesting in its preservation of the ostensible human form, the man bounded by skin and clothes, thus apparently whole and adequately protected from outside dangers. But within is mush, so the wholeness is illusory. The skin contains an inner compost of matter, which signifies the erosion of being, not its concentration or intensification, especially because containment inevitably fails, as in the imagery below, and the insides leak out:

> Yossarian ripped open the snaps of Snowden's flak suit and heard himself scream wildly as Snowden's insides slithered down to the floor in a soggy pile and just kept dripping out. A chunk of flak more than three inches big had shot into his other side just underneath the arm and blasted all the way through, drawing whole mottled quarts of Snowden along with it through the gigantic hole in his ribs it made as it blasted out.... He forced himself to look again. Here was God's plenty, all right, he thought bitterly as he stared—liver, lungs, kidneys, ribs, stomach and bits of the stewed tomatoes Snowden had eaten that day for lunch. Yossarian hated stewed tomatoes and turned away dizzily and began to vomit, clutching his burning throat.... It was easy to read the message in his entrails. Man was matter, that was Snowden's secret. Drop him out a window and he'll fall. Set fire to him and he'll burn. Bury him and he'll rot like other kinds of garbage. The spirit gone, man is garbage. That was Snowden's secret [pp. 449–450].

In the next image, the man within the skin is not even matter; he is nothing, mere space:

> It was, indeed, the same man. He had lost a few inches and added some weight, but Yossarian remembered him instantly by the two stiff arms and the two stiff, thick, useless legs all drawn upward into the air almost perpendicularly by the taut ropes and the long lead weights suspended from pulleys over

him and by the frayed black hole in the bandages over his mouth. He had, in fact, hardly changed at all. There was the same zinc pipe rising from the hard stone mass over his groin and leading to the clear glass jar on the floor. There was the same clear glass jar on a pole dripping fluid into him through the crook of his elbow. Yossarian would recognize him anywhere. He wondered who he was.

"There's no one inside!" Dunbar yelled out at him unexpectedly.

Yossarian felt his heart skip a beat and his legs grow weak. "What are you talking about?" he shouted with dread, stunned by the haggard, sparking anguish in Dunbar's eyes and by his crazed look of wild shock and horror. "Are you nuts or something? What the hell do you mean, there's no one inside?"

"They've stolen him away!" Dunbar shouted back. "He's hollow inside, like a chocolate soldier. They just took him away and left those bandages there" [pp. 373–374].

First, Heller directs our *disgust* toward what is inside: mush where there should be human structure. Next, he directs our *horror* to what is inside—*nothing*—which means the being has been overtaken entirely. Thus the normal function of disgust, to protect from outside threats, has failed entirely. The being is no more.

Finally, we come to the matter of death, the endpoint of serious illness or catastrophic injury. Rozin et al. (1997) see death as a primary stimulus for disgust. I am less persuaded than they that disgust is inevitable in confronting death. Disgust toward death often occurs when death is animated as a form of horrid, decayed life. When Menninghaus (2003) states that "every book about disgust is not least a book about the rotting corpse" (p. 1), we should note that his emphasis is not on death or on the corpse itself, but on the rotting corpse. Sebald (2002) illustrates this phenomenon as he considers the devastation wrought on German cities during World War II. He moves us into the realm of disgust and also horror concerning aspects of death. In so doing, he highlights ghastly life:

> Apart from the distraught behavior of the people themselves, the most striking change in the natural order of the cities during the weeks after a devastating raid was undoubtedly the increase in the parasitical creatures thriving on the unburied bodies. The conspicuous sparsity of observations and comments on

this phenomenon can be explained as the tacit imposition of a taboo, very understandable if one remembers that the Germans, who had proposed to cleanse and sanitize all Europe, now had to contend with a rising fear that they themselves were the rat people [p. 73].

Sebald goes on to quote Hans Erich Nossack, author of "Der Untergang" ("The End"), an account of the destruction of Hamburg:

The rats, bold and fat, frolicked in the streets, but even more disgusting were the flies, huge and iridescent green, flies such as had never been seen before. They swarmed in great clusters on the roads, settled in heaps to copulate on ruined walls, and basked, weary and satiated, on the splinters of the windowpanes [p. 73].

The rats and flies represent the life force gone wild; they are grotesque gluttons that will binge on anything that nourishes. Were the death or horrid life silently, odorlessly overcoming life, overtaking it stealthily but relentlessly, then we would enter the realm of horror, but this buzzing, malodorous world of slime, seepage, and gluttony is ground prepared for disgust.

A more commonplace example of the disgusting life often contained in images of death came from a man who traced an odor of decay to his basement, where he encountered a pail of water in which two mice had drowned. As he puzzled over the intensity of disgust he felt at the discovery, his attention turned away from death per se to the narrative he associated with his finding. He saw the mice attempting to escape their drowning deaths and failing in their efforts and, worse yet, he observed that one mouse had half-eaten the other. It was this story of attempted survival leading to bizarre cannibalism that organized his disgust. He commented that he commonly finds mice dead in traps and thinks nothing of disposing of them. The strong odor of decay had been an initial trigger for disgust in relation to the drowned mice, and the scene he discovered intensified his emotion.

When we turn to the cold corpse, if disgust occurs it likely is not the qualities of the thing (stillness, weight, coldness) that elicit the emotion, but the significance of those qualities. They signify the end of the life and consciousness of another, and they remind us of the possibility of such a state for oneself. Disgust toward the waxy-skinned corpse or the dry skeleton is the effort to refuse this monumental change of state, to reject it as a possibility. In this context, the idea of life outside normal boundary is expressed not through slime or alien life-forms, but through the sudden meaninglessness of the human body as a container for life. Life has fled the body and gone elsewhere or, worse yet, has simply gone. Earlier examples of disgust for nature, illness, or difference portrayed disturbing life positioned at the threshold of body and self. Death alters the equation by presenting us with the image of life that has already succumbed to destructive forces and is no more. There is no more self to protect, no more boundary to defend. Disgust at death is our last, desperate attempt to defeat such a disturbing occurrence through denying, refusing, or attempting to undo what has already transpired, to reestablish the simple and comforting imagery of a person defending his or her boundaries. It would be interesting to investigate whether such disgust over death occurs more frequently at certain ages (in youth, perhaps) or in certain groups (religious people whose belief in an afterlife is failing).

The awfulness of death is also its power to deprive us of a specific individual who is loved deeply or on whom we depend. Disgust may play a part in such experiences. Recently, I had to euthanize a beloved dog. Watching life leave the body I'd known and loved for 13 years, I recognized death in the alteration of the animal's eyes, which became lax and watery. I felt a slight twinge of disgust toward those dead eyes, which I would not have felt toward another creature but felt then because of my fight against the thought that I would never again see and be seen by my pet's warm, attentive, fully alive brown eyes. Again, the material condition—the wet, slack eyes—mattered little. What it signified mattered greatly. In this case, the disgust signified not a direct threat to my own life but a jarring recognition of the end of another life.

Confronted with a body no longer living, especially that of a person or animal who was meaningful in one's life, a person must suddenly traverse a complex psychological ground and make a series of major revisions in his or her understanding of the world. One considers the world that has been and the world that suddenly has begun, absent the life lost. The dead body itself—not breathing, not responding—signifies this massive change and catalyzes the recalculation of one's world. It is the *idea* of death that is at times horrifying and that we seek to refuse through disgust at the physical particulars of death.

Chapter 12
Final Comments

> Though we seek to create order, we do not simply condemn disorder. We recognise that it is destructive to existing patterns; also that it has potentiality. It symbolises both danger and power.
>
> —Mary Douglas, *Purity and Danger*

Whether the discourse concerns nature, nations, or noses, disgust addresses the relations between what we consider self and what we count as Other, and it stirs, along with its neighbor emotions, as we negotiate the critical problem of how to invigorate and enrich the self through contact with "otherness" without risking our sense of security. This paired set of desires—to expand and to safeguard—is served by discriminately allowing or interdicting movement across the self boundary. Disgust serves as the psychic equivalent of the cell wall in its ability to exclude those influences judged to be more damaging than beneficial, while admitting what seems safely nourishing. Disgust becomes of interest through this endless dialectic between the need to protect the self from intrusion and the desire to allow access to body and mind in order to admit emotional, spiritual, intellectual, and sexual nourishment. Whatever we encounter in our worlds has to be quickly but astutely evaluated for costs and benefits: Will it diminish more than it enhances? Do we meet it with aversion, with faint interest, or with fascination?

Disgust represents one of a number of tools humans possess for limiting the anxiety of existence. It depends on our ability to assert, "I am apart and boundaried." A boundaried being can exclude the things that frighten, and thus be safe. The boundaried self is a construct. If we believe in it as the moment's reality, it offers us the power and comfort of extrusion by way of disgust, but also the burden of securing its safety and worth. Disgust represents the opposite of the Buddhist philosophy, which teaches that there is no ego, no boundaried being called self. Nor are there matters so fixed in form and enduring that distress and extrusion are needed. Life is like the ocean's waters, always in flux. We need not call things to us, or hurl them away in disgust.

In our relations with nature, disgust stirs if we feel dwarfed by the vigor of the not-self, which can make us feel less real, solid, and robust than we like. Millennia of Western culture have added extra challenges to our relations with nature by feeding a circular system of meanings within which nature is defined negatively (as dirty, unruly, inferior to spirit and godliness) so that we can measure well against it; but then we must fight contact even more energetically because contact now signifies contagion of the disgusting.

With regard to sex and intimacy, we encounter the special challenges that come with relations with beings resembling ourselves. The similarities between one human and another intensify our longings for connection and our intuition of connection's possibilities, but also in some instances enlarge the threat of identity diffusion by revealing us to be much like everyone else, thus treasured images of individuality are disturbed. Reproduction brings some of the greatest challenges to boundary management. People are impelled to join intimately but such joining means loss of singleness. Indeed, nature's primary aim with regard to such coupling disregards the two individuals entirely in the interest of creating a third individual, who is neither one nor the other, though related to both. Sexual connection brings fantasies of expanding the self by joining with another, perhaps producing a third, but also losing the singular self. Normal disgust over certain of the sensations, smells, and sights of another's body can be suspended and replaced with pleasure in such intimacy, but disgust remains on the alert, ready to reinforce boundaries if an excessive threat to self-security appears. Such threats can begin with the nose, eyes, or tongue and flow into the meaning we attribute to the sensory information we collect. For example, we might react with disgust to hair, urine, or blood because of what those body elements have come to mean to us over the years. Alternatively, disgust can begin with the interpersonal and flow back toward the senses. For instance, fear of a partner's enveloping love may lead to heightened sensitivity to her loud voice or his hairy chest, which then becomes the immediate object of disgust.

In family groups, disgust helps to delineate the family as a social unit by informing its members of what behaviors are unacceptable for

Final Comments

those within. Disgust also operates between individuals, especially in high-conflict families where it is used to elevate one person over another, to pressure a person to modify his or her behavior, to dilute intimacy by underscoring difference, and to strengthen an individual's sense that he or she is unique or superior. Disgust prevails at times of developmental transition, when the conflict between increased self-definition and full immersion in the family group intensifies.

Science and art open the possibility of greater than normal expansion of the self through generation of startlingly new experience, new conceptions, and new and communicable representations of experience, for example, in graphic art, music, text, or scientific paradigms. These explorations also create risk of encounter with experience that may so alter the individual's perceived identity that he or she may draw rejection from others, or even self-rejection as in the case of a fiction writer who follows fantasy sequences deep into a disquietingly murky or violent world, or that of a photographer who cannot deny an inclination to view and record erotica.

Relations between groups of humans often are replete with disgust imagery, in part because threats from other groups near to one's door can seem great, but also because the hostile component of disgust is less inhibited in group interactions than in individual response. Lewis Thomas (1974) explores such disinhibition in his essay on Turnbull's anthropological field study of the aptly named Iks, an isolated, socially displaced, and stunningly antisocial Ugandan tribe, whose hallmark—as viewed by outsiders such as Turnbull—was the openly sadistic and selfishly individualistic attitude most Iks showed toward others in the group. In his characteristically adept prose, Thomas makes sense of the Iks' vileness:

> The solitary Ik, isolated in the ruins of an exploded culture, has built a new defense for himself. If you live in an unworkable society you can make up one of your own, and this is what the Iks have done. Each Ik has become a group, a one-man tribe on its own, a constituency.
>
> Now, everything falls into place. This is why they do seem, after all, vaguely familiar to all of us. We've seen them before. This is precisely the way groups of one size or another, ranging from committees to nations, behave. It is, of course, this aspect of humanity that has lagged behind the rest of evolution, and this is why the Ik seems so primitive. In his absolute selfishness,

his incapacity to give anything away, no matter what, he is a successful committee. When he stands at the door of his hut, shouting insults at his neighbors in a loud harangue, he is city addressing another city.

Cities have all the Ik characteristics. They defecate on doorsteps, in rivers and lakes, their own or anyone else's. They leave rubbish. They detest all neighboring cities, give nothing away. They even build institutions for deserting elders out of sight.

Nations are the most Iklike of all. . . . We haven't yet learned how to stay human when assembled in masses [p. 110].

Groups organized around religious principles speak to our efforts to find a secure place in the larger cosmos that includes all of creation, a naturally dwarfing span. We want to feel substantial and significant but we strive to be realistic as well, which requires some acknowledgment of our relative puniness. One solution lies in well-chosen affiliations. If we ally with the mightiest of forces, we may gain standing. If we cast our lot with godliness and purity, destruction may pass us by. Through disgust and the various concepts of pollution, degradation and sin that accompany it, the religious try to position themselves on the side of the angels. When such affiliation takes dangerous turns it can foster the free venting of hostility, unreasonably elevated self-regard, and inner certainty in the face of the daunting behavioral choices life requires. When less driven by insecurities, religion may foster the experience of awed merger with the grandeur of the cosmos, which belongs with the other boundary diffusions human beings desire and enjoy.

Horror takes us beyond disgust into a world in which disgust as "cell wall" has failed and we must cope with the invasion of a force we construe as alien that threatens to substitute its being for our own. Horror movies sometimes thrill us because they transport us to the edge of psychic implosion and back again to safety. Horror is the evil cousin of sexual passion in that both portray the dissolution of the individual, with sexual fantasy generally animating the exciting aspect of such connection and horror conjuring its demons. Both "carry us away," altering the sense of self.

In the realm of health and sickness, humans guard their images of a safe, well-functioning, and attractive body. The body's vital importance and its unity with the self motivate such vigilance. Images of ill health can be taken as external signs of spiritual deficiency and, as

Final Comments

such, come into company with racial, ethnic, gender, and physiognomic identifiers to which we too often attribute a core connection to inferior or superior status. In all spheres, disgust's function is complicated by the fact that we often do more than passively encounter things, and judge whether to admit or repel them. We actively draw things into the sphere of the self, only to label them disgusting, or to label them such while simultaneously showing them off to a friend or partner as something repulsive that person must please hurry over to share.

In all these domains and in others that have not been investigated here, disgust helps individuals and groups define and protect the self and delineate the relationship between self and Other. In disgust situations, the nature of the essential threat that is faced is effectively masked by our focus on a material condition that attracts and organizes the emotion. So we focus disgust on soup dribbling down a man's face but do not quickly recognize an underlying fear of intimacy—linked in the moment with a wish and fear of kissing the man—that motivates disgust toward his manners and face. This symbolization process is an important feature of disgust's operation as an ego defense. It allows us to launch a passionate attack without being subject to the greater vulnerability that would attach to full knowledge of the danger we face.

Disgust works in concert with emotions such as contempt and fury—adding its own special imagery and coloration—and in opposition to affiliation and incorporation. It is a formidable element in conflicts among groups large and small and an influential justifier of destructive action. Not all its effects are detrimental to human relations, however. Disgust over immorality or harmfulness, if tempered by the holder's own morality, has led to social reforms that enhance group harmony and the quality of human life.

References

Abraham, K. (1921), *The Selected Papers of Karl Abraham*. London: Brunner-Routledge, 1979.

Albee, E. (1973), *A Delicate Balance*. New York: Simon & Schuster.

Alexander, F. (1948), *Fundamentals of Psychoanalysis*. New York: Norton.

Angyal, A. (1941), Disgust and related aversions. *Journal of Abnormal and Social Psychology*, 36:393–412.

Anthony, J. (1986), The contributions of child psychoanalysis to psychoanalysis. *The Psychoanalytic Study of the Child*, 41:61–87. New Haven, CT: Yale University Press.

Arnold, E., reporter (2002, August 22), Fish-cleaning [Dirty Work series]. *Morning Edition*. National Public Radio.

Augustinus, A. (n.d.), *The Confessions of Saint Augustine*, trans. E. B. Pusey. Mount Vernon, NY: Peter Pauper Press.

Bear, G. (1997), *Slant*. New York: Tom Doherty Associates.

Bearak, B. (1999, April 21), Crisis in the Balkans. *New York Times*.

Benedict, E. (2001), *Almost*. New York: Houghton Mifflin.

Boone, S. L. (1999), Unvarnished truth: The chemistry of shame in Primo Levi. *Judaism*, 48:72–83.

Bowe, J., Bowe, M. & Streeter, S., eds. (2000), *Gig: Americans Talk About Their Work*. New York: Crown.

Boys Don't Cry (1999), Film. Twentieth Century Fox.

Brody, S. (1974), *The Disease of the Soul: Leprosy in Medieval Literature*. Ithaca, NY: Cornell University Press.

Channel4.com (2000, August 15), The anatomy of disgust.

Cooper, C. (1995), *Noises in the Blood: Orality, Gender, and the "Vulgar" Body of Jamaican Popular Culture*. Durham, NC: Duke University Press.

Cunningham, M. (1998), *The Hours*. New York: Farrar, Straus & Giroux.

Curtis, V. & Biran, A. (2001), Dirt, disgust, and disease. *Perspectives in Biology and Medicine,* 44:17–31.
Darwin, C. (1872), *The Expression of the Emotions in Man and Animals.* Chicago: University of Chicago Press, 1965.
Davey, G. C. L., Buckland, G., Tantow, B. & Dallos, R. (1998), Disgust and eating disorders. *European Eating Disorders Review,* 6: 201–211.
Denby, D. (1997, July 21), In Darwin's wake. *The New Yorker.*
Douglas, M. (1966), *Purity and Danger.* London: Routledge, 1984.
Drescher, J. (2001), *Psychoanalytic Therapy and the Gay Man.* Hillsdale, NJ: The Analytic Press.
Ekman, P. (1984), Expression and the nature of emotion. In: *Approaches to Emotion,* ed. K. Scherer & P. Ekman. Hillsdale, NJ: Lawrence Erlbaum Associates.
Ekman, P. & Friesen, W. V. (1975), *Unmasking the Face.* Englewood Cliffs, NJ: Prentice-Hall.
Ekman, P., Friesen, W. V., O'Sullivan, M., et al. (1987), Universals and cultural differences in the judgments of facial expressions of emotion. *Journal of Personality and Social Psychology,* 53:712–717.
Elliott, D. (1999), *Fallen Bodies, Pollution, Sexuality, and Demonology in the Middle Ages.* Philadelphia: University of Pennsylvania Press.
Franzen, J. (2001), *The Corrections.* New York: Farrar, Straus & Giroux.
Freud, S. (1905), Three essays on the theory of sexuality. *Standard Edition,* 7:125–245. London: Hogarth Press, 1953.
Freud, S. (1923), The ego and the id. *Standard Edition,* 19:3–66. London: Hogarth Press, 1961.
Gide, A. (1970), *The Immoralist,* trans. R. Howard. New York: Bantam Books.
Gilman, S. L. (1995), *Picturing Health and Illness.* Baltimore, MD: Johns Hopkins University Press.
Goldberg, M. (2000), *The Bee Season.* New York: Random House.
Haidt, J. & Keltner, D. (1998), Culture and emotion: Multiple methods find new faces and a gradient of universality. Manuscript under review.
Haidt, J., Rozin, P., McCauley, C. R. & Imada, S. (1997), Body, psyche, and culture: The relationship between disgust and morality. *Psychology and Developing Societies,* 9:107–131.
Heaney, S. (1998), *Opened Ground.* New York: Farrar, Straus & Giroux.

References

Heller, J. (1961), *Catch-22*. New York: Dell.
Herzog, D. (1998), *Poisoning the Minds of the Lower Orders*. Princeton, NJ: Princeton University Press.
Hobb, R. (1996), *Assassin's Apprentice: The Farseer Trilogy, Book 1*. New York: Spectra.
Hochberg, A. (2000, October 27), *All Things Considered*. National Public Radio.
Hoeg, P. (1995), *Smilla's Sense of Snow*. New York: Bantam Doubleday Dell.
Hurd, B. (2001), *Stirring the Mud: On Swamps, Bogs, and Human Imagination*. Boston: Beacon Press.
Izard, C. E. (1971), *The Face of Emotion*. New York: Appleton-Century-Crofts.
Jackson, M. R. (1984), *Self-Esteem and Meaning: A Life Historical Investigation*. Albany, NY: SUNY Press.
Jones, E. (1938), *Papers on Psycho-Analysis*. London: Bailliere, Tindall & Cox.
Kernberg, O. (1976), *Object Relations Theory and Clinical Psychoanalysis*. Northvale, NJ: Aronson.
Kingsolver, B. (1998), *The Poisonwood Bible*. New York: HarperCollins.
Kleinman, A. (1989), *The Illness Narratives*. New York: Basic Books.
Kolnair, A. (1929), Der ekel. *Jahrbuch für Philosophie und Phänomenologische Forschung, Vol. 10*, ed. E. Husserl. Halle & Saale: Max Niemeyer, 1974.
Kristof, N. D. (2003, May 16), Alone and ashamed. *New York Times*.
Krummel, R. (1985), *Looking Good*. New York: Michael Kesend.
Kuznets, L. R. (1988), *Fiction International, Vol. 18, No. 1*, ed. H. Jaffe. San Diego, CA: San Diego State University Press.
Laufer, M. E. (1986), The female Oedipus complex and the relationship to the body. *The Psychoanalytic Study of the Child*, 41:259–276. New Haven, CT: Yale University Press.
Lee, G. A. (1996), *Leper Hospitals of Medieval Scotland*. Dublin: Four Courts Press.
Leithauser, B. (1993, March 22), Cattails: A marsh in March. *The New Yorker*.
Levi, P. (1988), *The Drowned and the Saved*, trans. R. Rosenthal. New York: Summit Books.
Lewis, M. (1992), *Shame: The Exposed Self*. New York: Free Press.

Lidz, T. (1973), *The Organization and Treatment of Schizophrenic Disorders.* New York: Basic Books.
Magee, M. & Miller, D. D. (1997), *Lesbian Lives: Psychoanalytic Narratives Old and New.* Hillsdale, NJ: The Analytic Press.
Malson, L. (1964), *Wolf Children,* trans. E. Fawcett, P. Ayrton & J. White. New York: Monthly Review Press, 1972.
Marty, M. E. & Appleby, R. S. (1992), *The Glory and the Power.* Boston: Beacon Press.
Matchett, G. & Davey, G. C. L. (1991), A test of a disease-avoidance model of animal phobias. *Behaviour Research and Therapy,* 29:91–94.
Mathis, J. (2003, February 11), Nude rec has a certain "ick" factor. *Ann Arbor News.*
Mayman, M. (1974, September), The shame experience, the shame dynamic, and shame personalities in psychotherapy. Presented as George Klein Memorial Address at annual meeting of the American Psychological Association. Also presented to the Topeka Psychoanalytic Society, September 1975, and the Albert Einstein School of Medicine, December 1977.
Menninghaus, W. (2003), *Disgust: The Theory and History of a Strong Sensation,* trans. H. Eiland & J. Golb. Albany, NY: SUNY Press.
Merton, T. (1988), *Zen and the Birds of Appetite.* New York: New Directions.
Michaels, A. (1996), *Fugitive Pieces.* New York: Random House.
Miller, S. B. (1986), Disgust: Conceptualization, development, and dynamics. *International Review of Psycho-Analysis,* 13:295–307.
Miller, S. B. (1993), Disgust reactions: Their determinants and manifestations in treatment. *Contemporary Psychoanalysis,* 29:711–735.
Miller, S. B. (1996), *Shame in Context.* Hillsdale, NJ: The Analytic Press.
Miller, W. I. (1997), *The Anatomy of Disgust.* Cambridge, MA: Harvard University Press.
Morrison, A. P. (1997), *Shame: The Underside of Narcissism.* Hillsdale, NJ: The Analytic Press.
National Public Radio (2000, September 4), Americans and their jobs. *Talk of the Nation.*
Nissenson, H. (1976), *My Own Ground.* New York: Farrar, Straus & Giroux.
Oz, A. (1993), *Fima,* trans. N. de Lange. New York: Harcourt Brace.

Pagels, E. (1988), *Adam, Eve, and the Serpent.* New York: Vintage Books.
Pagels, E. (1995), *The Origin of Satan.* New York: Random House.
Phillips, M. L., Young, A. W., Senior, C., Brammer, M., Andrew, C., Williams, S. C. R., Gray, J. & David, A. S. (1997), A specific neural substrate for perceiving facial expressions of disgust. *Nature,* 389: 495–498.
Pilkey, D. (2002), *The New Captain Underpants Collection.* New York: Blue Sky Press.
Pineda, C. (1986), *The Frieze.* New York: Viking.
Pinker, S. (1998), *How the Mind Works.* Harmondsworth, UK: Penguin.
Quigley, J. F., Sherman, M. & Sherman, N. (1996, March), Personality disorder symptoms, gender, and age as predictors of adolescent disgust sensitivity. Presented at annual meeting of the Eastern Psychological Association, Philadelphia, PA.
Renou, L., ed. (1962), *Hinduism.* New York: George Braziller.
Repacholi, B. M. (1998), Infants' use of attentional cues to identify the referent of another person's emotional expression. *Developmental Psychology,* 34:1017–1025.
Rice, A. (1976), *Interview with the Vampire.* New York: Ballantine, 1993.
Rozin, P. (1976), The selection of food by rats, humans and other animals. In: *Advances in the Study of Behavior, Vol. 6,* ed. J. Rosenblatt, R. A. Hinde, C. Beer & E. Shaw. New York: Academic Press, pp. 21–76.
Rozin, P. (1999), Food is fundamental, fun, frightening, and far-reaching. *Social Research,* 66:9–30.
Rozin, P. & Fallon, A. E. (1987), A perspective on disgust. *Psychological Review,* 94:23–41.
Rozin, P., Haidt, J. & McCauley, C. R. (1999), Disgust: The body and soul emotion. In: *Handbook of Cognition and Emotion,* ed. T. Dalgleish & M. Power. Chichester, UK: Wiley.
Rozin, P., Haidt, J. & McCauley, C. R. (2000), Disgust. In: *Handbook of Emotions,* ed. M. Lewis & J. M. Haviland-Jones. New York: Guilford Press, pp. 637–653.
Rozin, P., Haidt, J., McCauley, C. R. & Imada, S. (1997), Disgust: Preadaptation and the cultural evolution of a food-based emotion. In: *Food Preferences and Taste,* ed. H. MacBeth. Providence, RI: Berghahn Books, pp. 65–82.

Rozin, P., Lowery, L. & Ebert, R. (1999), Varieties of disgust faces and the structure of disgust. *Journal of Personality and Social Psychology,* 66:870–881.

Saint Catherine Church (n.d.), 5 Shore Acres Avenue, Middletown, NJ. Website: www.stcathek.org/default.htm.

Sartre, J. P. (1948), *Anti-Semite and Jew,* trans. G. J. Becker. New York: Schocken Books.

Schore, A. N. (1994), *Affect Regulation and the Origin of the Self.* Hillsdale, NJ: Lawrence Erlbaum Associates.

Sebald, W. G. (2002, November 4), A natural history of destruction [trans. A. Bell]. *The New Yorker.*

Shakespeare, W. (1948), *The Tempest.* In: *Shakespeare: The Complete Works.* New York: Harcourt Brace World.

Shapiro, V., Fraiberg, S. & Adelson, E. (1976), Infant–parent psychotherapy on behalf of a child in a critical nutritional state. *The Psychoanalytic Study of the Child.* New Haven, CT: Yale University Press, pp. 461–491.

Shelley, M. W. (1831), *Frankenstein.* Philadelphia, PA: Running Press, 1987.

Sontag, S. (1977), *Illness as Metaphor.* New York: Farrar, Straus & Giroux.

Spence, D. P. (1982), *Narrative Truth and Historical Truth.* New York: Norton.

Sprengelmeyer, R., Young, A. W., Pundt, I., Sprengelmeyer, A., Calder, A., Berrios, G., Winkel, R., Vollmoeller, W., Kuhn, W., Sartory, G. & Przuntek, H. (1997), Disgust implicated in obsessive-compulsive disorder. *Proceedings of the Royal Society: Biological Sciences,* B264: 1767–1773.

Stallybrass, P. & White, A. (1986), *The Politics and Poetics of Transgression.* Ithaca, NY: Cornell University Press.

Thandeka (1999), *Learning to Be White: Money, Race, and God in America.* New York: Continuum.

Thomas, L. (1974), *The Lives of a Cell.* New York: Viking.

The Torah (1962), Philadelphia, PA: Jewish Publication Society of America.

Turnbull, C. M. (1972), *The Mountain People.* New York: Simon & Schuster.

References

Turner, V. W. (1970), *A Forest of Symbols*. Ithaca, NY: Cornell University Press.

Updike, J. (1996), *In the Beauty of the Lilies*. New York: Ballantine.

Warner, W. (2002, September 4), Other voices. *Ann Arbor News*.

Webb, K. & Davey, G. C. L. (1993), Disgust sensitivity and fear of animals: Effects of exposure to violent or repulsive material. *Anxiety, Coping, and Stress,* 5:329–335.

Weiner, E. (2001, July 9), *Morning Edition*. National Public Radio.

Wilbur, R. (1988), *New and Collected Poems*. New York: Harcourt Brace Jovanovich.

Wilson, R. A. (1968), *Forever Feminine*. New York: M. Evans.

Wrye, H. K. & Welles, J. (1998), *The Narration of Desire*. Hillsdale, NJ: The Analytic Press.

Wurmser, L. (1981), *The Mask of Shame*. Baltimore, MD: Johns Hopkins University Press.

Index

Abraham, K., 41, 91–92
abuse survivors, 94–95
Acre family
    cleanliness and order, 126
    disgusted rejection responses, 128
    process notes, 129–132
    Virginia, 125–127
        adolescent phase, 129–131
        revulsion to fish, 130–132
        rule-breaking, 127–128
adaptation, 49
Delicate Balance (Albee), 171
Adelson, E., 86–87
adolescence, 96
    physical experiences of, 62
    development in, 106
    treatment, sexual content and, 33
aesthetic violations, 145
affect-theorists, 12n
afterbirth, 107
age (aging), 38, 60, 94, 178
aggression, 80–81
AIDS patients, 183
Albee, E., *A Delicate Balance,* 171
Alexander, F., on anal phase, 86
Alice
    cleanliness issue, 133–134
    creativity, 133
    depression, 132–133
    inclusionist stance, 135
Alien (Ash), 172–175
Almost (Benedict), 43
Al Qaida, 166

anality, 61–63
    reaction-formation, 86–87
Andrew, C., 85
anger, 185
Angyal, A., 2, 49–52, 112
animal nature, relationship to, 48–49
Ann Arbor News, 32
anorexics, 83–85
Anthony, J., on anal phase, 86
anticipatory mind-set, 75–76
anti-Semitism, 180
    French, 163–164
    reasoning in, 164
artificial intelligence, 149
artistic inhibition, 143
Assassin's Apprentice (Hobb), 79
attachment, 119
Auschwitz, 157
autonomy
    conflict over, 83
    threats to, 98
aversion–attraction, 185–186

Bearak, B., 154
Bear, G., *Slant,* 148–150
Beauty of the Lilies, In the (Updike), 164–166
Bee Season (Goldberg), 97
Benedict, E., *Almost,* 43
Berrios, G., 85
Berry family, Alice, 132–135
biological protection, 56
biological theories, 2–4

Biran, A., 2–3, 49
bird poop, 62–63
birth symbolism, 101
blood
    image of, 173–174
    mixing, 156–157
    Red Cross draw, 28
    symbolization, 24–25
bodily disgust, 41, 68
bodily integrity, 7–8
bodily presence, 36–37
bodily separation, 41–43
body damage images, 28
body–environment boundary, 8
body orifices, 37–38
body part dislocation, 30
body-threat, 49
Book of Watchers, The, 157
Boone, S. L., 157
borderline personalities, 80–81
borrowed disgust, 40
boundaried self, 191–192
boundaried state, 16–17
boundaries, 20, 160–161
    in disgust and horror, 174–175
    sacrosanct, 148
    self-protective, 154
    sense of, 55
    transgressed in art, 145
Bowe, J., 185
Bowe, M., 185
Boys Don't Cry, 113
Brammer, M., 85
Brody, S., *Disease of the Soul,* 181
Brooklyn Museum of Art, 138
Brown, Laura, 100
Buckland, G., 83
Buddhism, 166
Budima, J., 154
bulimics, 92
Burke, E., 155

Calder, A., 85
cancer image, 178
cannibalism, 174, 188

Captain Underpants, 61–62
Cartesian cognito, 15
Catch-22 (Heller), 186
categories, breached, 21
Catherine, Saint, 183
"Cattails: A Marsh in March"
    (Leithauser), 134
Channel4.com, 15
children
    developmental achievement, 61–62
    socialization, 50–51
Christ, 184
Christian images, art and, 138–139
class anxiety, 156
class systems, 166–167
cleanliness, 126
clinical medicine, 148
Clinton, President, 20–21
closeness
    ambivalent, 116–123
    danger of, 121
coal waste slurry, 175–176
cognitive maturation, 11
collective disgust, 15
collective self, Japanese, 169
compulsive cleanliness, 43
condoms, used, 109
consciousness, modern, 15
contagion
    anxiety, 32, 73–74
    nakedness and, 32
    principle, 73, 178
contamination, 15
    fantasies, 35
    threat, 183–184
context, 34–35
Cooper, C., 107, 155
    The Jamaican Body, 184
coprophagic impulses, 86
coprophilic impulses, 86
Corrections, The (Franzen), 23, 34–35, 125
coupling relationships, 98–99
creative inhibition, 145
creative people, 138

Index

creativity
  associations and, 139
  psychoanalytic literature on, 144
Crisco, 54
Cunningham, M., *The Hours,* 100
Curtis, V., 2–3, 49

Dallos, R., 83
Daniel, V., 167
Darwin, C., 10n, 49
  catalogued emotions, 2
Davey, G. C. L., 83, 95
David, A. S., 85
death, 185–189
Death of a Naturalist (Heaney), 141
defiance, self-validating, 122
Denby, D., on Galápagos Islands, 53–54, 135
depression, eating disorders and, 83–84, 92
desire
  human body and, 104–112
  reaction-formation against, 110–111
developmental disgust, 59–60, 63
Diana, Princess, 183
dietary proscriptions, 24–25
difference, treatment of, 159
disease
  anticipation of, 182
  Nazi metaphors, 177
  preoccupations with, 178
Disease of the Soul (Brody), 181
disgust
  analysis, 57
  vs. anxiety, 167–168
  categorization, 38–39, 160
  costs of, 77–78
  desire and, 111–112
  developmental line, 10
  directing, 67–68
  dynamics, 143
  effects, 195
  emblematic, 40
  as emotion, 1–2
  experiences of, 27–28
  forms and functions, 1–2
  horror and, 171–173
  human body and, 104–112
  intergenerational war, 9
  late appearance, 5
  major muscle groups used, 10n
  paradox of, 17
  as protective agent, 70–71
  as reaction-formation, 161
  rejection and, 153–154
  relevant language, 158
  responses, 36–37, 77, 142
  toward self. *See* self-disgust
  shared, 61–63
  situation characteristics, 77
  stimulus, 176
  syndrome, 93
  terrain elements, 39
  transmission, 3
  types and subtypes, 38–45, 111
  understanding, 2
disgusting material, 74
Disgust Scale scores, 86
disidentification, 104
dislocation, 30, 33
distance, 8–9
distaste, 10
  reinforcer of, 53
distrust, 144
doctrinaire polemics, 154
dog devotees, 172–173
double-jointedness, 33–34
Douglas, M., 20, 21, 107, 109, 150, 160
  on dirt, 56–57
  Purity and Danger, 191
Drescher, J., 113
duality, of mind and body, 5–6

eating, 38
  disorders, 81–83
  psychological significance, 11–13
Ebert, R., 10n, 88
eckel sein, 120–121
ego defense, disgust as, 195
Ekman, P., 10n

Elliott, D., 107, 184
Ellsberg, Daniel, 20
emotion, boundary-managing, 88
empathy, 19
encopretic children, 133
"End, The" (Nossack), 188
erotic bond, 117
ethnic hatred, 164
externalization, 75

Fallon, A. E., 2, 10, 32
familial intimacy, 116
family groups, 192–193
fastidiousness, 85
fear, in intimate dyads, 99
fellatio, 110
feminine sexuality, 107–108
Fima, 116–119
fistulas, 178
fit, between artist and audience, 143–144
food aversions, 14
foreign element, 153
Forever Feminine (Wilson), 178
Fortson, B., 12n
Fournier, J., 107
Fraiberg, S., 86–87
Frankenstein (Shelley), 138, 146–147
Franzen, J., *The Corrections,* 23, 34–35, 125
free expression, 139
French Revolution, 155
Freud, A., 79
  on anal phase, 86
Freudian view, 21
Freud, S., 4–5, 110, 175
  reaction-formation concept, 57
Friesen, W. V., 10n
Fugitive Pieces (Michaels), 18–19

Galápagos Islands, Denby on, 53–54
gender, 180
Genesis, 6, 141, 157
genetic predisposition, 26
Gide, A., *The Immoralist,* 59, 179

Gig (Bowe, Bowe, and Streeter), 185
Gilman, S. L., 175
  on disease and health, 179–180
  on revulsion, 180
Giuliani, Mayor R., 138
gluttony, sin of, 84
Goldberg, M., 41–42
  The Bee Season, 76, 97
goodness, ideas of, 142
Grapes of Wrath (Steinbeck), 69–70
Grauballe Man, 141
Gray, Dorian, 172
Gray, J., 85
Grimstone, Friar John, 177
group organization, 194

Haidt, J., 2–5, 10, 10n, 13, 25n, 26–28, 70, 93, 96, 166–169, 187
Heaney, Seamus
  Death of a Naturalist, 141
  Opened Ground, 139–140
  "Personal Helicon," 1
hearing, 9
hell, of earthly condition, 166
Heller, J., 186
Herzog, D., 151, 155–156
Hinduism, 166
  view of body, 185
hip-hop song, 140
History of Jamaica (Long), 154–155
Hitler, Adolf, 118
Hobb, R., *Assassin's Apprentice,* 79
Hochberg, A., 175
Hoeg, P.
  Smila's Sense of Snow, 54
Holocaust, 77, 185
  child survivor, 141–142
Holy Virgin Mary, The (Ofili), 138
homosexuality, 114
horror, 194
  disgust and, 171–173
  sexual surrender and, 173
  of stimulus, 176
Hours, The (Cunningham), 100
house sparrows, 64

Index

human being
  composition of, 48
  form, 186–187
  insecurity, 51, 179
  intimacy, risks of, 98
  meaningless of, 188–189
Hurd, B., *Stirring the Mud,* 137
Hussein, Saddam, 121
Husserl, E., 52
hypercleanliness, 120
hypochondriacs, 178

idealization, 76–77
ideational disgust, 41
identification, 93, 104
identity, 135–136, 193
ignorance, 19
Iks, 193–194
Imada, S., 10, 25n, 26, 28, 70, 166–169, 187
Immoralist, The (Gide), 59, 179
impermanence, 179
impermeable systems, 185
individuality, 113
infancy
  absence of disgust in, 3
  food reactions, 9–10
  organizing behaviors, 11
infidelity, 115–116
infirmity, 178
innovation, 151
insula, 85
intention, 71–72
interpersonal response, 50
interpersonal transmission, 50
Interview with the Vampire (Rice), 174
intimacy
  breaches, 114–116
  couples, 97–104
  identification and, 105
  nonsexual, 116–123
  older woman, 101–102
  self-disgust and, 122
intuitive microbiology, 2–4
Izard, C. E., 10n

Jackson, Michael, 120
Jackson, M. R., *Self-Esteem and Meaning,* 153
Jains, 166
Jamaican Body, The (Cooper), 184
Jamaicans
  body concepts, 184
  Jonkonnu festivities, 155
Jones, E., 144
  on anal phase, 86
Justin, 47
juxtaposition, 35

Keltner, D., 10n
ken'o, 169
Kernberg, O., 11
Kingsolver, B., *The Poisonwood Bible,* 106
Kleinman, A., 185
  on Indian society, 167
Kolnair, A., 21, 57
  "Der Ekel," 52
kosher meat, 173–174
Kristof, N. D., 178
Krummel, R., 84
Kuhn, W., 85
Kuznets, L. R., 84

language, 12n, 13
Larson, G., 72–73
Laufer, M. E., 82–83
Lechter, Hannibal, 174
Lee, G. A., 175, 185
Leithauser, B., "Cattails: A Marsh in March," 134
lepers, 181–183
  power of, 135
Levi, Primo, 157
  stranger as brother, 162
Leviticus, 131, 184
  isolation, 107
  prohibitions, 40
Lewis, M., 50
Lidz, T., 160
life-boundaries, 55–56
Long, E., *History of Jamaica,* 154–155

Index

Longley, M., 1
Lowery, L., 10n, 88

mad scientist, 148
Magee, M., 113
Malson, L., 11, 26
Mapplethorpe, Robert, 139, 142
marginal, 160
　group, 164
Marty, M. E., 166
masochistic need, 80–81
Mathis, J., 32
Mayman, M., 79
McCauley, C. R., 2–5, 10–10n, 13, 25n, 26–28, 70, 93, 96, 166–169, 187
Mengele, Josef, 147
Menninghaus, W., 52, 120, 153, 187
menstruation, 60, 107–108
Merton, T., 15
messiness, 134
miasma, 47
Michaels, A., 141–142
　Fugitive Pieces, 18–19
　on Nazi psychology, 162–163
Miller, D. D., 113
Miller, S. B., 4, 13, 89
Miller, W. I., 12n, 21, 51, 54–55, 57, 111
　too much life, 119
mind/body duality, 5–6
Montaillou, women of, 108
moral disgust, 14, 25, 39, 59, 63–68
　aggressiveness of, 65
　science and, 146
morality, 68–70
mouth, functions of, 109
Muslims, 166
　extremists, 158
My Own Ground (Nissenson), 107

narcissism
　compulsive, 89–92
　disorders, 79
National Public Radio
　coal waste pond, 175–176

　on noodle-slurping, 9
　on Smithers occupation, 185–186
natural selection, 49
nature, 18–19, 56
　challenges of, 47
　distance from, 48
　love of, 133
　messy, 134
Nazis
　disease metaphors, 177
　as emblem, 119–121
　extermination of "undesirables," 64
　period, 162–163
negativity, 26
New Guinea, Hua of, 168–169
New Yorker, Denby on Galápagos Islands, 53–54
Nissenson, H., *My Own Ground,* 107
Nixon, President R., 20
noodle-slurping, 9
Nossack, H. E., "Der Untergang," 188
nude recreation, 32

obsessive-compulsive character organization, 84
Ofili, Chris, 138
Old Testament, 108
olfactory disgust, 26–27
Omphalos, 149
"One Mike," 140
Opened Ground (Heaney), 139–140
oral revulsion, 4–5
O'Sullivan, M., 10n
otherness, 158–159
　sense of security and, 191
outsiders, 161
Oz, Amos, 116–119

Pagels, E., 47, 157, 158
Palestine, 118
partial disgust, 39–41
passive-to-active defense, 103
permeable systems, 185
"Personal Helicon" (Heaney), 1
Phillips, M. L., 85

Index

physical form
   impermanence of, 47–48
   vulnerability, 29
Picasso, P., 35
Pineda, C., 55
Pinker, S., 2, 7
Poisonwood Bible, The (Kingsolver), 106
poop, 88
   bird, 62–63
   talk, 61
power, response to, 99
Practice, The, 67
prohibitions, 25
Protestantism, 151
proto-emotion, 88
Przuntek, H., 85
psychic integrity, 7–8
psychological self, 5
Pundt, I., 85
Purity and Danger (Douglas), 191

Quigley, J. F., 86

race
   categorization, 156
   hatred, 164
   laws, 157
   speech, 154–155
reaction-formation, 21
   anally directed, 86–87
   theory of, 49–50
Reformation, 151
rejection, 34
   disgust and, 153–154
relatedness, ambivalent, 105–106
religion
   on moral goodness and evil, 65–66
   pure and impure in, 166
Renou, L., 166
Repacholi, B. M., 50
rescue workers, 182–183
Rice, A., *Interview with the Vampire,* 174
Rozin, P., 2, 4–5, 10, 10n, 13, 17, 25n–28, 32, 54–55, 70, 88, 93, 96, 109, 166–169, 187

Saint Catherine Church, 183
Sartory, G., 85
Sartre, J. P., on anti-Semitism, 164
Satan, concept of, 157
scary life, 55
Schnee, Seefa, 149–150
science
   fiction, 148
   moral disgust and, 146
scientists, work inhibitions, 146–148
Sebald, W. G., 187–188
   "A Natural History of Destruction," 171
security, 6–7
self
   body and, 194–195
   expansion, 193
   other and, 191, 195
   protecting, 5–6
   relationships and, 106–107
   vulnerability of, 4
self-awareness, 15
self-boundaries, 14–15, 24–25
   challenge, 113–114
   horror and, 175
   protection, 4
self-disgust, 67, 82–83, 90–91, 184
   badness and, 133
   intimacy and, 122
Self-Esteem and Meaning (Jackson), 153
self-protective disgusts, 70, 80
self-protective reactions, 13
self-regard, 92
self-security, 7
self-symbols, 7
Senior, C., 85
sense experience
   imagery, 122–123
   response to input, 7
   taste, 23–25
separation
   sense of, 179–181
   threats to, 98
sexuality
   approach to, 33

contact, 38
  disgust toward, 60–61
  identification, 102–103
  intercourse, 109–110
  orientation, 113–114
Shakespeare, W., *The Tempest,* 141–142
shame, 51, 93
  personality, 79
Shapiro, V., 86–87
Shelley, M. W., *Frankenstein,* 138
Sherman, M., 86
Sherman, N., 86
Shoah, 185
Shore, A., 50
Shweder, R., 167
sickness, contact with, 182
sight, response to, 29–31
Sikhs, 166
singleness, loss of, 192
sins, illnesses and, 181
skin, 17–18
  as symbol, 7
Slant (Bear), 148–150
Smila's Sense of Snow (Hoeg), 54
Smithers, N., 185
Sontag, S., 177
  cancer image, 178
sound, 36
Southey, R., 155
speech, dirty, 37–38
Spence, D. P., 22
Sprengelmeyer, A., 85
Sprengelmeyer, R., 85
Stallybrass, P., 111, 129, 160
Steinbeck, J., *Grapes of Wrath,* 69–70
stimuli, 49
Stirring the Mud (Hurd), 137
Streeter, S., 185
substance, sense of, 55
surprise, 34
sympathetic magic, 13

tampon-toucher response, 31
Tantow, B., 83
taste, 23–25, 36
  imagery, 24
  objective reality of, 28
Tatian, 47
Tempest, The (Shakespeare), 141–142
terror, 29
terrorism, war on, 156
texture, sensitivity to, 8
Thandeka
  on projective identification, 159–160
  race laws, 157
  on race-mixing, 159
  on white racial self-hatred, 156
Third New International Dictionary
  (Webster), 47
Thomas, L., 48, 146, 193
toddlerhood, 87–88
Tollund Man, 141
"too much life" thesis, 52
touch, meaning and context of, 29–30
Tourette's syndrome, 150
trauma, 94
tuberculosis, 179
Turner, V. W., 160, 175

Ugandan tribe, 193–194
unconscious mind, metaphor for, 19
untouchables, 180
Updike, J., *In the Beauty of the Lilies,*
  164–166

values, disgust and, 44
vampire tales, 173
vampirism, 174
Virginia. *See* Acre family
Vollmoeller, W., 85
vomiting, 42–43
vulnerability, 34

Warner, W., 158
Webb, K., 95
Webster, D., *Third New International
  Dictionary,* 47
Weiner, E., 9
Welles, J., 7, 117

Index

White, A., 111, 129, 160
white pride, 156
white supremacists, 155
Williams, S. C. R., 85
Wilson, R. A., *Forever Feminine,* 178
Winkel, R., 85
Winnicottian playspace, 139

Wrye, H. K., 7, 117
Wurmser, L., *Mask of Shame, The,* 123

Young, A. W., 85
yuck, 87–88

zombie, 175